T0247770

Storylife

Storylife

On Epic, Narrative, and Living Things

JOEL P. CHRISTENSEN

Yale UNIVERSITY PRESS

New Haven and London

Published with assistance from the Louis Stern Memorial Fund.

Yale University Press books may be purchased in quantity for
educational, business, or promotional use. For information,
please e-mail sales.press@yale.edu (U.S. office) or sales@yaleup.co.uk
(U.K. office).

Set in Minion type by Westchester Publishing Services.
Printed in the United States of America.

Library of Congress Control Number: 2024935413
ISBN 978-0-300-26923-9 (hardcover : alk. paper)

A catalogue record for this book is available from
the British Library.

This paper meets the requirements of ANSI/NISO Z39.48-1992
(Permanence of Paper).

10 9 8 7 6 5 4 3 2 1

For Aalia, Iskander, and Layla and all the lifetimes their stories have already made

Contents

Preface ix

Introduction. Stories About Origins and Design 1

ONE. Scripts for Life: From DNA to Poetic Formula 22

TWO. Recombinations and Change: Ring Structures
in Nature and Speech 57

THREE. Crabs and the Monomyth: Parallel Evolutions
and Mythical Patterns 88

FOUR. Going Viral: Big Deeds and Bad Fame 113

FIVE. Symbiosis and Paradigm: What Stories Do
in the World 142

Conclusion. Inoculation and the Limits of Analogy 179

Suggestions for Further Reading 193

Notes 199

Bibliography 211

Acknowledgments 225

Index 227

vii

Preface

If you are reading this book, you probably know how precarious human civilization is at this moment. And yet, depending on your perspective, you might believe that this has always been the way of things, that life itself has been a remarkable experiment in precarity, billions of years in the telling. Nevertheless, recent generations have seen an explosion in access to knowledge worldwide, a transformation in the way we engage with each other and information that few of us are in a position to fully comprehend.

This book is a product at once of the COVID-19 pandemic and of my years of thinking, writing, and teaching about what stories do in the world. I have long experimented with biological metaphors for narrative in the classroom, but the spread of COVID-19 and (mis)information about it accompanied by political upheaval and racial (re)reckonings provided the context and the impetus to push the analogies farther. In part, *Storylife* is an extended metaphor, an exploration of how to think about stories if we externalize them, by which I mean if we imagine them as something separate from ourselves that act upon us with external agency. I use Homeric language and poetry primarily because of my own familiarity with them and because their dissimilarity from modern forms of narrative makes it easier for most contemporary readers to see them differently; but make no mistake, I see Homeric poetry as functioning metonymically (in a part-for-the whole relationship) with regard to narrative at large.

One of the questions I posed to myself before and after writing this book is how I would answer my own children's (potential) future question: What did I do when the world was ending? I wrote a book about viruses and stories, selfishly in part, trying to help myself understand the world around me, but also in the hope that it might contribute in a small way to helping us understand how our collective action against existential threats is complicated and undermined by our relationships with narrative. I completed the book proposal while recovering from a COVID infection and finished the book at a time when the world seemed ever more unsettled.

In this book I use examples from Homeric poetry and myth to explore both where poetic and literary ideas come from and their impact on the audiences that enjoy them, as well as the force the audiences have on the ideas themselves. I have set out to write something that would be appealing and provocative to specialists and general readers. In doing so, I have no delusions about writing the final word on the subject; instead, I hope to be part of that larger ecosystem of thinking about story, about authorship and ownership, and about how we as human beings forge a future together intentionally, loving and living alongside narrative in world that has space for all of us.

Storylife

Introduction

Stories About Origins and Design

The second-century BCE Greek authors Pausanias and Plutarch tell a story about an Olympic boxer named Kleomēdēs.[1] Kleomēdēs was victorious in his bouts but was ultimately stripped of a prize over an accusation of cheating. He returned home in a rage and brought down the roof of a school containing more than sixty children, killing them all. He then took refuge in the temple of Athena and vanished. When the families of those who were killed sent a herald to the oracle at Delphi to ask what had happened, the oracle responded, "Kleomēdēs the Astupalaian was the last of the heroes—Honor him with sacrifices since he is no longer mortal."

I have this story in my head when I think about the burst of heroic narratives in popular culture over the past two generations, from *Star Wars* to *Avengers: End Game*. Why is Kleomēdēs called a hero? Why is he the final one? Other Greek heroes, such as Achilles and Odysseus, have been back in the minds and on the lips of audiences in a way I never would have imagined just twenty years ago. What drives our interest? What do they do for us?

The questions that stalk me the most are about how selective our memories for heroes can be. We often miss one of the most important features about their stories: the harm they do to their own communities. Achilles and Odysseus, for example, are both like Kleomēdēs. They go out in the world and achieve greatness, only to turn against their own people with violence. Achilles prays to Zeus to punish the Greeks for dishonoring him, and as a result thousands die. Odysseus returns home to find suitors in his palace, and he, their king, slaughters them all and readies himself to murder their families until Athena intervenes. The heroic narrative in the full forms provided by Homer in the *Iliad* and the *Odyssey* invites us to see how these exceptional individuals threaten their communities instead of saving them. Yet most of us miss the point.

Why? Heroic narratives—along with the wonderful variety of stories that shape our culture—follow familiar patterns that correspond to stages in human life and echo and reinforce social structures and practices. But how do they develop, and who shapes them? What kind of influence do they have on the people who tell them? How do we understand something that is essentially both a product and a producer of culture?

The *Iliad* and *Odyssey* are complex appropriations of Homeric narratives that ask and answer many of these questions. And along the way, they can help us understand both what heroes do in the world that makes them and why it might have been better if Kleomēdēs had truly been the last hero of all.

To begin to answer these questions, we need to look away from heroes and from what we think we know about where stories come from. We need to think about narrative and its environment, and how both change over time.

Imagine a complex symphony or suite of interconnected melodies: as you listen, these melodies rise and fall over time, movements come and go and return again, sometimes changed, sometimes syncopated, sometimes just an echo of what they once were. But some three- or four-note sequences are more insistent than others—they press through the sound and are emphasized first by this instrument and then by those. Our impression of the symphony's character is wholly dependent on which part of it we give our attention to.

But sometimes it is difficult to pay attention, because the different melodies sound like multiple tracks playing at once. As you listen, you think of other melodies, and your reverie changes the symphony. The resulting music is beautiful but terrifyingly hard to follow: when you pause, you realize you have been listening to one line of melody when three or four others were going on at the same time. It is hard to start again because you do not want to lose track of the one you you are listening to. But you are already thinking about that brief gasp of melody that escaped you. And if there are a hundred people listening along with you, they have heard at least a hundred different songs.

The sixteen thousand lines of the *Iliad* and twelve thousand lines of the *Odyssey* are like twenty-four and eighteen hours of polyphonic music, played by musicians in separate rooms who cannot hear one another but are somehow working in concert. The audience stands someplace apart. If we relax and let the composition fall over us, we can get some idea of the whole. But when we listen closely, we can get lost in the depth of each passing strain.

This shifting, symphonic nature makes it hard to translate Homeric epic or even interpret it well. Each line has melodies full of resonant meaning that echo differently, based on who the audience is and what they have heard before. When someone tells you the *Iliad* is *about this* or the *Odyssey* is *about that,* that person is following one repeated series of notes for their movement and resolution, and necessarily leaving others aside. The total density of the soundscape of the poems and the generations of potential meanings within them makes them impossible to understand or explain in "real time." When I hear people talking about what an epic means, sometimes I feel as if they are talking about a different epic altogether. I have been listening to other movements, contemplating different themes.

The Homeric Question

The so-called Homeric Question is one of the most well-known academic problems of ancient literature—and, in all truth, it is not even a single issue. The Question goes something like this: Since we are unclear about the material conditions of the composition, performance, and circumstances under which the *Iliad* and *Odyssey* were committed to text, are the poems we have the ones that people experienced in antiquity, are they by the same "author," and are they, as we have them, unified and whole? The Homeric Question has inspired many different answers over time, generally rooted in assumptions about authorship and creative production that prize individuals over communal experiences, center a producer with little regard for audiences, and place far too much faith in the fixity of interpretation and understanding in the transmission of a written word. These problems may seem particularly and inextricably Homeric, but they represent issues that attend the discussion of literature and art across many disciplines.

Debates concerning the genesis, coherence, and meaning of texts from antiquity are in essence about how meaning is made, and what acts and processes we credit most for their character. There is an implicit connection between who and what we value in the creative process and how we think of ourselves in the world: the author model that has dominated our thinking about creativity sees poetic creation as akin to a god creating a universe, placing little value on the communities of audiences who shape the work by their reception or on the experiences and cultural trends that made the work, if not inevitable, at least possible. Theoretical approaches to authorship run almost parallel to the study of ancient texts, but they emphasize many of the same issues, from the intentional fallacy to the construction of authorship as a fiction, to the far greater importance of reader response.[2] Homeric scholarship provided modern readers with an early opportunity to think about these problems by introducing comparative studies in oral composition and performance as other ways to think about the creative process. But many of the suggestions and conclusions reached over time have not received wide acceptance because they have so thoroughly challenged fundamental cultural assumptions about individual independence and ownership.

Indeed, there are both cultural and cognitive reasons why, despite the existence of multiple frameworks to undermine conventional notions of authorship, the traditional model remains dominant. As with most cultural assumptions, however, it is a grave mistake to universalize our beliefs. Even early Greek poets like Homer and Hesiod (an epic poet whose tradition is considered basically contemporaneous with Homer) are best understood as metonyms, or stand-ins, for kinds of poetic traditions, in terms of both form and content. In fact, even though we see an obsession with authorship (as ownership, in a way) emerging from ancient Greece, early Greek poetry defers authority to divine inspiration, to the Muses. The Homeric narrator denies the power to sing the catalogue of the Greeks who came to fight at Troy (even as he does it) and the Hesiodic narrator claims that the Muses verbally abused him and declared, "Fools, we know how to speak lies that sound like the truth / but we can speak the truth when we want to."[3]

One of my favorite metaphors for poetic creation from ancient Greece centers on the Muses as well. In the Athenian philosopher Plato's dialogue *Ion*, Socrates debates with a performer of Homeric poetry (Ion, the rhapsode, or singer), who claims he has special knowledge about Homer. Socrates compares this special knowledge to the force exerted by a magnet on connected metal rings. Just as the magnet confers its power through each ring, Socrates suggests, so too does the Muse transmit the power of inspiration to a poet, then a performer, and then the audience. By this argument, the emotional and intellectual responses to a poem are in part a feature of the original inspiration. While Socrates implies that a divine force initiates all this, I think the metaphor functions just as well if we understand the Muse as the collective experience of audiences shaping and reshaping traditional performances over time. That magnetic Muse is culture and history and art, the quivering soul of humanity's heart.[4]

While the ancient Greeks had the metaphor of the Muses to help them understand where ideas come from, most of our discussions about creative production have emphasized the special dispensation of inspiration given to an individual and the perspiration necessary to bring it to life. Too infrequently do we see the import of serendipity and context, or acknowledge the critical interventions of privilege, power, and chance. Postmodern approaches from psychoanalysis through deconstruction and reader response theory have tried to de-emphasize the importance of the author and emphasize cultural movements, yet too often the message does not come through clearly enough. There is, to my mind, only a difference of extent and imagination between the Homeric Question and our approach to creative production in general: ideas, expressions, even structures and messages are shaped by traditions and conventions, interpreted and framed by audiences, and transmitted and revised by communities of meaning.

Our confused notions of authors and texts impoverish our understanding of what stories do in the world and how they live alongside, through, and sometimes in spite of the people who tell and hear them. While this book contains examples from Homeric poetry and Greek myth that help us explore the development of narrative and how it both shapes audiences and is shaped by them, it also functions as a case study in how stories live alongside and through human communities. I explore both how Homeric poetry works and how story functions in general by inviting readers to rethink the relationship between stories and audiences through comparisons of Homeric poetry and myth to living and quasi-living things like parasites and viruses on structural, developmental, and functional levels. Thanks to the particular place of Homer both through time and across different cultural frameworks (e.g., literate vs. oral, sacred vs. secular, and so on), the *Iliad* and the *Odyssey* offer something like a stratigraphy of narrative's recent evolution. Along with myth, the Homeric epics are useful test cases, moreover, because they are familiar enough in form and content to be comprehensible to general audiences, but distant and strange enough to many readers to provide fertile ground for experimental thought.[5]

The Question of Design

We face two primary obstacles when we start to think about where ideas and stories come from and how they operate in the world. The first is cultural: the dominance of cultural metaphors for stories' creation that focus on credit, blame, and ownership. The second, partly in support of the first, is cognitive: we are hardwired neurologically to respond to our immediate circumstances and our own experiences and as a result are rather poor at thinking in the aggregate.

Human minds have a limited capacity for attention: when I am out running, I can visualize a tenth of a mile and sometimes a quarter, but a full mile or more is abstract and becomes a feature of the passage of time rather than a describable space. Even when we create something on our own, we lose track of the minutes and hours that go into composition and craft, and at the end we have an object whose genesis has been reduced more or less to a series of type-scenes and anecdotes in our memories. Extensive study of these features of human memory systems by psychologists and cognitive scientists has shown that our past memories become stories we tell ourselves rather than faithful recordings stored on some kind of a biological hard drive. We remain poor judges of the fidelity of our own memories, almost incapable of imagining the aggregate impact of memories and narrative on generations of human beings.[6]

To make the cognitive challenge even more severe, not only are our memories stereotyped and easily manipulated, but our cognition is also biased toward sense and meaning. One of the most important things I have learned from reading theories of narrative and cognitive science is how our brains endeavor to make sense of the world—to the point that they will fabricate details in order to generate meanings that cohere with our prior assumptions.[7] We impose order on the world. We are often even viscerally uncomfortable when explanations are not available. These forces have sometimes very different outcomes. Our cognitive need for closure, for example, can lead us to accept the most common or easily comprehensible explanation for events, whereas certain emotional frameworks can prompt us to reject widely accepted beliefs in favor of exceedingly complex and tenuous conspiratorial explanations.[8]

We are especially vulnerable to teleological arguments, in which the appearance of order or the effective application of a function causes us to assume design or a designer. The famous watchmaker analogy provided by the Christian philosopher William Paley in 1802 is a useful example of teleological thinking: Paley argues that a person who happened to find a watch lying on the ground would have to assume that its function necessarily implied a designer. Following this analogy, Paley and others insisted that the complex structures of nature, along with their function, were such that they demanded a design and a designer. Processes that create complexity in structure and specificity of function are needed to countermand such arguments. Indeed, many authors in the nineteenth century saw Darwinian natural selection as a strong defense against Paley's teleological argument: it provided a framework for understanding how it is possible for the appearance of design to develop over time. In the twentieth century the teleological argument was applied to evolution in "intelligent design," and advances in evolutionary science made it clear that our cognitive bias toward teleology could turn evolution itself metaphorically into a "designer."[9]

Our preference for teleological explanations may be rooted in an anthropocentric view of the world. When it comes to evaluating nature especially, studies have shown that human beings are more likely to identify design and intention in systems or events that privilege human beings and human survival. Thus popular understandings of evolution see natural selection as necessarily yielding the *best* solution or ideal form in response to environmental challenges. In reality, evolution yields whatever adaptations develop and work well enough at a particular time in a particular context. Changes that are random and contextual in the moment can appear over time to be pointed and meaningful because we see neither the dead ends nor the intermediary steps. We see design because we are conditioned to see it. Yet as studies in complex systems in nature have shown, coordination and complexity develop as a mathematical necessity. As my colleagues at Brandeis University Michael Hagan and Aparna Baskaran have written, active systems of particles and swarms or flocks of animals that appear to move by direction or design are actually governed by rules of physics, moving in concert and order owing to thermodynamics, rather than undetectable communication (for animals) or external design (for particles).[10] It is not that order emerges out of chaos at a large enough scale but that foundational rules of physics create order without intention, whereas human brains are structured to identify order and attribute design and intention to it.

My main point in thinking through design and evolution is to underscore how some of our approaches to literature and culture are animated by cultural beliefs and cognitive biases. Our attachment to viewing the creation of stories in a particular way is both emotional and structural. We need to find ways to think differently if we are to have any hope of living individual lives of intention and meaning, and of acting collectively to meet the challenges of the information age, political polarization, and climate change. From early education through political propaganda, narrative shapes the lives we live alone and together; how we adapt to or *with* narrative will in part shape whatever future remains.

What would art look like if we were more rational, more synoptic? Over the past few years, artificial intelligence (AI) processes that were developed for commercial and experimental uses may have begun to answer this question as they generate visual art (and fake photographs) and forms of writing from letters to poems. The revelation that learning programs can generate "unique" works on spec has triggered panic about plagiarism, fear of AI savants stealing the jobs of human "creatives," and existential concern about the future of art (and work) as we know it. But if we think through our own relationship with stories, we may find that these concerns are misplaced.

In its initial stages, it is clear that ChatGPT and other AI applications are good at imitating fairly mediocre art and writing. While it is almost certain that the products of these processes will improve over time, they are limited by the corpora they search and the algorithms that instruct them to select one form or expression over another. In a way, they are like human minds searching through the specific models they know and relying on implicit understandings of forms and meanings to cobble together new statements. They differ from humans in applying aesthetic judgments. They differ in who their audiences are. We write, sing, and compose for other humans, our peers.

I spent some time with colleagues in computer science discussing how ChatGPT works and why they think we should be worried about it. Part of their warning comes from a belief that Moore's law—a famous dictum from the 1960s noting that computing power doubles every two years—will apply to AI applications as well. When I asked ChatGPT itself how it works, I received the following answer: "ChatGPT is based on the transformer architecture and is trained on a massive amount of text data using unsupervised learning. The model generates a response to a given prompt by predicting the next token in the sequence, one token at a time. The model uses the attention mechanism to weigh the importance of different parts of the input when making predictions. The final generated text is post-processed to ensure coherence, fluency [as we can see], and consistency."[11] Indeed, there are two features of how these applications operate that will inevitably work better over time: the processing power, accuracy, and speed of the AI driver and the size and adaptability of the corpora of languages and texts that driver uses.

The intelligence portion is rooted in Natural Language Processing (also called a Large Language Model, which uses machine learning to create programs that can interpret, translate, and generate human languages), which provides the architecture for familiar programs including text-to-speech applications, automated phone operators, and Google Translate. The bot's own explanation about where its words come from—"a massive amount of text data"—and what it does with those data (it makes predictions) strikes me as just similar enough to what happens when we speak and write to indicate a rather simplistic sameness between the two. When we articulate an idea, we draw on a broad experience in languages, conversations, and cultural inputs and deliver utterances that, in many cases, are in fact predictable and iterable. Different people say similar or the same things in similar contexts.

But the same words do not always generate the same meaning. Context and audience matter. The "poems" that ChatGPT delivers tend to be rather superficial. In its versions of the stories of Achilles and Odysseus, for example, the basic details are present (Achilles is angry; Patroklos is dead; Odysseus blinds Polyphemos and returns home to Penelope), but they give no sense of complexity or depth. Sure, the *Iliad* is driven by the rage of Achilles, but his story embraces so much more. In its versions of the *Odyssey,* ChatGPT focuses on the legendary events of Odysseus's own story in books 9–12, such as the adventures with the Cyclops and Circe. These events are as capably echoed in "Home Sweet Homer," a 1987 episode of the animated show *DuckTales.*

ChatGPT is not reading Homer. Instead, it is "reading" a corpus that refers to Homer and predicting as significantly "Homeric" the details that achieve the most "hits." This reminds me of the oft-quoted thought experiment in which an infinite number of monkeys eventually produce *Hamlet* on their infinite typewriters. None of the monkeys—nor, it seems, the typewriters—would recognize the form or quality of a *Hamlet.* Audiences—in this case, human ones—see *Hamlet.* To any observer without the historical and cultural framework, Shakespeare is merely dark marks on a formerly blank page, no more significant than the printed phone books of the twentieth century.

One of the reasons I am interested in how ChatGPT and similar programs work is that it helps us explore the limits of the analogies provided by Natural Language Processing for the way language and narratives function in our embodied minds. Words on a page are nothing without someone to read them and create their meaning. The meaning is not intrinsic to the words themselves and readers or viewers create a meaning based on their own experience. When we read a ChatGPT composition, it has been crafted by an AI system created by human beings to predict human-like articulations, but *we* create the meaning through our own interpretation. Our embodied experience provides nuance to what we do with texts and what they do to us in turn.

While there are certainly many objections to my stance on where meaning comes from, the most common—and perhaps most cutting—concerns quality. No one I have shared the ChatGPT compositions with needs to be told that they are bad. We recognize this because of a shared aesthetic system that is far more difficult to codify than how to write a letter of resignation.

Plato's metaphor of the magnet can be useful for the ChatGPT conundrum. Plato uses the analogy to challenge the performer's special authority to speak about a work of art. He attributes inspiration instead to a divine force. This magnetic power relies in part on the language everyone knows, the traditions of songs and stories that make each new performance legible, and the shared aesthetic frameworks that support the songs' form. But the machine-searchable frames that make language legible are not the same as those that trigger associative meaning.

Perhaps some of the ineffable difference between "good" art and "bad" comes from the mystery of human consciousness. If we see the importance of art as coming from our engagement with it and the production of meaning by audiences, I think much of the panic about AI proves to be anxiety over employment and the further consolidation of capital in the hands of those who control the technology. Human consciousness, as described by philosophers like Daniel C. Dennett, is not a program inserted into hardware; it is a product of the engagements among our senses, our memories, and the world over time.[12] Each response to each work of art is different and contributes to collective evaluations that over time function to exert a force as seemingly invisible and magical as Plato's magnet. If we think poetry can be mechanical, it is because we are focusing too much on its production, engaging in "supply-side" poetics, not thinking

about its reception: how each engagement creates something new.

If an AI were to generate "original" sui generis poetry, it
would have to be defined by the experiences and reflections of
that artificial intelligence itself. We might not even recognize
it as art: there is a dangerous solipsism to the assertion that an
application imitating humans, even well, is replacing them. If
AI becomes aware and creates something of its own, its meaning will be something unique to that AI and its audiences.
Perhaps humans will have their own interpretations; but these
will be something else altogether, a hybrid-cyborg art.[13]

Metaphors for Meaning

A first step toward rethinking how narrative works *with* our
brains is defamiliarizing ourselves with what we think we
know about where stories come from, how they act upon us,
and what happens when they are over. For me, this is one of
those difficult tasks, like imagining the color of a smell or the
taste of a sound, that may be possible only through metaphor.
There are, of course, limits to how far any analogy can work,
but I have found aural and arboreal metaphors useful in highlighting aspects of Homeric poetry that we conventionally ignore. This book came about when I added a virus to the mix.

One of the things that always strikes me when I talk to
people about Homer is how rarely we encourage *readers* to
consider the way listening to a work of art differs from silently
absorbing it. As an anecdote from Saint Augustine's *Confessions* in which he notes the oddness of seeing his mentor Am-
brose reading silently implies, narratives of all kinds functioned
as scripts to be re-breathed into life in the ancient world.[14] This
resurrection of the word, moreover, was often not solitary. Authors like Pliny often had enslaved people read aloud to them.

Aural engagement proceeds at a different pace and cadence from silent reading; it activates different parts of the brain; it triggers memory differently.

When I try to think about this difference and how it applies to the way we conceive of epic poetry, one of my first recourses is to music, in part because Homeric poetry was recited and sung, and in part because music plays on the memory differently from the written word. Each of the Homeric epics is a song, but with an extremely long duration and of surprising sophistication. I started this introduction by invoking a symphony and its complexity. I imagined separate rooms populated by different musicians but said nothing about where their sheet music came from. I also did not mention that none of them had access to the total song and that audience members pieced a different song together as they wandered from room to room, guided by their taste, their memory, and chance.

We make meaning differently based on our sensory inputs and our cultures of performance and reception. The bias positing that oral literature is in some significant way "less than" literate work is rooted in our own cultural experiences. And it can change quickly: even a literary Greek like Aristotle saw a "writer" in Homer where he should have found a singer.

I emphasize song and aurality here because Homeric epic developed and flourished outside the constraints of a page. When a translator or interpreter tries to make sense of what is on the page, it is like a conductor looking at a score for a symphony written in a different system of notation, with many sections unclear. Because of the polyphony of Greek epic, it is charged with meaning: the lines of song exist through time and carry many meanings at once.

I find the music metaphor compelling because it recenters the importance of sound, helps us think about performance and the importance of time and attention. But part of what is missing from this analogy is the poem's ability to expand on its own, as a product of nature and cultivation over generations. We know that the Homeric epics we possess developed over many generations, under the influence of audiences in different contexts, and at the "hands" of performers and translators. Here is where I find an arboreal metaphor useful for rethinking and modeling complex relationships. If you can, get someone to read the next few paragraphs aloud. Close your eyes and listen.

> Take a minute and imagine a tree in a manicured park or private garden. Make it a really lovely tree, one you would notice and remember if you lingered on it a bit, one that has been well situated in its environment. Think about the tree's imperfect symmetry, the way it occupies its space. Has it grown in odd angles to meet the sun's changing rays over the seasons or in response to persistent winds? How deeply is it rooted?
>
> Now think about this: someone planted the tree; others tended to it and trimmed it; more people spent generations selecting this domesticated tree from its ancestral stock. Think about the uncountable hands that made this tree possible, the saplings transplanted, the varieties combined over time. What were their lives like? What stories did they tell? What were trees to them?
>
> Then think about the tree's beauty, its aesthetics. What makes us set this tree apart from others? What is essential about it? Our appreciation is based on other trees we might not remember as well as an entire "grammar" of human beings and the environment. Like any other native language, you

learned its basic syntax without trying. You have a
sense of the way trees should be. You probably judge
a tree differently from a shrub for historical aesthetic reasons. You have expectations of what trees
should do, how they should look, and how they relate to the world around them. For the most part
you are not cognizant of these assumptions. But
you almost certainly have different notions about a
shrub or a bush.

Now, if you have been listening, open your eyes, but keep the
tree in your mind. If someone asks you who is responsible
for the tree, what do you say? Is it the person who designed
the park? Is it a gardener? Is it the first person who imagined a
tree in the garden? Any single answer ignores those countless
hands, minds, and environments that contributed to the *tree-
ness* of this tree. It also ignores the salient fact that you are the
one judging the tree and that your gaze is shaped by non-tree
things: your body, your memories, your beliefs about the relationship between yourself and the world around trees.

I have found it useful to consider the ways the Homeric
epics are like that tree. They come out of a complex relationship between performance traditions, new technologies, and
aesthetics that are both products and producers of the same
song culture. The reception and transformation of this ancient
song culture into something fixed and reanalyzed as a text with
an author has shaped our own culture too. How we respond
to "arboreal" questions is keyed into individual psychology and
cultural discourse. We always simplify our interpretation of
where the tree came from because our minds are too small to
understand that we are part of mind-networks and our lives
are too abbreviated to trace time's larger sweep. We impose
simple origin stories on art and human products because it is

hard to escape our own single experience of culture and see how it works in the aggregate.

These individual psychologies are shaped as well by cultural prejudices I mentioned above: First, our search for meaning in the empty universe encourages us to argue that design necessitates a designer. Second, our system of values and credit under capitalism emphasizes the metaphor of authorship as an opportunity for creating and maintaining value. The two aspects are part of a shared problem: we assign meaning to the world we see based on patterns and human-mirroring things. We recast the pattern as a design and in that an intention we assign to authority and authors. So group activities that result in notable patterns are reanalyzed as communications of some type of an authorial intention.

In searching for "Homer," most people find what they want to find. (This is a point the Homerist Casey Dué makes regarding the invention of Ossian, a narrator and author alleged for the collected Scottish epic poems published by James Macpherson in the eighteenth century.) My experience of teaching, reading, and writing about the epics for over two decades is that people cleave almost painfully to what they believe about authorship and art before they really listen to the Homeric poems. This is also why I keep thinking as much about who is thinking about Homer and why.

The two metaphors I have mentioned so far are useful in different ways: the symphony helps us to re-center the aural nature of narrative and consider how much our experience of a given work relies on how and when we are listening to it. The metaphor of a tree or garden refocuses the question of creation and time. In this metaphor a poem can be seen as a cultivation from a tradition of work, relying on a genetic pattern that has been shaped by people over time, both intentionally and unintentionally. Neither of these metaphors, however, provides ways of attributing agency and intention to narrative itself. In addition, neither of these metaphors helps us see how the human participants are changed and shaped by the creation. As the literary critic Terence Cave writes, "Humans live in a cognitive ecology."[15] We change the ideas we engage with *through* language, but we are changed *by* it too. If we derive agency and intention from this relationship, what can we say about *stories?*

Suggesting that language should be at least analogically understood as a kind of living thing is not new. Indeed, it is a return to a somewhat dated and largely dismissed approach. As early as the beginning of the nineteenth century, the German linguist August Schleicher, who introduced the tree model to the study of historical linguistics, saw languages as having families and genealogies with branches developing and dying out. Although the tree model is in some way hierarchical, he also argued for language developing in many different places: along with similar hypotheses, his *polygenesis* theory stood against single-language ideas and in a way may have anticipated modern arguments about biological language capacity. Unfortunately, Indo-European studies developed these ideas alongside a developing cultural chauvinism: for Indo-Europeanists who followed Schleicher, such as Max Müller, evolutionary models of language *and* culture became favorite frameworks for explaining cultural superiority.

Of course, social or cultural Darwinism is teleologically compromised and looks at cultural change without thinking about power and chance. The complexity of culture and language is well modeled by a school of thought related to Schleicher's vision: organicism, an approach to complex systems that posits that their complexity arises not from one set of elements or another but from the reactions in the system. (This theory has been used in biology, neuroscience, and elsewhere.) And organic metaphors for language and language development are far from on the wane—instead, they are changing as general knowledge of biology and genetics changes too.[16] While the language-as-organism metaphor is clearly attractive to me, I am also interested in language's metastasis as narrative and in imagining the force behind the development and spread of some narratives over others.

The scholar Dan Sperber argued a generation ago that the circulation of ideas may be best described through what he called "an epidemiological theory of cultural representations." Such a theory, he explained, should help explain why "some representations are more successful than others."[17] In large part because of the first few months of the COVID-19 epidemic, I began to think of narratives as viral in a nonmetaphorical way, especially as I witnessed the spread and hardening of conspiracies and mistruths about the disease. I learned all too quickly in speaking to doctors and scientists, however, that viruses are not, strictly speaking, alive. And yet they develop, they expand, and they overcome by engaging and responding to their environments.

This book unfolds as a reexploration through Homeric poetry of the analogy of narrative and its parts as living (or quasi-living) things. Throughout, I emphasize a concept borrowed from organicism—that everything in a complex system contributes to and depends on the complexity of that system and operates on analogical rules with the other components in that system. Thus, language and narrative emerge out of and through human audiences and their responses, and reflect processes akin to their biological nature. The weak form of my argument is that this analogy helps us understand the complexity of meaning making; the strong form is that narrative has an agency and purpose of its own, and we are merely part of its environment.

1

Scripts for Life

From DNA to Poetic Formula

O ne of the most intriguing challenges of how we enjoy art—whether reading a short story, listening to a piece of music, or responding to a painting—comes from figuring out how it works. We are generally comfortable with the understanding that French theater from the nineteenth century demands different skills of a modern English reader than an article from the *New York Daily News*. Yet we too often ignore that our ability to decode even a simple piece of printed news is based on a set of competencies that include our language as well as the cultural information required to contextualize it. Our ability to listen to music or enjoy visual art is similarly shaped by our cultural backgrounds (including social status, religion, language) and individual experiences. In each of these cases, "language" and "story" are part of what we bring to the interpretive project, and yet the forms each takes are clearly not the same. And the interpretive process is more complicated than a simple translation. To interpret a thing requires historical and aesthetic framing, neither of which is always easily attained.

The language of Homeric epic offers a good test case because it differs from modern languages in its form and some of its governing aesthetics. It is a language that has metrical shape as part of its structure and an assumed associative set of meanings that can give each word surprising depth and historical resonance. Yet I think it is not qualitatively different from other languages in this respect; it is merely difficult to explain to those who do not know Homeric Greek (and to some who do!) what the implications and effects of this system are. So in this chapter, we consider how much Homeric language works like an organism on its own, with independent structures unfolding into larger ecosystems of meaning.

Homeric DNA

As I mention in the Introduction, what Homeric poetry is and how it works were the subjects of some fairly strident debate in the nineteenth and twentieth centuries. Among the many pressing questions posed are two I would like to highlight. First, the poems' language and content are at times internally inconsistent: the language presents very different forms from distinct dialects, and the action includes heroes who die more than once or events that seem illogical, such as a duel between Paris and Menelaos in the tenth year of the war. Second, since the end of the eighteenth century at least, when Friedrich August Wolf composed his *Prolegomena ad Homerum* (something like an "Introduction to Homer") and outlined all the problems with the origins of epics and their transmission, scholars have questioned how works the length and complexity of the *Iliad* and the *Odyssey* could be composed and transmitted faithfully.[1]

These two issues—the alleged inconsistencies of the poems and questions about their origins and transmission—were judged by many to be connected. According to this logic, the poems' aesthetic and formal problems are a result of ambiguous composition followed by faulty transmission. For some time, Homeric scholarship split into opposing camps of Analysts and Unitarians. The former used the new scientific approach to scholarship popularized in the nineteenth century to search for the original and oldest parts of the epic, while the latter used more holistic and thematic argumentation to advocate for the unity of the poems. The onslaught from the Analysts was so effective that by the beginning of the twentieth century most scholars saw the epics we have as imperfect collages, pieced together by performers and editors over time.

Many of these conclusions were driven by an approach to philology that considers any textual dissonance a problem to be fixed by human reason. It took interdisciplinary efforts to help people see Homer differently—in particular the development of modern linguistics and the beginning of anthropological field study in oral poetry. At the intersection of these fields, we find Milman Parry and his student Albert Lord. Parry was an American Homerist who went to Paris to study with the linguist Antoine Meillet. Meillet worked in comparative and Indo-European linguistics and had been influenced by scholars like Ferdinand de Saussure (whose theories I'll discuss below). Under Meillet, Parry developed his ideas about Homeric language as a formulaic system. His work with language demonstrated that evidence of formulaic composition was a feature of an orally transmitted poem. At Meillet's suggestion, Parry took his student Lord to study living oral traditions in Bosnia, where the two observed the local heroic epic tradition and developed their theory of composition in performance.

The difference between the way we think about Homeric poetry and other kinds of literature starts with what we consider the basic unit of composition, the word. A naive understanding of language sees it functioning the way some of us diagrammed sentences in grade school: each word is independently put together, with a specific grammatical function and a more or less clear meaning. But many words have special meanings in conjunction with others and are used in some conditions more than others. Contemporary linguists who examine conversations or discourses as a whole often consider utterances or phrases as the basic units of language. What Parry first identified is that words worked together to fill the metrical/compositional needs of Homeric verse. Later authors have noted that a line of epic poetry can fall into three basic parts; these scholars see phrases—sometimes called units of utterance or intonation units—as the true building blocks of Homeric poetry.[2]

The details can be confusing, and I suspect that a significant reason why oral-formulaic approaches to Homeric poetry have not gained broader acceptance is that they seem so different from what we casually assume is true for language. It is worth summarizing some of the details on the way to other arguments.

One of the significant features of Homeric poetry is the repetition of nouns with specific modifiers: think "rosy-fingered Dawn," "Zeus, father of king and men," or "horse-taming Hektor." A long-standing, albeit untested, belief was that these "epithets" were in some way mnemonic (used to facilitate faithful memorization) and thus less than significant when it came to meaning. Parry's study of Homeric epithets demonstrated that they were in fact systematic to a certain degree and connected to meter. The *systematic* part means that for the different possible grammatical functions of what Parry called "an essential idea" there were specific forms for different positions in the metrical line. So if we take the case of Hektor, the son of Priam and leader of the Trojans, we find a series of combinations of modifying words and phrases with Hektor's name for every part of the line.

To help explain this a bit: the metrical term for Homeric verse is dactylic hexameter. That means there are six feet, or segments, to each line and that each of these segments can be occupied by a dactyl (a long syllable followed by two shorts) or a spondee (two long syllables). While there are many scholarly "laws" about how words are arranged across syllables, the only mostly fast rule is that each line ends with a dactyl followed by a spondee: think aloud "shave and a haircut" for the rhythm. (Nearly all rules in languages are tendencies rather than laws.) The result is that lines are made up of phrases of different metrical shapes crossing those boundaries between the feet in various ways.

This description is a little opaque for modern English speakers because the rhythm of our language is based on where the accent falls in a word rather than the length of the syllable. I have found that music provides an easier illustration. Epic verse offers a performer six measures that can be broken into either two or three beats each, but with the same duration per stanza. So if you know musical notation, consider a quarter note followed by two eighth notes as a dactyl: the two eighth notes occupy the same temporal space as one quarter. Indeed, many problems identified by scholars since antiquity come from imposing a visual/literary model on phrases that developed to be sung aloud.

The analogy from music continues to be useful if we think about the relationship between the "measures" (feet) and words: just as in music you will find few compositions where the lyrics and the musical measures are rigidly aligned, so too in Homeric poetry words or phrases need not be confined by single feet. Instead, Homeric lines tend to fall into two or three groupings. These groupings often correlate to "sense" units, producing a noticeable aspect of early epic verse: each line of poetry tends to be a full unit of meaning. It may not be a full sentence in a modern sense but each verse does tend to relate a more or less complete meaning. (To be fair, a modern grammatical sentence actually turns out to be a pretty poor guideline for evaluating ancient poetry.)

The earliest ancient Greek was not written with punctuation, and modern editors treat the opening seven lines of the *Iliad* as a single sentence. But this "sentence" is made up of several ideas united around what is arguably the main goal of the opening verses: situating their listeners in mythical space and time and preparing them for the kind of story they are about to receive. Here is a translation that attempts to preserve the sense of each line (but not the word order):

> Goddess, sing the rage of Achilles, the son of Peleus,
> The ruinous [rage] which made countless griefs for the
>   Achaeans
> And sent many stout souls to Hades
> And made the heroes' bodies pickings for the dogs
> And all the birds, while Zeus's plan was being fulfilled,
> From the time indeed when those two first stood apart
>   in conflict
> The son of Atreus, lord of men, and shining Achilles.

From a simple grammatical perspective, this song starts with a command to the goddess to sing of rage; that rage then becomes the subject of horrible actions for more than three lines until an assertion is added that this is happening according to Zeus's plan. We end with a specific time-targeting request, further framing the rage as issuing from a conflict with specific participants. In terms of ancient Greek style, commenters often describe this compositional technique as *paratactic* (additive) rather than *hypotactic* (subordinating), and this has come to be considered a syntactic hallmark of oral poetry.

When relaying this information, however, I always like to caution that while the *constructions* may not be heavily hypotactic, the ideas are interdependent and linked to each other. (An outwardly simple construction in no way denies complexity of thought.) Even with the enjambments of thought in lines 2 and 5 (where the ideas are both grammatically and semantically connected to what came before), each line can make sense on its own. My translation here has intentionally highlighted the connectives that bring these lines together. While ancient Greek was not written with punctuation, it did have *particles,* small, somewhat untranslatable words that direct us how to "hear" the lines and communicate the interrelations among them. (In addition, ancient audiences had tone and gesture to direct their interpretation.) In a way, the enjambments show that while a base structural principle of Homeric poetry is the six-foot line, the narrative that emerges on the frame of this structure weaves in and out of lines, like lyrical verses crossing over measures in a song.

As someone who is passionate about the intricacies of Homeric verse, I could go on about even just these seven lines. What I want to emphasize, however, is that, analyzed systematically and statistically, epic poetry exhibits a complex character, but it remains a language for which meter or rhythm is an aspect rather than a restriction. Parry's descriptive presentation of Homeric verse-making eventually led to an understanding of a *generative system*—that is, a language whose basic architecture includes (and therefore yields) metrical shape and length as part of its structure. It was only after witnessing performances of singers in the Balkans that Parry and Lord developed the idea of composition in performance, but that is in part because modern linguistics was still in its infancy.

In the early days of Parry's theories, he noted additional features of oral formulas: first, he identified a principle of economy, the tendency for there to be only one noun-modifier combination for each idea in a particular portion of the line. Second, he suggested that traditional epithets were primarily *functional* in the language, leaving only limited room for them to have particularized or context-specific meaning. This inaugurated several generations of debate among scholars who rushed to embrace oral formulaic theory and those who saw the identification of such a system as limiting creativity, innovation, or authorial intervention. Many critics derided the oral-formulaic approach as a kind of poetry by committee or mechanistic explanation for poetic inspiration. From this angle, by reducing epithets to mere "ornaments," we were denying Homeric poetry some of its character and power. (Indeed, many epithets also have ritual and sociocultural origins that render their resonance stronger than an average word.) And many proponents of the theory did not bring interpretive nuance to the argument at all, focusing instead on "proving" the theory by rooting out every aspect of the language that could possibly be framed as formulaic.

Absent in this debate until the later part of the twentieth century is the centering of the audience instead of the performer. Later writers following in the footsteps of Parry and Lord, like Gregory Nagy, John Miles Foley, and Egbert Bakker, saw the dichotomy of function ("the traditional epithet") and meaning ("particularized" modifier) as false, born of the prejudices of a literate culture and an obsession with the production of the poem rather than its reception. Many of these

assertions, however, are hard to digest without a fuller understanding of Homeric Greek and modern linguistics.

Where did this system come from? Here is where biological analogies can be really helpful. I want to start with the
suggestion that the longer articulation of a phrase—or what
some have called a "unit of sense"—whether filling an entire
line or part of it, may function like a strand of DNA to which
each sound element (word, particle) contributes.[3] Each "gene"
(or word) has potential expressions, conditioned by the elements around it and the larger environment in which it is embedded. When scientists study gene expression, they explore
how the information encoded in a gene eventuates into something that that gene does. The genotype (sum total of potential expressions) eventually yields a phenotype (the traits or
characteristics we see). The possible genetic information of
DNA contained within the genotype in some way produces a
particular instantiation that can be called an *interpretation*. Ri-
bonucleic acid (RNA) molecules and other proteins can serve
to activate a particular gene and also guide how much of its
character or its function is exhibited. Expressions (transcrip-
tions) are shaped by three basic processes, including direct engagement or copying of the DNA, modulation or control
from other signals or factors in the biological system, and
epigenetic effects (non-DNA interventions that generally alter
the control function of other proteins in the environment).

In the case of a word in a line of poetry, the different
shapes that words can take given the grammatical context of
the line provide a good opportunity for analogy (a morphological perspective). Words are not just about their forms;
sounds also have sense. Semantics are at play as well. If we were
to suggest that in a given cultural system a particular sound
develops a regular and repeated basic meaning, the activation
of this meaning could be modeled as the direct copying of

DNA, but it is this simple only if we imagine sounds as having *innate* semantic fields. Instead, meaning comes out of an interplay of function and context. If we take the analogy farther, syntax activates and limits the functions of a word under the pressure of the rules of the system as environment might shape the translation (or transcription) of DNA. Consider a simplistic example: your DNA contains information that informs the shape and size of your body, but factors such as nutrition, exercise, and climate had an impact on how your basic genetic inheritance was expressed. More aptly for this current discussion, within biological cells the single-stranded proteins called RNA can modulate how genes are expressed too, suppressing or augmenting features in response to other factors. Any individual heritable element, then, to some extent relies on other characteristics in the development of its form. So if we return to the first line of the *Iliad,* "Goddess, sing the rage of Achilles, the son of Peleus," the shape of each word is motivated by the words' grammatical relationship: the first word in Greek, "rage," has its accusative ending because it is the object of the imperative "sing," and so on.

While we still need to account more fully for the interplay of semantics, it is useful to linger a minute on the question of form. Like DNA itself, language is incredibly flexible and adaptable, activating some forms and suppressing others, depending on the needs of the particular moment of expression. Different combinations of words produce different forms by responding to one another's traits in more or less predictable ways. To an extent, we might argue that the function of words—to encode and relay meaning—is in part intrinsic to their form and then expressed in part by their relationship with one another. Such an articulation, however, skirts the critical fact that this function cannot exist without external witnesses to recognize words' meanings.

Homeric Greek provides good material for this model because it developed over time across multiple dialects, picking and choosing forms as the rhythm of the meter developed. The variety of forms available in the Homeric dialect helps demonstrate both the flexibility of the Homeric language and also the advantage of using biological models to make sense of it. The Homeric dialect also developed across different Greek dialects and seems to have selected (or preserved) variants during its evolution that would not be expected in the same dialect. A simple form like the active infinitive (think "to do"), for example, has three or four different possible endings in the *Iliad,* drawn from different Greek dialects (*-ein, -men, -nai, -menai*), allowing for each instance to be expanded (or contracted) to fit the need of the line or unit in question. Verbs that have vowel contractions in later dialects can preserve them or not. Augments (signs of past tense) can be present or not. The length of the same vowel combinations can change depending on both position and use. There is also variation in case endings to provide different metrical shapes.

The entire picture of Homeric Greek is not of a system that was developed rationally but instead of an accumulation of features selected for both their rhythmic functionality and their sensibility to audiences. While many of the variations selected in Homeric Greek are not those common in later Attic or Koine (the "common Greek" of the New Testament), they are still forms which would be "legible" and grammatically functional for most audiences. One easy way to see how this system works is in the variations of proper names for three of the most important figures in Homeric poetry: Achilles, Odysseus, and Zeus.

As with the example of Hektor (above), each of these names has a full system of epithets for different grammatical needs in the Homeric line. Both Achilles and Odysseus have stem variations in their names that allow them to start with a

Declension of the Names Achilles, Odysseus, and Zeus

nom.	Akīlleus / Akhileus	Odūsseus / Oduseus	Zeus
gen.	Akhīlēos / Akhilēos	Odūssēos / Odusēos	Dios / Zēnos
dat.	Akhīllēi / Akhilēi	Odūssēi / Odusēi	Dii / Zēni
acc.	Akhīllēa / Akhilēa	Odūssēa / Odusēa	Dia / Zēna / Zēn
voc.	Akhīlleû / Akhileû	Odūsseû / Odūseû	Zeû

Note: nom. = nominative; gen. = genitive; dat. = dative; acc. = accusative; voc. = vocative.

short-long or short-short structure. Zeus's name is even more interesting: Homeric Greek uses two different stems for the name of the king of gods and men. Zeus (single syllable, long) can thus end a dactyl, start one, or occupy part of a spondee. This flexibility means that it is possible to have the names Achilles, Odysseus, and Zeus appear at nearly any place in the verse.

Throughout both the Homeric lexicon and its morphology hundreds—if not thousands—of examples of word forms appear that do not belong on the same synchronic plane, or are morphologies developed by analogy, or are archaic forms alongside "neologisms," or are forms and roots that occur only once or twice. Years of study leave me with the impression not only that such a system would never have been designed by a single person or group but that the only explanation is one akin to that of the variation and selection for function that occurs in the natural world. In part, I am inspired by models from parallel evolution where the same trait will develop in particular species under the right conditions. This, however, is not a perfect analogy, since for the most part scientists see parallel evolution as occurring in species that are unrelated.[4] Many of the variations acceptable in Homeric Greek developed from dialects that have diversified in a (relatively short) period of time.

What makes the evolution of this particular ecosystem fascinating is that parallel linguistic developments yielded distinct morphologies, yet the rhythmic needs of the Homeric line allowed these parallel developments to coexist. But any serious scholar of Greek will tell you that the system is not complete or wholly efficient. Again, thinking about evolution has helped me make sense of this. The process of evolution capitalizes upon the materials at hand (the genome, the ecosystem), and the process allows for whichever available traits in a system facilitate survival and reproduction within that system, even as it changes. The interplay between both the randomness of diachronic survival and the vicissitudes of ecological change can produce species that function well enough in their niches. This same interplay, however, can also yield less effective results and baffling vestigial structures (flightless birds, mammalian male nipples, the appendix). So our ecosystems tend toward specialization and economy, but they never really become fully efficient. When I look at the range of options in Homeric poetry, I see a system in which most of the forms have both rhythmic and grammatical/lexical function, but where the variety and history of the language leaves room for some doubt. One famous example of a "vestigial structure" in Homer is the digamma, a letter that had virtually passed out of use in our earliest examples of ancient Greek.

The digamma (ϝ, F) is a "glide" or semi-consonant closest in sound to the English "w" in *width* or *wine*. As late as the classical period in ancient Greece, some dialects still used the digamma, and it shows up in inscriptions, even though it fell out of use in most dialects centuries earlier. Certain words and combinations are conditioned by the sensed absence of that sound. In the first seven lines of the epic, for example, we have three instances where this letter's former presence still impacts the rhythm: words that have vowels together that would ordinarily be a diphthong (one sound) instead of multiple syllables usually once had a digamma (as in the trisyllabic *Aidi,* "Hades," which may have been pronounced something like *Awidi*). In other cases, words that once began with digammas will still not elide (that is, combine with or replace a previous short vowel).[5]

The digamma is an interesting case because its importance to Homeric meter was not understood in mainstream European scholarship until Richard Bentley (1662–1742) figured it out while beginning (he never finished) an edition of the *Iliad.* He noted many metrical "irregularities," by the standards of later forms of Greek, and demonstrated the impact of the missing digamma. Bentley did not have recourse to oral formulaic scholarship, but he did have the sense to see what was missing from a system. When I look at the "missing digammas" now, I do not see a silent letter function, but instead a series of flexible metrical "rules" shared and preserved as the digamma faded from use. In essence, it left a series of vestigial options in different situations, providing even more variations to an already flexible language.

A short summary of what I am suggesting is not altogether radical: the Homeric dialect developed over time by selecting elements from other dialects to fit the needs of its rhythmic shapes. The different morphologies possible in this system had to be familiar enough by analogies to other forms or sensible enough within the articulative context for audience members to make sense of them.

Epic Epigenetics and Ecosystems

The brief description I have offered has been more formal, *morphological,* than functional. When it comes to language, function is not merely the outputting of form; it is also the conveyance of meaning. What I find especially interesting about comparing language to life-forms lies in the potentiality of genes and words. Anyone who has cultivated plants or raised children knows that there is no guarantee that an extant gene will be expressed as a particular trait or characteristic. Some interplay of different genes in combination occurs, but environmental features condition development and growth as well as gene expression. Beyond the classic interplay between nature and nurture in a biological entity, gene expression is also shaped by epigenetic effects, those non-DNA interventions that generally alter the control function of other proteins in the environment. To cut to the chase: the morphological evolutionary model I have offered so far is incomplete without consideration of the semantic meaning of words. This meaning develops from an interplay of use/function and language's environments: its speakers and listeners.

Epigenetics as a category of changes that occur during gene expression covers both what happens during cellular differentiation and what can occur as a result of interaction between DNA and its environment. Epigenetic changes are not mutations or permanent alterations to the genes but rather distinctions in expression that might not be predictable from an examination of genes in isolation. In the twentieth century several definitions were developed for epigenetics, but a consensus has built around a definition that allows the study of epigenetics to include nearly anything that shapes the development of an organism beyond predictable changes in a DNA sequence. (Epigenetics has also been used to describe in psychological development the multidirectional relationship between inherited characteristics and social environment.)

Epigenetic effects are crucial to the development of complex organisms, but they have also been linked in humans to particular diseases. Epigenetic effects are considered to be behind the lifestyle choices (diet, smoking) that can increase risks for heart disease and cancer. While many scientists now recognize that epigenetic effects can shape heritability of disease risk, recent studies have also shown that trauma can have a transgenerational epigenetic effect on gene expression. This has been a particularly important revelation in considering the multigenerational impact of racial trauma and poverty.[6]

One primary takeaway from adding epigenetic factors to our analogy is that the potential meaning of a given word or sequence of words relies in great part on factors that are not characteristic of those words themselves. The analogical lines become a bit blurry with this next step, but it is a crucial one. If a sequence of words has a function that is expressed in a particular environment, then that environment must include the audiences within it who "decode" the words just as proteins and other influences shape gene expression. Audience activation of meaning is conditioned by a cascading array of factors including context, prior knowledge or exposure competence, and attention, to name a few. The more people who are involved in making sense of words, the more potentially varied and complex the meanings of those words may be.

When it comes to Homeric poetry, as I mentioned in the Introduction, audiences would come to a particular performance with other performances in mind, as well as varying states of knowledge or familiarity with the meaning of words and other possible usages. The performance context was charged in addition by its occasion and potential ritual implications and the words themselves were marked by their register: Homeric Greek was an intelligible but different dialect from the day-to-day language.

Let's return to the first line of the *Iliad* to see what difference this audience participation makes. If, as a reader, I consider just the formal aspects of the first line of the *Iliad* (in

Greek, *Mēnin aeide Thea Pēlēiadeō Akhilēos*), that is, its basic
DNA, I can make sense of the grammatical relationships
among the words. To do more, I need to have a rough idea of
their basic semantic content: Goddess, sing the rage of Achilles, the son of Peleus. But how much sense is there in merely
translating the words? A reader or listener who also has experience in the performance environment and the larger language senses a different potential in each word and through
reception and interpretation bears witness to a different expression. Each word contains overflowing potential activated
by audience knowledge and engagement in sequence. The word
mēnis, for example, is marked as "rage" only for divine figures,
consumed by anger over a disordering of their cosmos, as my
first Greek teacher, Lenny Muellner, argued.[7] The imperative
aeide in combination with the invocation of the goddess conveys cultural information about the performance, the importance of song, and the deferral of authority to an external
divine source. And each of the final names is potentially connected to a whole range of stories about Peleus and Achilles in
addition to possible wordplay based on etymologies about their
names. The full expression of any one of these words happens
in the minds or conversations of audiences as the lines are
presented in sequence and the character of each expression
changes by how much each audience member knows.

And, of course, the epigenetic effects of performance unfold and change over time: subsequent lines are shaped in reception by the words we have already heard, and what we think
we know about the song is reshaped by what comes later. In
addition, the conditions under which we hear the song, the
number of times we hear it or versions of it, and the people
who experience it with us all shape how we interpret it. If the
words undergo epigenetic effects, the series of effects and interpretations occur within what I think of as a narrative's

ecosystem. We might also want to concede that we have some of this backward: because we place the text first rather than the system that generated it, we see the Homeric poems as bodies and their words and traditions as genes. But the contexts that activated and shaped them may have been more primary in calling them into being. The analogy may thus break down usefully, helping us to re-center the context as part of the genealogy. Such tension may arise from biological confusion in genetics and epigenetics as well.

To pause for a moment before considering how this ecosystem shapes a story, I have argued so far that the basic building blocks of Homeric poetry are illustrated well by the analogy of DNA expression. This analogy can be useful in understanding language exchange in general. In fact, a great deal of my own attraction to this model may come from an early training in historical linguistics. When applied effectively, studies in historical linguistics can help us understand language change over time and the relationships among different language groups. The limitations of such study, however, reside in our unwillingness to see complexity and randomness. Language develops over time in chaotic ways, and diachronic studies of language are useful for describing how they change but problematic if applied to a synchronic example. Contemporary speakers do not often know where words come from or sense semantic shifts from one generation to another. Indeed, I now think of the difference between a historical linguist and a sociolinguist as like that of a person who studies prehistoric evolution and one who studies a modern virus. Diachronic knowledge can inform modern study and is deeply useful, but the interests and outcomes of the studies are different.

A problem shared by both approaches is available data. In studying languages historically we are limited by the evidence that has survived over time. When it comes to a language like the Homeric dialect, we have several dialects and a wide array of forms that have evolved into one functional system. Our studies of this system have been in part practical (how does the system work?) and in part historical (where did it come from?). Too many of these studies, however, have sought to establish antiquity and priority of forms. To my mind, this is misguided. Imagine if we considered the oldest DNA in our bodies to be our authentic character, rather than some element that has persisted over time, contributing in ways we do not always understand to who we are now. This is what it is like when scholars identify "older" parts of Homeric language and attempt to date poems relatively or in some way downgrade and privilege aspects of language by mere comparison. It tells us nothing true about the whole.

Language and Minds

One of the primary difficulties in accepting the linguistic system I have outlined so far is our limited view of how language works. Our notion of language has changed a lot over the past century, and I think the developmental psychologist Michael Tomasello gives us a good start when he suggests that "language is a form of cognition."[8] We can ask, fairly or naively, where the system came from and how it functions. But we necessarily have a blinkered view of language on a daily basis because we have only our own language use and individual reflections to rely on. As mentioned briefly in the Introduction, biological models for language are nearly as old as the discipline of linguistics itself. A significant subplot in the story of scholarship on language and literature of the past two centuries is how linguists have viewed the relationship between individual, discrete utterances and the larger "language" in general. This story has no small impact on Homeric studies.

The development of ideas about Homeric poetry happened both in concert with and parallel to modern linguistics. In the tension between Milman Parry's emphasis on function with the "traditional epithet" and the importance of interpretation and expression (in quasi-biological meanings) in the "particularized epithet" we may also find a central concern of linguistics for the relationship between a language in abstract, as a describable coherent system, and its particular uses. To recast the question: Can we see a language as a genotype of potential expressions that yield a phenotype we actually observe?

There are several approaches to linguistics that arguably echo this analogy. The idea of *langue* and *parole* from the work of the linguist Ferdinand de Saussure is an essential starting point. Milman Parry's understanding of language changed during his study with Antoine Meillet in France: as he moved from focusing rather narrowly on the compositional figures of Homeric verse to studying linguistics in Europe and then beginning fieldwork in the Balkans, his model shifted from the functional aspects of Homeric formula to the cultural and performative contexts that supported the technical developments. Parry's work with Meillet was influenced deeply by Saussure's recent publications.

While Saussure was at the time probably best known as an Indo-European linguist, the ideas explored in his posthumous *Course in General Linguistics* helped frame conversations in Europe for several generations. This was a rather mild counterweight to the historical linguists' tendency to genealogize all forms, but it pairs well with his distinction between *langue* (language) and *parole* (speech). For Saussure, *langue* is the potential product of the collective minds of a linguistic group;

parole is then the individual examples created in language usage. Langue and parole are ultimately both products of culture shaping the individuals who engage in the latter, and thus also producers of culture over time.

Saussure's work was tremendously influential on the Prague School of linguistics, on structuralism (especially the anthropological work of scholars like Claude Lévi-Strauss), and among postmodern philosophers like Jacques Derrida. Conversations in the United States, however, moved in somewhat different directions, emphasizing empirical study and psychology. In the United States a conflict arose in the twentieth century between psychological approaches to language (e.g., the work of Leonard Bloomsfeld), sociolinguistic approaches like those of William Labov, and the later, ultimately dominant work of generative grammar, led primarily by Noam Chomsky. Saussure's work is reconcilable with Chomskyan universal grammar, with some caveats.

Recent advances in cognitive linguistics have shifted some of these debates, but the terminology and the differences within the fields can obscure the general agreement on the model of an abstract, nebulous range of potential language activated and particularized through use. Remaining disagreements, as I see them, have to do with a belief in an essential language faculty as opposed to language as operating in the same parts of the brain and through similar functions as metaphor and imagery (here the linguist George Lakoff and the cognitive scientist Mark Turner are important). Where Chomskyan linguists might see some core aspects of syntax as innate and adaptable in use, cognitive linguists see a complex adaptive system of sensemaking that includes image, gesture, sound, and story. There are those who find a middle ground, of course, arguing that language capacity overlaps but is not entirely coterminous with other ways of thinking. In the cognitive cases, especially, we still have much to learn about the flexibility of human neurology and the fixity of neurobiological function.

My own inclination is to lean toward cognitive linguistics, even though it is abundantly clear that the *idea* of generative grammar has been an important metaphor and model for developing Natural Language Processing, while the insight from cognitive linguistics that language and meaning are *embodied* in our personal experiences, and larger cultural references will be needed to produce more nuanced and human-like AI language exchanges. Nevertheless, I have taken the time to start from Saussure's approach because his articulation is one of the first I remember reading that echoes what we think is going on in Homer. The notion of a generalized system that becomes particularized in specific examples is also crucial to the structuralist approaches of Lévi-Strauss and akin, if not directly related to, cognitive models that admit metaphor and embodied information into the discussion.

A critical distinction I would like to make between using biological analogies for language and some tenets of generative grammar regards its heritable aspects. While some evolutionary psychologists (and linguists) argue that human language has a biological component, meaningful differences can be distinguished in what they mean by this. It would probably be ridiculous to assume that our capacity for language has no root in our DNA, but the extent to which any particular aspect of language is biologically determined is unclear. If I may take recourse to a different (imperfect) analogy, language as we know it is more akin to a reprogrammable computer program, while our DNA creates minds and bodies capable of "running" said program(s) to various degrees of competency.[9]

But the most important takeaway, I think, is that language exists only conceptually across different minds, expressed into concrete examples that stand in a *part-for-whole* relationship to the whole. Following cognitive linguists, I believe that narrative exists in the same way and that the minds that engage with it should be considered part of the narrative ecosystem, where words and the stories they tell are "triggered" to deploy their meanings.

Swift Feet

To explore this larger, more abstract idea, it is useful to disaggregate again, to get back to the particular. Any word or phrase, as I have discussed, contains in its linguistic DNA the "genes" of its semantic range and grammatical function. Any particular aspect can change over time or be activated by different circumstances. The important thing is that words and phrases, like genes or strands of DNA, have a range of potential meaning until they are expressed in a particular context.

Let's get back to noun-epithet combinations and consider again the relationship between language development and use in Homer. As Parry demonstrates—and many others have confirmed—Homeric language used modifiers in part to create a compositional system within the parameters of epic rhythm. Over time, this system led to a tendency toward "economy," a habit of having only one way to say, for example, "swift-footed Achilles" in a particular grammatical use in a particular spot in the line. This tendency is not unique to Homer: most languages shy away from exact synonyms in meaning and use. We do not notice this economy so much because we are accustomed in the modern world to larger pan-dialects that expose us to local differences in use but again tend to reduce differences in favor of mutual comprehensibility. In addition, since at least the Hellenistic period of ancient Greece, the rhetorical style of Mediterranean and European languages in artistic and academic settings has tended toward variation over repetition. In a smaller, closed system like Homeric epic, as a result, we are oversensitive to repetition and economy.

A long-standing objection to Parry and Lord's approach to Homer—that a "formula" renders contextual meaning impossible or deprives the author of the ability to innovate—misunderstands both how the theory developed and how language functions. The case of the combination "swift-footed Achilles" can help illustrate this. The "problem" of Achilles' traditional epithet in the *Iliad* is the tension between diachronic meaning (or evolutionary function) and contextual use (or, let's say, adaptation). What happens when we consider the deployment of this inherited feature in the single narrative of the *Iliad*?

Achilles receives a series of epithets in the *Iliad,* but the first time he is invoked as "swift-footed" is when he stands up to speak among the Achaeans at the beginning of the epic.[10] At this moment, he intervenes on behalf of the Achaeans against Agamemnon to suggest a response to the plague that opened the epic. The phrase is repeated throughout his subsequent argument with Agamemnon and his complaining about it later. It even vividly stands in contrast to the epic's description of him as "raging while sitting alongside the ships, the god-blessed swift-footed Son of Peleus *was no longer going* into the man-ennobling assembly or to war, but he *was eating away* at his heart, staying there, and he *was longing* for the war cry and battle."[11] In Greek, this passage highlights the tension even more. Each of the verbs uses an iterative stem (that is, a morphology that indicates an action is ongoing, without end), whose force I have tried to convey with the English imperfect.

A simplistic reading of the epic would posit that "swift-footed" here is merely a traditional epithet; yet the accumulation of uses in book 1 and the contrast in this passage leave audience members with a sense of dislocation: Achilles may be swift-footed in his form, but in this context swiftness is of no avail.[12]

Achilles' swiftness may be ironic in the epic—indeed, many have wondered how his swiftness can be praised when he needs a god to intervene after he has chased Hektor around the walls of Troy three times in book 22. While audiences may sense this irony, it builds in part on the semantic range of the combination "swift-footed." Swiftness in the larger context of myth and poetry is a marker of physical excellence, of the type of figure capable of heroic violence. It is also, moreover, a marker of vitality, as preserved in the English contrast between the quick and the dead. Swift feet in particular indicate heroic physicality in the Greek mythical tradition, a fact underscored by Achilles' death from a foot wound and the way that a foot or leg mutilation sidelines some men from battle and often symbolically grants them excellence in intelligence instead. Somewhere within the narrative DNA of being swift-footed is its contrast with swiftness of mind. And as many scholars have shown, the *Iliad* and the *Odyssey* are deeply implicated in the Greek mythical exploration of the contrast between figures of intelligence (*mētis*) and those of strength (*biē*): Achilles is positioned as the quintessential hero of physical force in contrast to Odysseus, who exemplifies intelligence and guile.

One of the arguments I have made elsewhere with Elton Barker (*Homer's Thebes*) is that Achilles' traditional swiftness functions both compositionally and in acknowledging a particular tradition and a characteristic of heroes as insufficient for the challenges of the *Iliad*. This is why, we suggest, the epithet pops up so many times in Achilles' argument with Agamemnon: it enacts a disjunction between his heroic traits and the political conflicts that motivate the *Iliad*. Semantically, it may also resonate with his swiftness to anger and the brevity of his life, but at its core it echoes a narrative interest and strategy of the epic as a whole, which is to receive an inherited tradition, deploy it in a new circumstance, and explore the limits of its adaptability to a new world.

It may seem like a leap to imagine that audiences responded in real time to these semantic cues, but repetition within the epic and signs from without the epic tradition support the suggestion. And to be clear, we do not need to imagine that all audience members were sensitive to every cue for the potential meaning to matter. Broadly speaking, the language of swiftness resonates with concerns about the relationship between individuals and their community. In an early response to Homer, Xenophanes, a pre-Socratic philosopher, states: "Swiftness of feet, the thing honored most in all of man's acts of strength in the contest, could never make a city governed well."[13] While this passage reads now as a criticism of Greek elite athletic culture, it also communicates a shift in values from a tradition valuing a hero as swift-footed to one acknowledging swift feet as insufficient. Indeed, in isolation, the connection may seem tenuous, but a few other examples indicate just how deeply integrated the associations between swift-footedness and a certain kind of hero were.

The Spartan poet Alcman (ca. sixth century BCE) provocatively declared that he did not care about the dead, "Laukaisis, Enasphoros, or swift-footed Sebros / the violent one."[14] In the rest of the poem, he acknowledges—even celebrates— that these men, along with others, suffered because of their own evil plans: they transgressed the limits set for them by mortality. More subtly, in the *Odyssey*, when Odysseus tells one of his Cretan lies, he claims he had to flee the island because he killed the son of King Idomeneus, a man he calls "swift-footed

Orsilokhos, who surpassed all the grain-fed men / in broad Crete with his feet / because he wanted to deprive me of all the booty from Troy."[15] In this tale, Odysseus revisits some of the themes at the beginning of the *Iliad* and also echoes Alcman's fragment: the swift-footed hero is a figure of excess and transgression: he overreaches his bounds and disrupts order all around him.

Of course, it is difficult to make a positivistic assertion that when ancient audiences heard the epithet "swift-footed" in its Iliadic usage they responded with this interpretive range. Indeed, we can only state that it is possible, given the evidence of how the phrase functions within the epic and without. While this uncertainty makes many modern readers of Homer uncomfortable, what it indicates for me is how incomplete our understanding of epic narrative is without thinking more expansively about its audiences. To return to a biological analogy, it is like trying to make sense of the development of a single example of a species with only a partial fossil record and a limited picture of the environment(s) that shaped it.

Vestigial Meanings: Homeric Duals

In the case of the meaning of the epithet-noun combination "swift-footed Achilles," it is clear that any stark distinction between a traditional, conventional meaning on the one hand and a particularized, contextualized meaning on the other makes little sense if we center audience reception instead of poetic production. There are few aspects of language that are not in some way both functional and conventionally relevant. How different layers of meaning may be activated at different times, then, enriches our understanding. Not only are the potential meanings of an utterance shaped by the deep diachronic plane (the historical development and some total of uses), but they are also selected by the local meanings (how an item is positioned or activated in a poem) and curated in turn by the experience of an audience member interpreting the lines. Because there is always room for emendation and reflection, we have a truly complex picture: the interactions of three spheres of meaning, plus the adjustment that happens when the experience and reception of one audience member comes into engagement with another's.

The sophisticated and unpredictable outcomes of these engagements are in part why literary interpretations can (and must) take so many turns. It is also why biological systems provide stimulating analogies for the development of meaning: each element in an ecosystem has its own genetic and historical components, an ongoing engagement with other elements in the ecosystem, and a series of responses to the environment itself. Sometimes the possible myriad interactions cause earlier traits to be expressed or end up relying on surprising features. Sometimes structures that appear vestigial are simply less commonly activated; at other times, they might become important again in a new adaptation. I would like to introduce one example of this in Homer as a way of thinking about how latent features of composition (the function) and older patterns can be reused in the face of the challenge of making new meaning.

Ancient Greek developed from a language that had a full system of nominal and verbal endings for what we call the dual number. Generally speaking, languages like Latin, Greek, and Sanskrit inflect the endings of their nouns to show their grammatical function and number. We have some of this in English: subject pronouns "he"/"she"/"they" contrasting with pronouns "him"/"her"/"them" for the objects of the sentence. To add to the number distinction between singular and plural, both Greek and Sanskrit have a dual form to describe pairs of things acting together: eyes, twins, people, etc. In most cases the sound marking the dual is quite distinct: the combination *wo* in *two* and the long vowel in *both* are good examples of the vestigial dual persisting in English.

Classical Greek retained a limited use of the dual, and Homeric Greek preserves it here and there. The most striking place where it shows up in the *Iliad* is in the description of the movement of two heralds from one place to another. So when Agamemnon sends heralds to retrieve the captive woman Briseis from Achilles in book 1, we find dual forms for their pronouns and their verbal endings. It is very clear that the heralds, Odios and Eurybates, in this case are a pair and that the movement of heralds from one space to another is marked as a type-scene in Homer.

This introduces what I think of as the "three-body problem" of poetic meaning: the interaction of the conventional meanings of an utterance with its surroundings in the synchronic performance against the experiences and expectations of the audience. If we return to the duals in Homer, I am interested not in the vestigial function of the dual number, since this is truly still functional in Greek, but in how the vestigial functions of heralds as signaled by the marked use of a dual help to develop and highlight meaning in the poem we possess.

Let me start by setting out the problem. In *Iliad* 9, Achilles has been withdrawn from the conflict for eight books of the epic, and the situation looks pretty dire for the Achaeans. Agamemnon, at the advice of the elderly Nestor, sends an embassy to Achilles to plead with him to return, offering him compensation and further promises as inducement. Here is the passage, with relevant plural forms underlined and dual forms in italics:[16]

Let Phoinix, dear to Zeus, lead first of all,
And then great Ajax and shining Odysseus.
And the heralds Odios and Eurybates should follow
together.
Wash your hands and have everyone pray
So we can be pleasing to Zeus, if he takes pity on us.
So he spoke, and this speech was satisfactory to
everyone.
The heralds immediately poured water over their
hands
And the servants filled their cups with wine.
And then they distributed the cups to everyone
And then they made a libation and drank their fill.
<u>They left</u> from Agamemnon's, son of Atreus's, dwelling.
Gerenian Nestor, the horseman, was giving them
advice,
Stopping to prepare each one, but Odysseus especially,
How to try to persuade the blameless son of Peleus.
The *two of them went along* the strand of the much-
resounding sea,
Both praying much to the earth-shaker Poseidon
That <u>they might easily persuade</u> the great thoughts of
Aiakos's grandson.
When *the two of them arrived* at the ships and the
dwellings of the Myrmidons
<u>They found him</u> there delighting his heart with a
clear-voiced lyre,
A well-made, beautiful one, set on a silver bridge.
Achilles stole it when he sacked and destroyed the city
of Eetion.
He was pleasing his heart with it, and was singing the
famous tales of men.

Patroklos was sitting there in silence across from him,
Waiting for Aiakos's grandson to stop singing.
The *two of them were* walking first, but shining
    Odysseus was leading.
And <u>they stood in front</u> of him. When Achilles saw
    them, he rose
With the lyre in his hand, leaving the place where he
    had been sitting.
Patroklos rose at the same time when he saw the men.
As he welcomed those two, swift-footed Achilles
    addressed them.
"*Welcome* [*you two*]—really, <u>dear friends</u> *two have
    come*—the need must be great
When *these two* [*come*] who are <u>dearest</u> of the
    Achaeans to me, even when I am angry."

The embassy includes three speakers, Odysseus, Achilles'
older "tutor" Phoinix, and his cousin, the powerful warrior
Ajax, son of Telamon. The two heralds accompany them as
well. Yet the pronouns and verbal forms that describe them
move between dual and plural forms. The grammarian responds that this is incorrect because there are at least five entities involved here. Modern responses over the past century
have been:[17]

1. The text needs to be fixed, the duals have come
   from an older/different version of the poem that
   had a smaller embassy (with several variations).
2. The traditional use is imperfect, the dual is being
   used for groups. Some scholiasts (ancient scholars
   largely preserved in marginal notes to ancient
   manuscripts) suggest that audiences would have
   just used the dual for the plural.

3. The dual herald scene is merely formulaic and has been left in without regard for changes in the evolution of the narrative.
4. The text is focalized in some way, showing Achilles (e.g.) refusing to acknowledge the presence of someone he dislikes or focusing on two people he does like.[18]
5. The text is jarring on purpose, highlighting that something is wrong with this scene.

Ancient commentators seem less bothered by the alternation in forms: an ancient scholiast suggests that the first dual form refers to Ajax and Odysseus because Phoinix hangs back to get more instruction from Nestor.[19] Of course, this interpretation does not even try to explain what happened to the actual heralds who were sent along with the embassy. Yet the interaction of forms seems to give some support to a complex reading. The number and entanglement of the forms makes interpolation (by which I mean a later editorial addition) seem unlikely (if not ludicrous) as an explanation.

I have presented the responses in a sequence that I see as both historical (in terms of traditions of literary criticism) and evolutionary. The first response—that the text is wrong—assumes infidelity in the transmission from the past and entrusts modern interpreters with the competence to identify errors and interpolations and to "correct" them. The second response moves from morphological to functional, positing that ancient performers might have "misused" the dual for the present during a period of linguistic change. Neither of these suggestions is supported by the textual traditions which preserve the duals without significant exception and which show only a marked and appropriate use of the dual throughout Homeric epic.

The final three answers depend upon the sense of error explored in the first two: first, a greater understanding of oral-formulaic poetry extends the Parryan suggestion that some forms are merely functional and do not express context-specific meaning (option 3) while the fourth option, supported by Gregory Nagy and Richard Martin, models a complex style of reading/reception that suggests the audience understands the misuse of the dual to evoke the internal thoughts and emotions of the character Achilles in one way or another. The last explanation is harder to defend based on how integrated the dual forms are in the passage: the dual is used to describe travel to Achilles' tent, then the scene shifts to Achilles playing a lyre and Patroklos waiting for him to stop, followed again by dual forms with what seems like an enigmatic line: "The *two of them were* walking first, but shining Odysseus was leading." Ancient commentary remains nonplussed: Odysseus is first of two, the line makes that clear, and Phoinix is following some-where behind. Nagy's and Martin's explanations are attrac-tive, and they respond well to the awkward movement between dual and plural forms as well as Achilles' specific use of the dual in hailing the embassy with a bittersweet observation. I like the idea of taking these two options together, leaving it up to audiences to decode Achilles' enigmatic greeting.

Responses 4 and 5 are not necessarily exclusive. The fi-nal option builds on the local context of the *Iliad* and sees the type-scene as functioning within that narrative but with some expectation that audiences will know the forms and the con-ventions. As others have argued, the use of the duals to signal the movement of heralds is traditional and functional in a compositional sense because it moves the action of the narra-tive from one place to another. In the *Iliad*, the herald scene marks a movement from one camp to another, building on what I believe is its larger conventional use apart from composition, which is to mark the movement from one political space, or one sphere of authority, to another. When Agamemnon sends the heralds in book 1 to retrieve Briseis, the action as well as the language further marks Achilles' separation from the Achaean coalition. In book 9, the situation remains the same—Achilles is essentially operating in a different power-structure—but the embassy is an attempt to address the difference. The trio sent along with the heralds as ambassadors are simultaneously friends and foreign agents. Appropriately, the conventional language of epic reflects this tension by interposing the duals and reflecting the confused situation.

Most of the responses above except for the first two are valid from the perspective of ancient audiences. The first two explanations—that the text is wrong or the usage is wrong—either selectively accept the validity of some of the text but not that which they find challenging for interpretive reasons or assume a simplicity on the part of ancient audiences (and many generations in between). The subsequent responses, however, credit a creative intention rather than the collaborative ecosystem of meaning available to Homeric performance. In the telling of epic tales, it may well have been customary to manipulate conventional language through creative misuse; and yet if audiences are not experienced enough in the forms or attentive enough to the patterns, such usage would probably not be sustained. Audiences (like the ancient scholar) imagine Phoinix lagging behind, or Achilles focusing on just one character, or they sense the pattern of alienation and separation that makes it necessary to treat Achilles as a foreign entity and not an ally. So while the text relies on audience competency with epic conventions, this specific articulation also allows for depth of characterization in a particular moment: The final three interpretive options cannot be fully disambiguated. Although we may argue for greater weight to the typological argument—that audiences would understand the complicated marking of Achilles as a potential *enemy* through this disjuncture—we cannot dismiss the tension between that larger structural meaning and the immediate force of Achilles' speech, inviting us to see the use of the dual as a character choice.

It is useful to see this poetic interplay from a systemic perspective. A biological analogy helps us understand that this sequence of words, relying on diachronic development and the local pattern established in the text, offers a jarring use of a quasi-vestigial or at least developmentally rigid morphology to convey complex and ambiguous meaning. Audiences are the final part of the interpretive ecosystem: as they "decode" the meaning, the words and their story take on different forms in each mind, combining with and responding to the experience of each listener, yielding an expansive, multiplying ecology of meaning that reduces by turns as people respond to it, check each other's interpretations, and develop a shared understanding.

I worry somewhat that the metaphor comparing Homeric language to DNA is attractive because our language for evolution and the way we understand it have been implicitly shaped by linguistic metaphors. The word I have used so frequently in this chapter—*morphology*—is a borrowing first attested in discussing biology, not language. Nevertheless, a gap will always exist between the metaphors we use to talk about things and the things themselves. For me, the test of an analogy's efficacy is whether I understand something differently—if not better—than I did before. By resituating Homeric "problems" in an ecosystem of meaning, I believe we can better understand both their origins and why ancient audiences were probably not bothered by them.

2

Recombinations and Change
Ring Structures in Nature and Speech

I grew up in rural southern Maine, surrounded by pine forests that were only a few generations old. In 1947, York County, the southernmost region of the state, experienced a series of fires that destroyed tens of thousands of acres. The forests I wandered as a child were populated with trees that seemed immense to me, but were for the most part thirty to fifty years old, interspersed with the rare old growth and newer incursions made by logging. I learned to recognize the odd patches where newer trees had been cleared and a rapid growth of saplings emerged like an overgrown field beneath towering guardians. The forests told different stories of the impact of farming two centuries earlier, to the drought that led to the Great Fires of 1947, to the more complex relationship between renewed rural settlements and controlled logging. This world was both natural and human made.

Forests have stories to tell and are also in the midst of the telling. Most of us are familiar with the growth rings of trees, how time can be counted by the rings of a cross-section. It can be harder to see how these rings are part of a larger ecosystem, how the trees' bodies responded together to dry summers and winter snows. But a trained eye can begin to see the details. One of our challenges in thinking about the larger structures of Homeric poetry is that we tend to imagine epic as a singular object rather than a durative performance. By this I mean that we need to reconsider epic structure as a feature of time. Narratives unfold over time: if every measurable moment of this narrative time were more or less the same shape, then a structural analysis would show it to be something like the rings of a cross-sectioned tree. But as a narrative moves forward in time, it changes, adding new ideas and new functions, yet somehow must be contained in the same structure.

Epic—and narrative in general—encompasses more than single phrases or lines of poetry. Each combination of sound and meaning is joined with others to form the complex structure of longer poems. One of the chief questions about these longer compositions is how they can develop without the aid of writing and, in the case of Homer, without a single author to guide them. This question assumes that the appearance of design requires a designer. So a useful additional analogy from the biological world is the development of complex organisms from single-celled life. If we imagine for a moment that a formulaic phrase or line of Greek poetry is like a simple life form, examples from the natural world may help us understand the development of more complex structures.

One thing that emerges quickly from the comparison is that there are multiple pathways for movement from simple forms to structural complexity. And most complex organisms travel one of these paths through their lifetime: from fertilization to birth, mammals move from embryogenesis through cell and tissue differentiation into unique creatures. In recent years scientists have studied the development of multicellular organisms using advanced genomics. Genes that help single cells adhere are found widely throughout different species and are adapted for different functions as complexity increases. Current studies have suggested that multicellularity developed more than twenty distinct times in the biological record. Many of the same genetic building blocks end up being used in very different species with wildly different results. There are, of course, challenges along the way: individual cells must work collaboratively rather than competitively; cell differentiation does not necessarily follow the development of multicellularity. But differences in forms and function arise out of the interactions among genes, the environment, and cells under pressure to change.

A primary comparison I would like to draw is that morphology at a multicellular level is not necessarily predictable from an organism's base material; complex structures develop in large part in response to environmental demands. So if we return to thinking about epic language and what it does in the world, we can perhaps better understand some of its primary shapes. Epic has both compositional and propositional (or semantic and interpretive) pressures in its performance environment: its structures developed in such a way as to allow longer compositions that can both be articulated by performers and understood by audiences. To ensure audience uptake, epic also requires certain kinds of repetitions (both in the recurrence of phrases over time and in the reiteration of ideas). Repetition and variation are also important rhetorically: narrative aims to persuade. Drawing on natural models, we can envision a longer Homeric song as a complex, "multicellular" entity, made up of type-scenes and their variations, thematic and lexical repetitions, ring structures, and various kinds of doublets and triplets.

Complexity Without Design

The leap from seeing the *Iliad*'s complexity as being a result of
an organic development similar to a tree's rather than of intentional design requires first a recognition of its structures
and then an understanding of where these structures come
from. In his *Homer and the Heroic Tradition*, Cedric Whitman included a foldout chart of the themes of the epic, demon-
strating correspondences between ideas and problems explored
in books 1 and 24 and throughout, in a pattern that resembles
the design on a geometric vase. Whitman was not the first to
argue for this—previous Homeric disputes about the unity of
the *Iliad* and the *Odyssey* used analyses of intricate structures
and patterns to argue for design as an indication of a singular
Homer creating the unique *Iliad* and *Odyssey*. Some contem-
poraries were beyond skeptical: Frederick M. Combellack
suggested that "the cunning symbolism and subtlety which
Whitman finds in Homer are . . . almost entirely dreams" and
later added that scholars who see geometric structures in
Homer "have been unable to restrain their enthusiasms within
the limits of the plausible."[1] From this perspective, the design
detected by Whitman and others before him is a function of
their aesthetic assumptions and a result of a specific and targeted investigation, as if they were conspiracy theorists warp-
ing string and images on a bulletin board.

Yet in this tension we find again different implicit models of reading. Whereas Whitman finds structure because he
looks for it, Combellack refuses to acknowledge what Whitman points to as significant because he believes it implausible.
The latter's denial does not wholly undermine the former's
findings. In the Introduction, I used an analogy of a tree to try
to imagine Homeric poetry as developing a unique organic relationship between song and human beings over time. One of

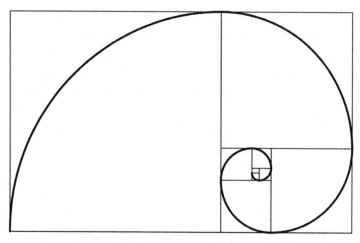

A Fibonacci spiral (Wikimedia Commons)

the clearest visual images I have from that experiment is the mirroring of a tree's root structures in the ground by the branches spread in the air: the doubling is functional (the root base supports the weight of the upper tree), but it is also imperfect: the branches and roots have grown in different directions based on the environments they encountered: rocky, uneven soil will push roots above the surface, just as a region with strong winds or specific sun angles will yield sparser or leaning branches. This image is useful for me in thinking about the way language and themes repeat in Homeric poetry and approach symmetry but deviate from it.[2]

When I consider the *Odyssey* from this perspective one of the important features of its metastructure is that almost all the significant plot and thematic elements from the story of Telemachus in books 1–4 are repeated in the rehabilitation of Odysseus in books 5–13. The resulting structure could be depicted as what some might call a logarithmic spiral. Fans of symmetry and order have long discussed the so-called "golden spiral" that grows increasingly wider for every turn it takes (and authors have seen this in early epic as well). I am not going to claim that the *Odyssey* is some kind of a mystical Fibonacci spiral; but I do think it exhibits a similar structure for the same reason that we find such spirals in certain galaxies and in mollusk shells: the structure accommodates growth within a general form—it serves to expand the function of the entity, rather than exhibit a particular formal aesthetic for an external viewer.

From Formula to Type-Scenes

The image of a mollusk's spiral shell can help us think back to Whitman's "geometric Homer" and Combellack's assertion that his intricate patterns are "entirely dreams." Imagine taking someone who had never seen the ocean to a beach to wander among the shells and debris. Given the fluid shapes of kelp, the deposit of rocks left by the ocean's movements, and the assorted detritus abandoned on the sea's edge, would it be entirely a wonder if our imaginary friend attributed some remarkable purpose to the shell or suggested that its shape was no accident?

In truth, the shell's shape is not an accident: it is a product of a cyclical process with potential for reuse. Human beings have found spiral designs aesthetically pleasing and have used them for adornment, inspiration, and even trade. As I mention in the Introduction, the case of Homeric poetry is different— as a product of human beings, selected by similar forces over times, it provides evidence of structuration from (1) the temporal restrictions of a performance that elaborates through expansion rather than subordination; (2) the rhetorical and cultural aims of a genre that responds to different levels of audience interest and ideology; (3) aesthetic expectations that shift but tend to rigidify over time; and (4) layers of alteration made by "editors" and compilers at different points in a text's history.

When Whitman and Combellack look at Homer together they generally see the same structures but imagine that they exist for different reasons. Combellack argues that epic's structure is necessarily a feature of its development and function: like the mollusk shell, it expands conservatively, growing regularly but protecting its form. Whitman sees its colors and history of use by humans and other species as well as how the form has itself altered the way its species have functioned over time and thus sees a different story altogether. The two rely on a different aesthetics, different stories about what form means.

What I would like to suggest is that Whitman and Combellack exist in a binary rather than a polar opposition. Combellack's approach to the shell tells us how it developed and functions against a tradition of arguing that there is only one explanation for its design (that there was a designer), while Whitman identifies complex meaning based on the existence of certain structures. The problem with this intervention, of course, is that Whitman probably attributed such complexities of meaning to intentional design as well.

In the Introduction, I provide a few examples of how complex structures and actions in the natural world can be grasped through an understanding of physics and mathematics. There are two important additions. First, accepting the natural order of design requires what we might think of as an aesthetic adjustment, shifting how we understand "design" and its purpose. But second, and more important, in the slippage between something having the appearance of design and being identified as designed lies the impact of human culture. Aesthetics are subject to an intense kind of circularity: we identify as beautiful or structured in the world objects and phenomena that adhere to previous notions of beauty and structure. We thus imitate the natural world in the creation of our own things; we appropriate the world around us, and we adapt it to our needs.

In a way, the mollusk shell's spiral tells a different story if we include human use and the impact of our intervention over time. The object occurs as part of a natural process, but we find its shape and near symmetry pleasing. We select for it. We attribute extrinsic meaning and value to it. We also do this with stories. This process is part of the larger narrative eco-system for an epic poem too: when we follow Combellack and worry primarily about the cause of a structure or element, we forget that audiences over time have privileged that object to give it different kinds of meaning.

Part of the hard task in bridging the gap between Com-bellack and Whitman described above is to learn enough about where the structures of Homeric poetry come from in a gene-alogical perspective. It may seem strange to compare an epic to a mollusk shell, but each is the product of multiple repeti-tive but unwitnessed processes. When we view their forms together, we are looking at things that exist *now* but have a record of their progress through time in their layers. Under-standing where *a* story comes from requires both an under-standing of where stories come from in general and the origin of the particular forms upon which any narrative is built. Natural analogies can help us think about these processes with less of an emphasis on authorship or agency.

When teachers describe the development of multicellu-lar life, they often present it as coming from four processes: the proliferation of cells, the specialization of their function, interaction among them, and movement among them.[3] If epic poetry has a basic "cell," it is the word-phrase combination; these phrases interact with their metrical shapes and their context to develop specialized functions, and so on. Above the level of the word, the phrase, and the line, people who study oral poetry have focused on what we call type-scenes.[4] Such scenes are a more complex kind of "cell," a building block that should be understood as contributing to a structure but functioning within it, like specialized organelles. Type-scenes are repeated patterns in what we might think of as conventional or repeated scenes: moments of dining, arming, onset and conclusion to speaking, and other kinds of near-ritualized performances, especially in sacrifices. Many modern scholars have seen type-scenes as evidence of what Albert Lord describes as "composition by theme."[5] These scenes can vary in length, but tend to present recurring actions. That is, they have a stock set of elements that can be altered to fit the needs of their narrative environment. As the classical philologist Sarah Hitch argues, type-scenes are like formulas: conventional material used innovatively through different combinations and variation within a specific pattern is the expected way to create meaning in an oral poetic context.[6] Type-scenes are made up of motifs and formulas the way multicellular life-forms are composed of individual cells: in each case the overall form can have a very different function from those of its constituent parts, and separate iterations of the "same" form will have different characteristics and functions based on their local environments.

Homeric poetry abounds in type-scenes, and they present enough variation that it can be difficult to see the pattern for all the changes. This is why it is doubly important to distinguish between compositional and semantic function, one occurring at the source of utterance and the other unfolding in its reception. One type-scene, discussed in Chapter 1, was the movement of heralds from one space to another, emphasizing certain actions (e.g., washing of hands) and relying on specific conventions (like the use of a dual) to set it apart from other actions. As Hitch explores in her book, while sacrifices are assumed to be rituals, and rituals are made up of repeated, regular actions, Homeric poetry shows rituals being adapted based on social relationships and the movements of the plot.

Just as linguistic morphology can be capitalized upon to serve both structure (grammar, prosody) and meaning, so too can thematic composition serve both structural and interpretive ends. (Indeed, it would seem strange if it were not so!) Such repeated actions, however, are often ignored as having merely structuring significance—that is, as moving us from one space to another in the plot, permitting a formulaic transformation that establishes a different tone and space for that movement (think of robots changing into vehicles in formulaic scenes in animated television shows), or as a latticework for the presentation of other information. In fact, type-scenes should be seen as flexible and adaptable multicellular elements of oral poetry. They are built from conventional language and they demonstrate a greater formulaic rigidity than other parts of the poem. Yet it is a mistake to imagine that this is all they are.

I have already shared some ideas about the use of formulaic language in *Iliad* 9's alternation between plural and dual verbs. This is, admittedly, an extreme case of adaptation, and it serves primarily to frame a particular movement and to set up the embassy in *Iliad* 9. Smaller differences, like vocabulary shifts in arming and battle scenes or a shifting in participants and detail in sacrifices, help characterize individual Homeric figures or convey nuance in the difference between the intimacy of a small group sacrifice and the performance of sacrifice in assembly.[7]

Another example I have emphasized elsewhere is a repeated scene of deliberation in the *Odyssey*.[8] A curious and frustratingly resilient notion persists among teachers of literature that Homeric characters have "no interiority"; and while it is certainly true that they do not present extensive monologues à la Captain Ahab in Melville's *Moby-Dick* to expose the inner workings of their minds, they do have variations on deliberations, or a pondering of options.[9] The narrative act of portraying a hero as having choice implies interiority in itself.[10] When Odysseus is trying to sail his raft to escape from Calypso's island, he is beset by squalls, high waves, and a displeased deity. Because the conventions of Homeric poetry rarely provide for the revelation of a character's thoughts, the epic workaround is for the characters to speak to themselves (or a part of themselves). The line that is deployed to do this in *Odyssey* 5 occurs four times and is followed by speeches that open with laments.

Here we have a good example of how larger composite structures are built of traditional parts.[11] Full lines of speech introduction and conclusion shape the structure of epic verse, but they also condition audience response. Odysseus's speeches, for example, are introduced by *okthēsas d'ara eipe pros hon megalētora thumon* (and then really glaring he spoke to his own proud heart). The first part appears frequently in speech introductions to characterize a speaker's anger, usually at social improprieties or cosmic disorder; the verb of speaking, *eipe*, is common in this position, but in combination with the preposition *pros* it denotes an utterance directed to a single recipient (as opposed to combinations that specify multiple addressees and onlookers); the adjective meaning "proud" can carry a positive or negative connotation, but in this specific combination it probably implies a nervous or overworking spirit—a surplus of emotions the speaker is struggling to address.

This same line of introduction occurs in book 11 of the *Iliad,* where Odysseus again stops and speaks to himself and worries about whether he should risk himself in battle: he fears being overtaken alone and considers fleeing, but restrains himself by reciting what sounds like conventional wisdom: "But why is my dear *heart* saying these things? / I know that cowards flee from war / and there is a great need for whoever excels in battle to stand his place bravely / whether he is struck or strikes another." Similarly, the same line introduces Menelaos struggling against his fear of Hektor as he protects Patroklos's body. It prefaces his working through his fear and concluding that he would be ashamed to retreat when so many others were standing still. He too asks why his *dear thumos* considers these things when he knows the danger he is facing.[12]

Given these examples, we can see a close interrelationship between the introductory line and the contents of the speech: each speech hinges on addressing the heart and on correcting its impulses based on social conventions or the facts at hand. In that remarkable sequence in the *Odyssey,* the formula shows Odysseus talking to himself and lamenting the situations he finds himself in. It combines the full line of introduction mentioned above with another formula often used for pondering two options ("but much-enduring, glorious Odysseus was debating . . .").[13] This two-line speech introduction—remarkable both for its combinations and length—also includes a three-word naming of Odysseus that focuses on his "much suffering" character. Unlike the examples in the *Iliad,* Odysseus does not ask why he speaks to his own thumos; instead, his speeches show him sizing up the danger, coping with his panic, and then deciding upon a course of action. This is a critical movement that increases Odysseus's sense of agency and prepares him to act in search of his homecoming, despite the privation it temporarily causes.

This type-scene has incredible potential depth available to audiences who experience it in sequence. We can imagine the Iliadic scenes of deliberation—or a shared exemplar—to be adapted to different circumstances in the *Odyssey* in order to showcase Odysseus's relative calm and reliance on his reason. Apart from the characterizing effect, type-scenes also build up the structure of the book. Such repetition in a short space with difference builds on the profile of conventional meanings to create emphasis and contrast appropriate to the context.[14] This kind of emphasis can only be inferred on the part of a performer by an audience member who notices those differences and interprets them within a frame that balances convention against execution: they need a manifold ecosystem for their fullness.

My point is that type-scenes are larger blocks of formulaic language that can be deployed and differentiated. They are structural features that can have significant interpretive range. If we miss out on this range, it is because we are focusing overmuch on their function.

Structure and Stance

One of the words for "wood" in ancient Greek, *hulē*, is also the word philosophers use for "matter" (the basic material of the universe). Yet as we know from modern science, a piece of wood is actually made up of different kinds of cells: the *xylem* moves waters and minerals through the tree; a *phloem* moves sap and nutrients; *parenchyma* provide structural support; and fiber bundles construct the walls. Trees expand and grow by moving materials through the cells, re-creating these basic forms, and building upon themselves.[15] To move from the individual building block of Homeric poetry to larger structures,

we stand first on formulas and then build a pathway through
type-scenes. One of the basic principles of Homeric poetry
pervading its structure and semantics is its metonymic nature.
What I mean by "metonymic" is that Homeric poetry exhibits
a *part for whole* correspondence in the way it builds both meaning and form. For some Homerists, "metonymic" indicates
the associative logic that organizes the telling of Homeric
narrative and myth. Metonymy often describes a part-for-a-
whole relationship, in which one element stands in for a whole.
We use metonyms as a part of everyday language: if I ask
someone to give me a "hand," I am requesting what the hand
represents, not a dismembered body part. Homeric poetry is
often said to be metonymic because of the way a bare mention
of a detail can introduce an entire narrative.[16] A small section
of either epic will evince structural features that will also be
operative in the whole, just as the themes of book 1 of the
Iliad return throughout the poem and help shape and direct
the plot that follows.

   One of the most significant structures in early Greek poetry is what many have called a ring composition. An idea,
theme, or motif occurs, other elements are explored, and then
the initial element returns for emphasis or closure. In the
speeches just discussed, the line of introduction specifies that
a character is addressing his thumos, and that fact is performed
during the speech itself. The line of performance redirects the
speech from emotional content to a weighing of factors for
a decision to come. Variations within the form allow for expansion of its components, or, in the case of Odysseus's self-
deliberation in the *Iliad,* compression and adaptation. Here
we see in smaller sections (ten to twenty lines) how features
that demonstrate the interdependence of structure, content,
and elaboration can be scaled up or "stacked" to create more
complex narratives.

The structure, however, also has semantic functions. Just as a formula answers the needs of both structure and meaning, so too do the larger structures beyond the line. It may help to describe the significant structures first. To start, in general, poetry like Homeric epic, composed and performed orally, tends not to subordinate ideas syntactically—it has an additive character as ideas are built upon one another. Of course, this is a tendency rather than a rule, but within this basic additive structure, performers can repeat and expand within the framework of that repetition. Such repetition is not homogenous: the linguist Roman Jakobson, in fact, sees building by parallelism as an essential way of building diversity within the appearance of uniformity, an essential feature of meaning in all languages.[17] In its repetitions and expansions, ring structure is actually a species of parallelism. It is especially useful because it is "scalable": that is, successive and interlocking repetitions can contribute to incredibly complex structures. When paired with rhetorical emphases like rising three folders or anticipatory doublets (discussed below), rings offer nearly endless options for varying, expanding, and contracting narrative forms.

Let's start with ring composition. Ring structures are found broadly throughout oral and literary compositions all over the world. The basic element is a mirroring in the way something begins and ends. A ring frames, providing opportunities for both structure and interpretation.[18] Such mirroring repetition helps to refocus or emphasize the beginning idea and invite audiences to reconsider the elements in between in light of such parenthetical reminders. Rings, of course, can be expanded with other rings within them or they can overlap each other, developing a complex latticework of links, reminders, echoes, and returns. The Homerist Elizabeth Minchin emphasizes that ring structures are a component of everyday

Cross section of a Papaw tree (©Wikimedia Commons)

speech. She argues that ring composition is an important cognitive component of storytelling. As the Homerist Erwin
Cook argues, further, ring composition is essential to how the
narrative helps guide reception. Cook explores five different
potential effects of ring composition: the enclosing of a section
of song creates a "self-contained whole"; rings can help anticipate the outcome of a section; information can be added within
the ring; the process of ring composition increases meaning
along the way, capitalizing on the paratactic nature of Homeric
poetry; ring structures may also increase what some have
called an aesthetic principle, creating pleasure through structural parallelism.[19]

As with most things in Homer, *all of these effects can operate at the same time.* It is also clear from Homeric poetry

that the emphatic function was known and felt consciously by performers and audiences. In book 9 of the *Iliad,* when Nestor is trying to persuade Agamemnon to appease Achilles, who has been sitting out the war since breaking with Agamemnon in book 1, he addresses the king and says, "Most glorious Agamemnon, son of Atreus, lord of men, *I* will end [*lēkso*] with you, I will begin [*arksomai*] with you / because you are lord of many."[20] After saying this, he makes a point about the importance of law and listening to good advice, before ending the introduction by saying, "Whatever begins hinges on you."[21] Note the play in the ordering here: Nestor inverts beginning and ending to start and ends with a reference to how things begin, all while embedding his chief message (listen to *good advice,* mine). This language of beginning and ending is common to ritual hymns. Similar phrases occur throughout the *Homeric Hymns* and in key passages of Hesiodic poetry.[22]

Ring composition binds, allows for expansion and interconnection, and provides different methods for emphasizing ideas. There are chiastic structures within complex rings (e.g., ABCBA) and variations that make even simple ring structures more complex.[23] The ring is, moreover, probably a self-conscious feature of Homeric rhetoric insofar as it is a regular structure of the speeches within the epic and is, as with the case of Nestor in *Iliad* 9, a conscious tool of emphasis in character speech. The metapoetic nature of the device—that is, the self-conscious use for specific ends shared by performer and audience—gives it additional weight, both for notice within the poems and for the implication that the larger structures of the poems share similar structural elements. The whole of the *Iliad* and the *Odyssey,* according to some accounts, are made up of various kinds of rings.[24] A central feature of ring structure is mirroring repetition coupled with iteration with difference. Ring structure announces a theme, takes audiences through different material that in some way relates to the theme, and then echoes that initial statement again. This second return, even if a perfect repetition of the first, is necessarily different for the audience because of the information they have received along the way. So, just as with formulas themselves, in larger structures formal repetition is not the same as simply restating an issue. The rings have a parenthetical function—they set the material they contain off from the text around them as something that is freestanding, independent. But they are more permeable than our punctuation: they invite us to consider how the *part* set apart by the repetition relates to itself and to material outside the ring.

Two similar structuring elements here build on the additive or "stackable" aesthetics of oral poetry. Paratactic composition—adding one element after another—may produce different expectations regarding the most emphatic element in a list. Where modern rhetoric among English speakers tends to assume that the first element is the most important, early Greek rhetoric privileges instead the final element. This develops in part, I think, because of the temporal experience of performance: each element in a list literally replaces the one before in space and time. In practice, Greek persuasive speech came to privilege rhetorical devices like the "rising three folder" (also called an "ascending tricolon"), which gives emphasis to the final element in a sequence of three by semantically and syntactically increasing each item.[25] Homerists have recognized this as an organizing principle at the level of the line; for instance, G. S. Kirk identifies a full line naming Odysseus as presenting an ascending tricolon: "god-born, son of Laertes, much-devising Odysseus."[26] In this line each element develops in length as well as in interpretive significance. Another example is the list Agamemnon offers at the beginning of the *Iliad* when he threatens to deprive another king of his property, "either Ajax, or Idomeneus, or divine Odysseus"; here again, we find an increasing syllabic weight or length to each element, with the final one receiving an adjective as well.[27]

Yet this sentence from book 1 is not complete, because it contains a fourth element as well. In the following line, Agamemnon continues and presents the lengthiest, weightiest element of all: "or you, son of Peleus, the most outrageous of all men." A rising tricolon may be attractive because it places a special emphasis on the number three or merely because of the length of the Homeric line, but it is by no means needlessly restrictive. Structures like this tend to end speeches for emphasis, but they can occur at different points and with various competitions depending on the rhetorical needs of the speaker.

This structural feature has ethical and semantic content as well. In looking at lists of friends and family, the Homerist Johannes Kakridis emphasized the rhetorical importance of what he calls "an ascending scale of affection."[28] This practice of early Greek poetry, to emphasize later elements in a list the most, is probably related to the ascending tricolon. But Kakridis emphasizes that it can be used to communicate values and relationships as well. In book 6, for instance, Hektor imagines his own death and says to his wife, "The pain of the Trojans does not concern me as much / nor that of Hekuba herself and Lord Priam / nor my brothers—the many good ones / who have fallen into the dust at the hands of the enemy—/ as of you, on that day when one of the bronze-girded Achaeans / will lead you off as you cry, stealing away the day of freedom."[29] Here we see how a simple rhetorical principle in one or two lines (a tricolon plus one) can be expanded to occupy several lines, providing both structural and interpretive gain. Hektor moves from those most distant to him (his fellow Trojans) through his parents and siblings, before capping the whole lament by turning to Andromache with two lines, and an inset narrative (as he imagines her taken into slavery). Note the variations on structure: siblings may be seen to be more or less close to Hektor than parents, yet they get elaboration where Hekuba and Priam do not. Here, I might even suggest that Hektor is moving not precisely in a scale of affection but also in one of time, as he imagines the end of his life from his origin (his parents) through his youth (his siblings) into adulthood and the present time (his marriage to Andromache).

Some kind of a correlative relationship exists between the length of the Homeric line, the paratactic nature of orally composed poetry, and the tendency to present arguments and lists in triplets. Here expanding structures and weighted meaning work together, as with formulaic features discussed in the previous chapter. Of course, triplets and tricolons (plus one at times) are not the only structural features that garner semantic weight. Doublets are also important: Homeric lines of action often contain doubling (see the repeated phrase "once they swore and completed an oath," and elsewhere in the *Odyssey*), and we find doubled subject phrases (e.g., "strength and hands").[30] While such doubling can be considered compositional and functional, just as with formulaic epithets it leaves considerable room for interpretation. Consider in the first example potential semantic differences between swearing and completing the oath or in the second one the move from an abstract to a concrete and the way the meaning together communicates the physical nature of the power currently being emphasized.

As with the tricolons, these examples of doublets in individual lines are echoed by doublets in larger structures. Many readers have found doublets in characters to elaborate and expand narratives: in the *Odyssey*, for example, Calypso and Circe are seen as doublets of each other thematically. A "narrative doublet" has been described as the repetition of themes and elements in a narrative, presenting different characters and events using some of the same motifs and plots. Such doublets can be local (two short passages) or more far-reaching (e.g., the doubling of the themes of the story of Telemachus in the narrative of Odysseus in the *Odyssey*). The philologist Bernard Fenik has seen in this structure a kind of increasing emphasis akin to what we find with the rising tricolon in what he terms the "anticipatory doublet."[31] Here we can imagine a theme or structure performed only to be repeated with additional elaboration and thematic weight. Such structuring primes an audience with a specific thematic template and then varies that template to introduce new meaning.

In our work on Greek epic, Elton Barker and I suggest that a version of the anticipatory doublet is at play both at the level of composition and at a broader conceptual level. In Hesiod's *Works and Days,* the poet introduces two kinds of strife: one (e.g., *conflict*) is destructive and bad for people while the other (e.g., competition) is productive and pushes people to be better. In scholarship there has been some debate about what it means for Hesiod to include two kinds of strife when he names only one in his poem on the creation of the universe (the *Theogony*), but we suggest that the two work as doublets: not only does the second position of the good strife emphasize its greater importance, but the second iteration qualifies its meaning and updates it.[32] In a way, this last phrasing helps us address the "problem" of strife being born twice in Hesiod: the conceptually later tradition is an update on the first. It does not erase it but instead adapts it and provides for new possibilities.

We also believe that the spirit of the anticipatory doublet animates Greek narrative on a macrocosmic scale. There is in Greek poetry—as in the lines of Homer themselves—a tension between traditional inheritance and the desire or will to adapt and innovate. This tension is productive rather than negative insofar as it exists within a competitive culture. For example, Barker and I return repeatedly in *Homer's Thebes* to additional lines from Hesiod's *Works and Days*. When the narrative tries to put its audience's world into some kind of a cosmic order, it explains that the race of heroes disappeared because of violent conflicts:

> Evil war and dread battle destroyed them,
> some [*tous men*] at seven-gated Thebes in the land of
>   Cadmus,
> when they fought for the flocks of Oedipus,
> and others [*tous de*] when it had led them in their ships
>   over the great deep sea
> to Troy for lovely-haired Helen.[33]

This is a clear doublet on a structural level: the Greek puts the heroes in binary sequence, "some" (tous men) the wars around Thebes wiped out, "others" (tous de) the war around Troy. The connection between the particles *men* and *de* can be contrastive or merely additive. Here the notional connection may be both: the first element is clearly significant, but by all narrative scale and emphasis the war around Troy surpassed those around Thebes. As an anticipatory doublet, then, Thebes and Troy are doing similar narrative work and can be seen in conjunction with each other, but Troy surpasses Thebes. Such a local contrast in structure and theme, moreover, can anticipate expansions in narrative as well, implicating shared themes and plots, and a shared, albeit ranked, position in cosmic significance. The effect is in part to make an argument (that the Trojan War was like the Theban Wars but more important) and to anticipate a narrative structure (one followed the other).

People who study oral poetry have long identified rings, doublets, and tricolons as features of orally composed and performed speech. Within these patterns, chiastic structures (mirroring patterns, such as A-B-C-C'-B'-A') add complexity and depth.[34] Studies have focused, however, more on identifying the features than on explaining how they work in the world (beyond their function). Returning to the framework of a continued debate between Combellack and Whitman can help us summarize and contextualize the relationship between structure and interpretation in Homer. Combellack, focusing on the compositional side of oral poetry, emphasizes that the structures we see are a result of the functional needs of a poet composing in (or near) the time of performance. The rings are features of emphasis and reminding, while doublets are a local way of sustaining, contrasting, and elevating topics and themes. Whitman looks at the larger structure and the relationship between thematic ring structures and repetitions and sees sophisticated—if not quasi-mystical—design and meaning. One might imagine Combellack retorting, not without reason, that Whitman is projecting onto the poem anachronistic expectations and aesthetics, and mistaking mechanical functions for clever design and ambiguity for allegory. While Combellack would certainly be right about Whitman's near-maniacal identification of subtle structure, he is fundamentally wrong about what the *appearance* of structure means.

Modern readers who looked for evidence of structure and design on the order of a Vergil or Dante in Homer have been frustrated and have either reached to identify repeated motifs and forms the way Whitman does or insisted that any identification of such is hallucinatory, following Combellack. Those who have tried to "fix" Homeric poetry to make it align with literate expectations look for human-made products to be

clearly so, to contrast with nature, like an Ionic temple standing squared and finely tooled against a wild landscape. But the
poems themselves show a structural growth that is accumula-
tive and spiraling. It is a naturalistic composition adapted to
the ecosystem of its performance in which audiences respond
to the structure and give it meaning.

Reading Meaning into the World

When we look at a mature plant or a full-grown animal, we
see a snapshot of its development and cannot fully grasp the
growth and series of changes that produced it over time. Replication and iteration are crucial to development and function.
Repetition is often viewed from a literary perspective as a naive
or simple device, yet it is an essential structuring feature of life:
from the micro-repetitions of a living body as it respirates and
regenerates to the larger "circles of life" that structure generations, repetition patterns time. In discussing the structures of
epic poetry in this chapter I have several times referred to their
potential impact on audiences without moving beyond bare
speculation. I have just suggested that an almost naturally occurring structure was integrated into epic poetry at every level
because audiences respond to it. I would like to close this chapter by exploring *why* this might be the case.

Recall my assertion that epic poetry has an essentially
metonymic quality. This quality operates in the domains of
both structure and meaning. So a single word or phrase can
evoke an entire world of meaning, while a structure—as in the
anticipatory doublet from Hesiod's *Works and Days* mentioned above—can anticipate both a larger structure of which
it is a part and a conceptual relationship of narratives or traditions that are being posed in an analogous relationship. For

me, then, repeated structures within epic can tell us something about the nature of the whole.

Let's return to the parenthetical structures mentioned earlier. One of the things I emphasized in discussing ring composition is how repetition sets apart a section of the epic as a thematic unit that exhibits some kind of completeness: ringed structures make propositions, they tell stories, they attempt speech acts such as persuasion and praise. But these rings are also part of the paratactic structure of epic poetry: they accumulate and advance meaning as they progress, and they invite audiences to compare the demarcated part with other sections and the larger whole.

Ring compositions are not the only structures or devices that create such subsidiary "epic pieces." In fact, so many structures exist for "chunking" epic into smaller pieces that more of each epic is bounded parenthetically than is not. Lines of speech introduction and conclusion, for example, help us transition into direct speech and out of it from narrative while also providing some information on how the speech is intended and received (or is *to be* received). These parenthetical structures have the important compositional function of framing and then demarcating direct speech from narrative, but they have also developed a cooperative function of inviting audiences to think about the characteristics of the speech in a particular way. Similarly, similes are bounded by "just as" and "just so" statements that separate narrative or speech from comparison, directing audiences to follow through the comparison at both its beginning and end. And as we will discuss in Chapter 5, these comparisons are rarely 1:1 and perfectly clear; they often shift and move from one element inside the simile (a vehicle) to a different corresponding element outside the simile (the tenor).

Is there anything that unites these framing strategies, and if so, what can it tell us about the aesthetics and reception of Homeric epic? In the shifts and interpretive demands put on audiences by narrative structures, speeches, and similes alike I see an echo, if not a confirmation, of a model of reading explored by Mark Turner in his book *The Literary Mind*. As Turner describes, when we hear (or read) a story, we do not actually experience the narrative created by the teller of the tale. Instead, the story unfolds in a cognitive blend in a space between the world of the narrative and the reader's mind. Narrative, the literary critic Paul Armstrong suggests, "help[s] the brain negotiate the never-ending conflict between its need for pattern, synthesis, and constancy and its need for flexibility, adaptability, and openness to change."[35] From this perspective, story is the instrument by which we make sense of our experiences, expectations, and current events. When we hear a story, we fill in details that are not expressed, but we are also guided in understanding the plot and its themes by our own experiences. When we hear narratives together in group settings, we each construct our own notional blend, one we adapt and shift as we reflect on it together. So not only is the "same" story not actually the same for different people, but the "same" story is different for the same person over time.[36]

The parenthetical framing strategies I have discussed all similarly mark the movement from a more concrete space to a blended one, from a simpler narrative to an invitation to make connections, to provide details, to experiment in the blended space between self and story. This happens within epic through mimetic speeches and challenging similes, but we can see characters engage in reading meaning into the world when discussing omens or experimenting with telling stories themselves. If we follow the *part-for-whole* structure of epic itself, then the interpretive invitation of a speech or a simile is in part a model

for the relationship between the audience and the whole
poem. Characters in the poem model anticipating responses
to speeches, encountering misinterpretations, and trying to
use narrative to understand their world; similes invite us as
readers outside the poem to compare the action of the narrative to different worlds and imagery. The process of witnessing the former and then engaging in the latter, I believe, helps
train audiences in the iterative and ambiguous task of applying epic narratives to the worlds around us.

To be clear, I am arguing that epic poetry provides models for its own interpretation within it—not as a clever puzzle
for audiences to decipher but as an outgrowth of its development over time. This structure, moreover, is not home to epic
poetry alone. Indeed, I think we find it as a central compositional principle of early Greek poetry, even when it is not explicit. Consider a famous example from lyric poetry, Sappho's
fragment 16 (composed around the sixth century BCE):

> Some say a force of horsemen, some say infantry
> and others say a fleet of ships is the loveliest
> thing on the dark earth, but I say it is
> the one you love.
> It is altogether simple to make this understood,
> since she whose beauty outmatched all,
> Helen, left her husband,
> a most noble man,
> And went sailing to Troy
> Without a thought for her child and dear parents.
> [Love] made her completely insane
> And led her astray.
> This reminds me of absent Anaktoria.
> I would rather watch her lovely walk
> and see the shining light of her face

than Lydian chariots followed by
infantrymen in arms.[37]

The poem starts out with a narrative conceit of an imagined
debate, at some level communicating the ancient equivalent of
"different strokes for different folks." The first four lines have
at times been characterized as being about poetic topics and
genres: talking about love, the argument goes, is the function
of lyric, while horsemen and cavalry are about war. Then the
speaker moves from the debate about the relative nature of
beauty and passion to a point of comparison from myth: Helen
chose her love for Paris over all else. The narrator closes the
comparison after twelve lines to turn back to her narrative
world, comparing Anaktoria both to Helen and to the "loveli-
est thing[s]" on the dark earth.

The striking poem offers a couple of important points
about parenthetical thinking and the cognitive blend. Note
how a structural ring that starts in the narrator's projected
"real world" circles around the world of myth. But as we move
from the outside in, then to the outside again, the narrator
accumulates detail: the world of myth "contaminates" the external world: Sappho (the narrator) is Helen, but Anaktoria is
Helen too, standing amid the Lydian chariots and infantrymen. The move from inside the myth back to the framing device is made through the self-conscious "this reminds me
of . . ." The resulting concatenation of myth detail with the narrative frame *performs* for the audience the kind of cognitive
blending that Turner suggests occurs in the reading of literature. Sappho's narrator is at once a singer commenting on the
relativity of beauty *and also* a besotted lover who sees in the
world of myth the longing and force of her own experiences.
As audience members witnessing this process, we recombine
the details, starting at first in the debate about beauty, then

trying to unpack and understand the jump to talking about Helen before moving all too quickly to follow the narrator's logic and blending in the closing sentiment.

Similar structures and interpretive challenges exist throughout Greek poetry, from the praise-songs of Pindar (a Theban composer of victory odes who lived in around the fifth century BCE) through the complex mirroring on the Greek tragic stage. And blending from lives outside the narrative shapes the stories that are told as well. Consider the long story that Phoinix tells Achilles in book 9 of the *Iliad*. When Phoinix arrives, he is trying to persuade Achilles to return to battle, and he recites the tale of the Calydonian boar hunt. But he frames this story with reference to Achilles: he says that it is right for a person to listen to the pleas of those who are dear to him, "just as we have learned previously from the famous stories of heroic men [*klea andrōn*] / whenever intense anger overtakes someone."[38] In doing so, Phoinix echoes the narrative's presentation of Achilles earlier, where it depicts him as singing through the klea andrōn to himself as the embassy approaches *and* it engages with the thematic situation at hand.[39]

The story that Phoinix tells, however, thoroughly twists the narrative of the Calydonian boar hunt. Traditionally, the tale is one of heroes banding together to kill a massive boar, devolving into a conflict over the spoils when Meleager, the young prince of the city, tries to give the boar's hide to the heroine Atalanta. In rage, Meleager's mother, Althaia, destroys a log that is connected to Meleager's life force, resulting in his death. In Phoinix's story, Meleager sits out the conflict until even his wife, Kleopatra—a clear inversion of Patroklos's name—asks him to join the battle. According to Phoinix, Meleager ignored the promises of gifts, had to fight anyway, and ended up laboring without recompense. Phoinix ends by urging Achilles to "think about this," warning him that he too will end up fighting without honor. Achilles replies that he does not care about the gifts and threatens to leave for home the following morning.[40]

Phoinix frames his narrative with explicit invitations to make comparisons between the experiences of his addressee and that of the central character in his story. He offers a specific interpretation that Achilles rejects because Achilles is taking a *different* lesson from the narrative (to stay out of battle because *he does not want* the goods or the social obligations they imply). This exchange, then, features both how storytellers adapt stories to the experiences of the audiences and also how audiences misread or reread the stories through their own perspectives.

The basic analogy I have offered of the movement from single cell to multicellular life is useful in helping explain the morphology of Homeric epic (its composition) and the appearance of design. The attractiveness of this analogy, of course, relies in part on the pervasiveness of metaphors about complexity and structure in a culture informed by scientific discourse, but only to a limit. The imaginary continued debate between the scholars Whitman and Combellack is a bit of a distraction because both authors equate complexity with design. Exploring the biological analogy shows that it is not strictly necessary to do so.

The structure of a cell or a song like Sappho's fragment is given value through observation; and this observation is often distantly secondary to the processes that created the structure. By looking at the larger context that conditions these structures—the biological ecosystem for a life-form or the fuller performance context over time for a poem—we can see the interrelationship between form and functions and begin to imagine how they might develop without intention.

But development without intention is not the same as preservation or survival. The model of the narrative ecosystem discussed in the previous chapter helps us to understand repeated structures. Repetitions in ring structures and the additive emphasis in doublets (and triplets) emerge in a narrative ecosystem that includes audiences who respond to rings and doublets and who may be conditioned in part to expect them. Rather than being incidental, these framing devices both imply that the task of poetic narrative is to prompt comparison and also reflect the deep connection between epic narrative's structure and its purpose. The living fabric of Homeric narrative anticipates and models its own uses. But this does not mean that it is successful in anticipating what happens after its story ends.

3
Crabs and the Monomyth
Parallel Evolutions and Mythical Patterns

Thus far I have been preparing a picture of how language and story develop together. One of the limits of this step-by-step presentation is that the overarching argument—that *narrative* functions analogously to a living thing—can get lost. Nevertheless, the risk of losing the thread is equal to the benefit of returning to pick it up again, as if in a ring structure examining what was said before in light of what has in the meantime been learned. In addition, laying out the foundations of language, structure, and the collaborative nature of meaning is necessary if we accept the basic proposition that the traits of language and human cognition that make us susceptible to—if not wholly dependent upon—narrative operate on multiple levels of form and function.

A second risk of my approach is that readers might get the impression that my arguments apply for the most part only to Homeric poetry. But if we look at patterns in stories, we can expand the focus from the Homeric poems. I am less specifi-

cally concerned with Homeric language than with the larger
categories in which epic takes part: heroic myth and narrative
in the broader culture of the eastern Mediterranean. These
categories move us from something more or less concrete to
more abstract patterns. Some concepts from parallel and convergent evolution will help us think about common structures
in myth and consider "genetic" relationships between the Homeric epics and the Gilgamesh poems, as well as the so-called
Greek Miracle.

Narrative Patterns: The Hero

Human minds lean on patterns to think, yet in our daily lives
we tend to overemphasize exceptions and aberrations. We are
also somewhat conditioned to attribute meaning and significance to pattern and repetition alike. Academic study is by no
means immune to this, and stories receive a lot of attention:
Google "TV Tropes" for a brief introduction into our continuing obsession with common themes and morphologies.

Certain patterns emerge as dominant in our cultural
narratives. If you have noticed that characters like Luke Sky-
walker (from *Star Wars*), cinematic versions of Peter Parker
(from *Spider-Man*), and Neo (from *The Matrix*) move their way
through rather similar plots, you have identified something of
the cultural immanence of the "monomyth," a term coined by
Joseph Campbell, most famously articulated in his *Hero with
a Thousand Faces*.[1] Campbell's book was, in fact, a significant
influence on George Lucas, the director of *Star Wars,* yet its
ideas have developed from many different places. At the core
of the argument about the monomyth is the observation that
a certain narrative pattern can be seen developing in many different places surrounding what we now often call a hero. Yet
central to the process of identifying tropes is dissecting a

functional narrative and examining its parts, as if taking a
living story and subjecting it to a kind of analytical death.[2]

Anyone who has read or studied myth to some extent
can understand the attraction of the monomyth: it explains
with near-magical success a wide array of repeated narrative
structures. Indeed, identifying similar plot patterns in heroic narrative appears to be as old as literary criticism itself:
Aristophanes, the fifth-to-fourth-century BCE Athenian comic
poet, mocks the heroic *katabasis* (trip to the underworld and
back) in his *Frogs,* and Aristotle identifies specific heroic arcs
for comedy and tragedy in the *Poetics.* Campbell's work, however, builds on the more recent observations of scholars like
Lord Raglan and Vladimir Propp, who noted common traits
in legends and folklore. Propp, especially, worked in the tradition of linguists and anthropologists like Lévi-Strauss and
Saussure, examining myth for common traits and morphologies to help explain how narrative worked. For folklorists and
anthropologists, examining shared narrative patterns is in part
about uncovering a grammar of narrative to assist in comparing different cultures and stories more effectively. One difficulty I have with work like Campbell's is that in emphasizing
the manifold stages of his vision of the monomyth he dimin-
ishes differences in the variations. Yet these differences are
crucial to understanding how and why the stories functioned
in their own contexts. The monomyth is in a way like a distil-
lation of many similar narratives into reconstructed DNA—
it rushes to shared origins without appreciating the living
species.

The broader intellectual work that supports Campbell's
approach is rooted in a kind of universalism that takes the
human context of storytelling more seriously. Another influential folklorist was Otto Rank. Rank's *Myth of the Birth of the
Hero* comments on common traits in the birth narratives of

all heroic figures, noting things like their birth to distinguished parents, strange sexual activities before a hero's birth, challenges due to prophecy, the dislocation of the child from his rightful social place, and so on. Moving on, Rank examines the stories of heroes like Moses, Oedipus, Jesus, Gilgamesh, and Herakles. As a practicing psychoanalyst, like Freud, Rank emphasizes the importance of therapy for helping people address their experiences to unlearn destructive ways of thinking. For Rank—and Freud—heroic myth was useful in helping us explore shared limitations from traumatic experiences like birth and growing up. Myth, in the Freudian sense, is evidence of a collective unconscious, exploring our anxieties and fears. For Carl Jung, the heroic pattern is a framework for various archetypes in the story of a lifetime.

These different approaches to heroic patterns share an emphasis on separable features of stories, the assumption that the members or elements of tales could be mixed and matched, and a basic assumption of their universality with an inconsistent consideration of how the stories functioned in specific contexts and how their function as discourse—connected to social and political power—contributes to their overrepresentation in certain genres. But how do we explain how closely their structures resemble each other?

Evolution and Convergences

Common cross-cultural features in words, rituals, and social structures often invite speculation regarding their origins. Observed parallels between two narratives—a device, motif, or plot point—elicit speculations about their cause: did one thing influence the other, is there some exemplar to which they are both responding, or is there another way to approach the problem? One of the principles that I have been emphasizing is that many of the literary elements in Homer can be seen as a product of the relationship between inherited forms and their context, advocating for the importance of the larger linguistic or narrative ecosystem. If context is critical to giving shape to every part of an epic poem, then it is likely that similar contexts will yield poems with similar shapes. Our habitual search for original articulations and authenticity, however, often prevents us from thinking about parallels in this way.

This is another issue for which a biological analogy can be especially useful. When as a graduate student I first thought about the problem(s) of cultural transmission, I used a somewhat inflexible and naive dichotomy of universalism (shared cultural traits are due to universal human characteristics) versus priority (temporal priority of a shared trait may imply direct or indirect influence) to talk about the relationship between common themes in the *Iliad* and the Gilgamesh poems.[3] This approach responds in part to cultural values that prize the new or original as authentic and the variant or inherited as somehow derivative. Thinking about even specific cultural similarities, however, such as the contents of two different poetic traditions, stands to benefit from some critical distinctions from modern evolutionary theory. The difference—and, indeed, interplay—between parallel and convergent evolution, for example, provides some important distinctions. Convergent evolution is when unrelated species with equivalent morphologies develop similar traits over time, whereas parallel evolution is when related but separate species develop similar traits unknown in their shared ancestor. A common example of convergent evolution is the wings of bats and insects: similar adaptations for flight evolved from different morphological roots. Old and New World monkeys are often offered as an example of parallel evolution: they descend from a shared ancestor, they were separated on distant continents for thousands of years, yet they still developed along common lines. Both frameworks ask us to consider what motivates developments that appear the same and the balance between what is inherited and what is encountered in the world.

These concepts may be especially useful because they do not collapse easily into the simple dichotomy mentioned above. The evolutionary frameworks do not necessarily countermand identifications of universalism or influence, but they do show that the situation is more complicated. If we take seriously the proposition that narrative is intimately connected to the activity of human minds (or, again, vice versa), then one explanation for shared narrative traits and patterns across different cultures is the "genetic" relationship between human bodies and stories. And yet the wide variety of narrative characters and functions undermines the romantic notion that the shared human condition accounts for stories' similarities on its own. Instead, as with most things, the picture is more complicated. To help us think through this, let's talk about crabs.

A famous and fascinating case in evolutionary biology is how crab morphology has developed independently at least five times to our knowledge (and has disappeared on at least seven other occasions).[4] There are tens of thousands of crab varieties, falling into broad groups of "true" crabs and "false" crabs, primarily showing a difference in walking legs and qualities like the relative position of antennae and eyes. The general crab body type, however (a wide, flat shape with a bent abdomen), developed repeatedly in decapod (ten-legged) crustaceans in a process that is now known as "carcinization" *independently* at different points in time and in different ecological contexts.

As discussed in the Introduction, a popular misconception about evolution is that it is in some way fundamentally economical *or* efficient. The language of "selection" may be partly to blame, since, at least in English, the action implies some kind of an agent. Selection for one set of traits over another is part of a responsive process, relying on available genetic material, mutation, and chance. So a basic explanation for the recurrence of the crab's form is its success in shared ecological contexts, while another is the influence of a shared genome. Both explanations present their difficulties. Neither exists in a vacuum.

Let's start with the crustacean genome and those distinctions between convergent and parallel evolution. Crabs as a group are not really a coherent family; they are a collection of distantly related families hailing from a shared ancestor that existed sometime between over 540 million years ago and under 20 million years (practically a blink of an eye on a geologic timescale). And their development shows movement in all kinds of directions, with expansion and contraction apparent on an evolutionary scale: a king crab can be said to have evolved from an ancient king crab exemplar into a hermit crab and then a hermit can evolve back into a king. While genetic information about crab families and carcinization is limited by the availability of genetic material and the spotty nature of the fossil record, the wide array of ecologies that are home to crabs makes it more difficult to explain their development by way of appeal to shared external pressures.

One reason for similar evolutionary developments is that similar environmental pressures lead different species to evolve common traits. A difference between convergence and parallelism is often seen as a case of inheritance. Convergent features are considered *analogous* features (those that developed similarly but are not fundamentally the same) but not *homologous* (developed from the same genetic place). Analogous features are not genetically determined by a near ancestor; homologous features can have very different functions. Consider the wings of birds and bats: they are analogous (because they developed differently) but homologous too because they are both forelimbs from a vertebrate genetic ancestor (to distinguish the pair from winged insects). Analogy is morphologically unrelated similarity of function; homology is similarity in form based on a similar ancestor.

In some cases what appears to be an example of a parallelism is actually a kind of ancient convergence, a "deep homology." Thus, even species extremely far apart in the genetic family tree could possess enough similarity in genetic mechanisms that, given the same external pressures, the development of similar traits is not surprising. This lends weight to the theory of shared influence of common genetic options and similar environmental challenges. Traits like the crab's low flat body and strong shell are useful against predators and may serve faster movement in mixed aquatic environments. Some scientists also encourage us to look to the elements of the crab body itself as influencing similar outcomes all the time, providing a useful reminder that an organism's other physical traits are part of the total environment that influences development. Phenotypic integration is "covariation" among body parts: basically, similar developments in related species because of the functional relationship among their body parts.

This discussion offers some useful distinctions and definitions to think with if we turn back to myth. Parallel and convergent evolution describe two ways of understanding how similar traits developed in different species. In the first, a shared genetic background allowed related species to develop similar traits based on homologous features (shared genes). These categories may apply to repeated narrative patterns in two significant ways: first, like the crab features, narrative patterns are complex and interrelated; second, despite the relative morphological complexity of the crab features, they developed independently due to a shared genetic core and

similar environmental pressures. Just as in the case of evolution, however, applying these categories to all forms of narrative presents difficulties. Parallel and convergent, even with a
perfect fossil record and complete genomic knowledge, are descriptive categories emerging from human observation: the
aggregate change in the real world over time is much messier
and unpredictable.

To turn from multiple crabs back to the monomyth . . .
What might it mean that narratives like the stories of Gilgamesh, Jesus, and Herakles have such similar characteristics? Let's think about ideas of parallel and convergent evolution
in conjunction with the dichotomy of universal and derivative.
These are, of course, categories from different disciplines that
map onto each other only uneasily, but there may be some use
in comparing them. Often when considering the relationship
of cultural features, we may ask simply whether shared traits
are a result of a common antecedent or cultural borrowing or
whether, in contrast, they are a feature of some kind of universal human nature. Parallelism and convergence supply
more complexity to such developments while also providing
more influence to shared contexts. One can imagine without
prejudice the argument that the narrative pattern under discussion was in a way culturally immanent in the eastern Mediterranean, providing just enough of a backbone to generate
different kinds of narratives with some essential shared traits.
While the mysterious or dislocated births of heroes like Herakles and Jesus are clearly similar, is this similarity strong
enough to claim that the narratives are in some significant way
"genetically" related? The plot function of a dislocated birth,
it seems to me, is to provide an explanation for significant social change (a conflict among the elites) alongside an etiology
for the power of an agent of change (the hero is still elite). Such
a function could conceivably develop in multiple cultures pro-

vided they had the right balance—or imbalance—of social power and order. From this perspective, we could position at least this part of the heroic narrative as an example of convergence: stories from different cultures have developed similar traits in response to similar cultural pressures. Here different versions of the monomyth may well be like independent developments of the crab body structure: a shared genetic core, developing similar responses to similar environments.

And yet our story is more complicated than this. Part of what makes the mysterious birth narrative so powerful is the miracle and opacity of birth. For one, as Telemachus says in the *Odyssey,* no one is witness to his own begetting.[5] None of us really knows much about the conditions of our conception and birth, and our passage from childhood into adulthood through the biological vise of adolescence can naturally create feelings of dislocation or disaffection cross-culturally. The human body undergoes a remarkable cognitive transformation from childhood to adulthood. Children are flowing with endorphins and serotonin, and the transition to adulthood disrupts and alters these levels. It is entirely unsurprising that audiences across cultures might respond to narratives that echo the confusion and uncertainty of such shifting experiences. For adults, this memory of change may be charged as well by the experience of childbirth and rearing. Prior to modern medicine, a large number of human pregnancies did not result in offspring who reached adulthood; the development of personalities, moreover, occurs over such a long period of time that the emergence of character in early adulthood may seem like a mystery too.

So there is an accord between human developmental neurology and the experience of life (and death) that can help us understand why certain kinds of stories may gain traction over others. If we accept an expanded understanding of the

relationship between narratives and human life, I believe we
can also make an argument for the *parallel* evolution of elements of heroic narrative. Recall that one of the main features
of parallel evolution is the development of similar traits on homologous (shared) morphology. If we can assume that certain features of human culture are rooted in responses to our
genetics and that stories relating to these features respond both
to our shared life cycles and the conditions of mortality, we
have, I think, something like an explanation for Freud's family
drama or Jung's archetypes. Similar stories have developed in
similar contexts because of the basic parameters of human life.

In large part, we can follow the psychoanalytic tradition
in seeing many of the primary features of the heroic pattern as
related to shared conditions of human bodies and human lives.
The multiformity of narratives available, however, probably
indicates more complicated relationships. Imagine, again, the
heroic narrative as a crab. Some species of narrative are more
closely related to each other, as certain crab families are clus-
tered around the five major evolutionary developments. There
are clear genetic relationships between narratives in the same
cultural and linguistic groups, as well as geographic distribu-
tions. The story of Herakles can be seen in the background of
the Homeric Achilles. The pattern of Moses's life may be less
implicated in the development of the narrative of Jesus, but I
suspect that cultural forces and traditions brought those two
more closely together than a Gilgamesh and an Achilles, while
on our modern big screen, heroes of fantasy and science fiction operate under something of a cultural accelerator, given
the modern economy and globalization.

From this perspective, pattern-seeking in narratives
across cultures can be more an exploration of how narrative
structures developed than an explanation of origins and priority. We must, of course, also account for the problem of what

happens when we look for patterns (we find them). In thinking about intricate narrative patterns like the monomyth, we may ask when similarities are examples of shared ancestors and similar pressures over time (convergence) and when they are due almost entirely to similar environments and needs. Here, again, phenotypic integration may be useful.

One of the popular aspects of Campbell's vision of the monomyth is its detail. What are the body parts of a heroic narrative? Let's keep some parameters in place: in the mythological pattern prized by Campbell and other male-identifying scholars, heroes are generally men (qua biological gender in a system tending toward the binary conceptually and yielding a basic patriarchal social structure); they occupy a space at the intersection between tensions of culture and wild, mortal and divine. If we add "ecological pressures," the narratives act as vehicles to explore these tensions, and these vehicles are defined in great part by their legibility to human audiences. To add more: the stories are told through marked language; they engage with and reflect the power structures of the world in which they develop. I imagine there are better ways to go about describing the shared body parts of heroic narratives, but just a few suggest that their similarities are as likely to be a result of a kind of phenotypic analogy as of some kind of genetic flow from one culture to another, with the reminder that phenotypic integration assumes some level of shared inheritance, however ancient.

The shared inheritance I would emphasize is deep in the history of the development of human language and culture, tens of thousands of years in the past, if not longer, made more likely by interconnections (contaminations?) over time and the shared environment (and influences) of the eastern Mediterranean, major historical trends, events, and a self-conscious cultivation of narrative. If we consider stories developing in ecosystems, like crabs, and exhibiting different features based on an interplay between their inheritance (genetics) and their environment, the pressure of human involvement adds yet another layer to this process. Long before humans started writing about narratives and identifying their parts, we knew that stories had power and cultivated them for it. Human intervention has shaped narrative in much the same way as we have shaped agricultural crops and domesticated animals. Evolution does not stop because of domestication; instead it moves at a different pace and *alters the agents of domestication as well.* Humankind and human culture have been inalterably changed by the changes we have wrought on other species.

The studies I have cited about carcinization rely in great part on thousands of individual investigations of crab morphology and speciation, just as studies of Indo-European poetics rely on a great deal of specific, technical investigations into morphology and synthesizing treatments of myth base patterns on countless variations. Commenting at length on the monomyth or heroic pattern from this analogy is difficult because they are both abstractions. Here is where the metaphor of domestication becomes important. If the material in this chapter so far has seemed rather speculative or untethered, it is at least partially due to the nebulous—even ambiguous—nature of the material. Exploring the narrative patterns of heroic myth is like reducing a range of species to general phenotypes and focusing on shared elements and characteristics without engaging in the specifics that define the individual species. This is why the analogy of crab evolution is useful but also why the discussion may come off as somewhat superficial.

Actual examples of narrative—whether we call them stories or literature—are bound culturally by the forms they take structurally and the purposes they serve in context.[6] They are not neat distillations of ideal patterns but messy manifestations within which general patterns can be hard to find. When Campbell (or others) selects narrative details from a poem or story to align it with patterns found elsewhere, he leaves behind the very traits that make that story *itself* and which allow it to make sense in its cultural environment. To explore more fully the aptness of the crab evolution analogy for thinking about the monomyth, therefore, we need to move back toward the specifics. I will stick with heroic myth—or at least examples used in talking about it—by looking at the Homeric epics and the eighteenth-century BCE Gilgamesh poems.

Cultural Transmission: The Gilgamesh Poems and the Homeric Epics

It is a common assertion that some of the oldest extant "literature" comes from ancient Mesopotamia. These texts boast the first alleged author in human history, and they also present narrative motifs and patterns that anticipate and possibly contribute to later traditions with which we are very familiar, such as the flood narrative in the Akkadian *Atrahasis*.[7] While I am reluctant to use the term *literature,* both for its resistance to any definition and its culturally bounded characteristics, I do think it is a fair enough usage since these narratives are *texts;* they seem to operate by generic rules that place them outside everyday speech; and they also seem to have occupied an elevated or elite position in their cultures.

The story of Gilgamesh in modern scholarship is rather exciting. While there is one ancient classical attestation of the name Gilgamesh in the work of the second-century CE rhetorician Aelian ("he was called Gilgamos and was king of the Babylonians"), European scholars remained ignorant of the story of the god-king of Uruk until the decipherment of the first cuneiform tablets with his story in the nineteenth century.[8] The translated narrative was sensational, telling the story of a "hero" who went out to fight a wild-man (Enkidu), only to befriend him and go with him on an adventure to the Cedar Forest to face a monster named Humbaba (or Huwawa). When Enkidu dies following this encounter, Gilgamesh is undone, mourning both the loss of his friend and his own potential death. Until Enkidu's passing, Gilgamesh had not fully conceived of his own mortality. In response to this experience, Gilgamesh goes on another quest, this time to try to defeat death. His journey takes him to Utnapishtim, a survivor of the great flood, who shares with him the secret of immortality (and the story of the flood!): a special plant. Gilgamesh finds the plant but loses it to a hungry snake on the way home, and in the closing moments of the story seems to accept his mortality and that he will live on in a way through the walls of his city, Uruk, which advertise, for all to see, his great deeds.

Given additional formal aspects of the Gilgamesh narrative—formulaic phrases, repetitions, ring compositions—the poems' rediscovery invited comparison to other Mediterranean traditions. The individual tablets were imagined to be part of a "Gilgamesh epic" seen as a possible forebear for Greek heroic narrative, if not the Homeric *Iliad* and *Odyssey*. And it is not difficult to understand why some might see the god-hero Herakles reflected in Gilgamesh's accomplishments (and failures), or why the close relationship between Enkidu and Gilgamesh might recall Patroklos and Achilles in the *Iliad,* especially since Patroklos's death sends Achilles into a second rage that requires him to accept his own death. Even more seductive are some of the "literary" traits that appear to draw the content of the Gilgamesh poem even closer to Homeric epic. Chief among these are metapoetic reflections about the power of narrative to confer fame and perpetuate a kind of life after death for its heroes. Homeric epic regularly points to its own ability to generate kleos, "fame," and Achilles himself notes in book 19 of the *Iliad* that "the Achaeans will remember our strife for a long time."[9] The final lines of the Gilgamesh narrative, in which he looks to the city and imagines how it conveys his accomplishments, both return through repetition to the beginning of the tale and also contain what some modern scholars have seen as a metapoetic hint: the language referring to the clay bricks that comprise the city echoes that used for the tablets on which the story of Gilgamesh was written.

From this brief summary, it should be clear why the translation of the Gilgamesh narrative caused such a sensation, which was sustained into the twenty-first century. The Assyriologist Tzvi Abusch, for example, writing in 2001, claims, "The Epic of Gilgamesh combines the power and tragedy of the *Iliad* with the wanderings and marvels of the *Odyssey*."[10] The problem, as is usually the case, lies in the details. Without even considering potential connections between the Gilgamesh stories and the Homeric epics, the *form* of the former complicates everything. For one, the story of Gilgamesh is not one narrative but many: when I teach about Gilgamesh, I say the *Gilgamesh poems* because what we actually have are around a dozen traditional Tablets from different language traditions (Old Babylonian, Sumerian, Akkadian, and the Indo-European Hittite starting before 1800 BCE) spanning over a dozen centuries with many variations. Abusch and others call the poem an epic because it deals with a hero and has a note of tragedy. Such thematic emphasis correctly aligns some of the spirit of Gilgamesh with the Homeric Achilles and Odysseus, but it elides genres that were very different in form and function.

To complicate matters further, we do not have much evidence about the role of the Gilgamesh poems in the world:

unlike Greek epic, which seems to have come from a living oral performance tradition and had real influence in the shaping of culture in the mishmash of polities and dialects we now call ancient Greece, the Gilgamesh poems present little evidence as to their cultural function. Some scholars believe that they existed for most of their history purely as scribal exercises, separated from the active narrative practices that were ongoing throughout the region.[11] As the Assyriologist Andrew George notes, some texts hailing from the same practices had known ritual uses (the even older *Enuma Elish* was read aloud at least twice a year as part of cult practice in Babylon), but we are only certain of the Gilgamesh texts being used for pedagogical reasons in scribal schools.[12]

Nevertheless, texts can have different purposes over time. So others believe that the Gilgamesh poems hailed from storytelling traditions, pointing to iconography uncovered in ancient sites, but the relative stability and antiquity of the narratives complicates the claims. Indeed, if our limited evidence of the Homeric poems makes it difficult to say anything certain about their genesis or performance, what we know about the Gilgamesh poems practically paralyzes us. One important generic detail remains, however: the language used in Akkadian to refer to the Gilgamesh narrative includes *shiru* or *zamaru*, which can mean "song" and points to the general idea that the texts are poems with origins somewhere in performance, most likely sung. Further, while there are debates about how to characterize or understand the genre of the Gilgamesh poems, the texts themselves imply that audiences are supposed to learn from them.[13]

Since the first translations of the Gilgamesh poems were published, readers have been drawn to the similarities outlined above. One of the sticking points was coming up with a model of transmission that made sense for the material at hand: ob-

stacles included time (the early versions of the Gilgamesh poems were much earlier than the Homeric epics), geography (the
distance between, say, Babylon and Athens), and cultural difference (work in Sumerian languages influencing Greek epic).
Further discoveries have weakened these obstacles: the existence of Gilgamesh poems in Hittite and now Ugaritic both
shorten the geographic difference between Uruk and Troy and
provide more direct cultural contacts: Hittite, as an Indo-
European language with clear evidence of engagement with
people from Mycenaean Greece, provides an attractive mode
of travel from one culture to another. Indeed, as Mary Bachvarova shows quite convincingly in her *From Hittite to Homer,*
there was ample adaptation and flexibility in the Anatolian
stories of Gilgamesh to provide cultural space for the transmission of themes and motifs from Mesopotamia to Greece.[14]
Further, recent studies have been more positive about the
existence of Gilgamesh narratives as "legends" or non-scribal
story traditions. The Gilgamesh tablets display a tendency
toward narrative coherence and integration that differs from
the accumulation of parallels and layering seen in later literary traditions.[15] In the late twentieth century, scholars were
readier to argue for ancient Near Eastern influence on Greek
culture, a fact indisputable from archaeological evidence as
well as from the history of ideas in early Greece.

Modern cultural forces that shape our inclination to
identify the Gilgamesh poems as forebears to Homer run in
both directions: on the negative side, cultural chauvinism (and
straight-up racism) has prejudiced many against seeing a relationship between Greek literature and the ancient Near East,
where scholars have usually been more attracted to privileg-
ing the "genetic" precedents of Indo-European language and
culture. Appeals to ancient Near Eastern models, however,
often arise out of an equally misguided notion of westward

progress, the idea that culture and human advancement have steadily moved from the Mesopotamian crescent to Greece, Rome, western Europe, and the Americas. Cultural distribution and change are, like linguistic change and biological evolution, much messier than either of those models. This is where the crab model makes things interesting.

Recall that before discussing the monomyth, I emphasized the difference between convergent and parallel evolution and also included the model of phenotypic integration. While parallel evolution is when species from a common ancestor develop similar traits to one another that did not exist in the common ancestor, convergent evolution, when species from separate lineages develop similar traits in similar environments, can be partly expressed through phenotypic integration—when similar structures across species influence the development of similar traits in similar environments. The timescale and the forms of the poems themselves are different enough to make Homeric epic and the Gilgamesh poems better fit for a convergent evolutionary analogy than a parallel one, with a strong emphasis on phenotypic integration.

Let me explore why. In that rather naive paper earlier in my career, I examined the similarities in the treatment of life, death, and the rhetoric of immortal fame in the *Iliad* and the Gilgamesh poems.[16] One of the shared themes focused on is a turn that happens in both traditions when a woman on the margins gives advice to the main character to enjoy life while it lasts. In the *Iliad,* Thetis interrupts Achilles' mourning to say:

> My child, how long will you eat your heart with
>   mourning and grief,
> not thinking of food or sleep? It is a good thing to sleep
>   with a woman too, for

you will not live long, since death and mighty fate
    already stand over you.[17]

In a fragment from the Old Babylonian version of the
Gilgamesh story, Gilgamesh recounts his experiences with Shiduri the innkeeper to the boatman Ur-Shanabi.[18] In the standard version of the story, the innkeeper/barmaid bars the door
and excludes Gilgamesh.[19] In the Tablet from Sippar dated to
the eighteenth to seventeenth century BCE, Shiduri listens to
Gilgamesh's lament and responds:

But you, Gilgamesh, let your belly be full,
enjoy yourself always by day and by night!
Make merry each day,
Dance and play day and night!
Let your clothes be clean,
let your hair be washed, may you bathe in water!
Gaze on the child who holds your hand,
Let your wife enjoy your repeated embrace.[20]

This passage, in a way, echoes the famous epitaph attributed to Ashurbanipal in the Greek tradition, "I keep whatever
I ate, the insults I made, and the joy / I took from sex."[21] And
it has a pattern familiar to what we see in the *Iliad*.[22]

Woman on sea/margins
Hears heroic lament
Gives advice about enjoying life (eating and sex)

The advice given about enjoying life also echoes senti-
ments from the biblical Enoch and Qoheleth (Ecclesiastes). So
we could imagine a general diffusion of the motif throughout
the eastern Mediterranean. Indeed, we find the invocation to

drink and be merry throughout early Greek lyric poetry and in the Syro-Mesopotamian wisdom text known as the *Ballad of Early Rulers,* which asks, "Where is Gilgamesh, who, like Ziusudra, sought the eternal life?"[23]

The pattern of ideas in the heroic context makes this comparison striking. A significant difference between the two scenes is the emphasis on children in the Gilgamesh fragment. Such an acknowledgement is not absent from the Homeric epics, but it is downplayed—perhaps pointedly—in the *Iliad,* where the loss of children and parents is repeatedly lamented. In addition to this difference, I would suggest that the similarities are due in part to what we might think of as phenotypic integration, namely, human mortality and our consciousness of it, and a Mediterranean trope of investing women with special knowledge about life and death. Consider, as a comparison, lyrics from John Prine's "Spanish Pipedream."[24] The narrative of this song presents a soldier who goes to a bar and encounters a dancer/stripper who gives repeated advice to his disenchantment:

> Blow up your TV
> Throw away your paper
> Go to the country
> Build you a home
> Plant a little garden
> Eat a lot of peaches
> Try an' find Jesus on your own

The chorus repeats between verses until on the third round it turns from the quoted advice into a statement of action:

> We blew up our TV
> Threw away our paper

Went to the country
Built us a home
Had a lot of children
Fed 'em on peaches
They all found Jesus on their own

Here the turning away from news and the noise is a withdrawal from martial life, from the chaos of worldly events. Prine's narrator moves on from his youthful uncertainty to a life of food, presumably sex, and caring for offspring. Each of the three examples provides advice about abandoning mourning, providing what has been called "a prescription for healing."[25] Now, while one might suggest that Prine was familiar with the Old Babylonian version of Gilgamesh or Thetis's advice in the *Iliad*, I would argue instead that his narrative is a reflex of "traditional" advice relying on a cultural structuration of gender and an attitude toward death that is similar enough to that of the ancient eastern Mediterranean to yield themes that seem familiar. These themes are more properly an example of a kind of parallel evolution (common cultural traits developing from a shared set of cultural milieus) or a kind of convergent evolution relying on shared phenotypical features (binary gender, fear of mortality, the enjoyment of food and family as an alternative to war).

To return to the question of the similarities between the Gilgamesh poems and the *Iliad,* another chief feature to consider is whether their forms are homologous or analogous. No casual viewer will look at the *Iliad* and the Gilgamesh poems and imagine that they are the same, but they share key characteristics that may influence their capacity to reflect and communicate similar contents. First, both are long works that by nature of their development and cultural position got absorbed and expropriated from other narrative traditions, reflecting contents that might seem at home more in settings we call "wisdom literature." Second, their status as poems that exist through time—and self-consciously so—means that they had the opportunity to gather accretions of motifs over time as cultures changed. Third, whatever the conditions of their reception, they both focus on issues of human life and mortality, specifically probing masculine behavior and violence. Fourth, in their relationship with political and cultural authority in their respective (and often successive) regions, these central themes are ideologically pitched to the ruling elite. Even if we accept the suggestion that the Gilgamesh poems developed out of a performance or song culture, however, the date is so far back in time as to make any proposal of a shared performance antecedent virtually impossible (other than human capacity for speech and responsiveness to narrative). The best description I can imagine is that these are analogous structures in similar complex environments.

This discussion has been useful in helping me think through the significance of the monomyth in light of available analogies. The monomyth is a decent example of parallel evolution in the short run (similar developments in parallel descendants from the same forebear) and convergent evolution in the long run (similar developments in unrelated species based on similar environmental challenges). The narrative ecosystems that yield some of the features emphasized in the monomyth are what we might consider core genetic features of being human (mortality and consciousness of it, the dislocating nature of moving from childhood through early adulthood), while others are more localized (emphasis on heroic individualism, patriarchal structures). I think it is also clear that narrative ecosystems overlap and cross-contaminate one another.

Nevertheless, there are two serious challenges to taking the monomyth more seriously than as a descriptive pattern. First, as we can see with the Gilgamesh poems and the *Iliad* and the *Odyssey,* our examples of the monomyth are embedded in compositions far more complex than the basic elements of the heroic pattern. If we reduce any of these narratives to its monomythic elements alone, we lose the forms altogether and many of the themes and motifs that make these works memorable. Indeed, we might go so far as to say that in this situation, reducing these poems to those patterns is the equivalent of taking three random mammals and emphasizing their shared traits as the most important things about them.

I do not believe that the Gilgamesh poems had direct influence on the shaping of the Homeric epics, but this is conditioned in part by my own desire to emphasize the complex systems that gave birth to them. As discussed earlier, there are *bad* reasons to emphasize either a genetic connection between the traditions (the false narrative of westward progress) as well as bad reasons for refusing them (cultural chauvinism, barring ancient Near Eastern influence on Western "miracles"). I think there are *better* reasons, based on our evidence, to see the cultural contexts of the eastern Mediterranean as supporting them both.

One of the most damaging and stagnant models for cultural development in the eastern Mediterranean is the discourse of the so-called Greek Miracle. This argument posits that there is something unique and intrinsically different about Greek language and culture that helped it give birth to what we now recognize as its literature, philosophy, and art. The argument arises largely from German philhellenism and if it is not directly implicated in subsequent Nazism and white supremacy, it at least comes from a common kinship. No one who studies language seriously, who studies history seriously, or who is deeply familiar with the region could hold this notion today. Greek science and philosophy developed first in contact zones with ancient Near Eastern cultures; the culture of larger Greece (Sicily, Italy, Ionian Islands, and more) was always enmeshed with other languages and peoples. The very geographical features that facilitated the development of a shared Greek culture without a unifying political framework for hundreds of years also allowed dynamic engagement with cultures over the sea. The Greek "miracle" is a product of cultural diversity.

There is a spotty history in using arguments for biodiversity from the natural world to advocate for multiculturalism; but there is a difference in observing what happened in the past and seeing biodiversity as a useful analogy. Theorists have argued that biodiversity provides some ecological-level insurance against plagues and extinctions, and have demonstrated that in limited settings—human agriculture for example—monocultures can have devastating effects on ecosystems.[26] Narrative monocultures can be slow to respond to cultural change and often require political force for their own persistence. Dynamic cultural environments provide more opportunities for combination and new growth as cultures share and develop together.

Of course, rich, dynamic environments, whether natural ecosystems or narrative paradigms, develop in ways we cannot anticipate. They develop neither in the best way (ethically), nor even in the most efficient way: they change based on individual encounters and in response to new pressures and combinations. If the danger of monoculture is oppression and stagnation, overabundance can be chaotic, disrupting systems and order. What remains to be considered are their potential dangers.

4
Going Viral
Big Deeds and Bad Fame

How do we begin to understand the importance of storytelling to the cultural ecosystem of ancient Greece? While we may at times overstate the reach of ancient Greek song culture, Greek epic creates a special place for song and stories. At the beginning of Hesiod's *Theogony*—a poem contemporaneous with our *Iliad* and *Odyssey*—the narrator sings that Zeus fathered the Muses with Memory (Mnēmosunē) to provide "forgetfulness of evils and a break from cares." Then the poem claims that the power of the Muses allows kings to resolve conflicts without violence through persuasion and just judgments, before asserting again that for those who have grief in their hearts, a singer (*aoidos*) will sing the "famous deeds of earlier people" (*kleia proterōn anthrōpōn*) so audiences will stop having negative thoughts and remember nothing of their pains:

> Thanks to the Muses and far-shooting Apollo
> People are singers and musicians across the land,

Though kings are from Zeus. The one the Muses love
Is blessed. For a sweet voice flows from his mouth,
And if anyone has pain in a newly aggrieved heart
and he chews over his thoughts in sorrow, then a singer,
the Muses' assistant, will praise the famous deeds
    generations
before and then the gods who live on Olympus,
and quickly that man will forget his troubles, he won't
    remember
a bit of grief. The gifts of the gods change us quickly.[1]

Here storytelling is both personal and political: it can address suffering in the spirit and forestall strife in a state. It also has a curious power to shape memory, somehow to replace pain recalled with heroic narrative. Narrative's control over memory thus directs audiences to certain kinds of stories while also distracting them from others. To think more broadly about humanity's relationship with story: the ability to control memory can help us address our experience of pain and trauma as individuals and groups. Memory creates and curates identities. But without proper bounds, too much memory or too much forgetfulness is damaging, if not fatal.

The passage from Hesiod about the curative power of narrative in early Greek poetry contains an impressive constellation of ideas: stories are seen as a kind of treatment for severe human emotions.[2] But as I anticipated at the end of the previous chapter, narrative has a negative potential too. This becomes clearest in the *Odyssey*, where storytelling appears to have a conceptual range similar to drugs. The *Odyssey* is, to a great extent, about the power of narrative to help its eponymous hero redefine himself and plan his return home. As a master of narrative, Odysseus uses the power of his story to get various characters to do what he needs them to and to test others. Narrative's dangerous potential is clear for the first time when Odysseus narrates his encounter with the Sirens, whose songs lure men to their doom. As Circe describes them:

> You will first approach the Sirens who truly bewitch
>   [*thelgousin*]
> All people who approach them—
> Whoever sails near in ignorance and hears the voice
> Of the Sirens has no wife and young children
> Standing by them or delighting in them when they
>   return home.
> No, the Sirens bewitch [*thelgousin*] with clear song
>   [*ligurē aoidē*].[3]

These Sirens *bewitch, cast a spell over,* or *enchant* audience members with their words, turning them away from their return home, a central motivating theme of the epic.[4] Homecoming, for Odysseus and others, is a return to life and light, a recuperation of identity and agency.[5] The verb *thelgō,* "bewitch," does not appear in the *Theogony* at song's creation. In the *Iliad,* however, song can trick people, while the *Odyssey* describes how Agamemnon's wife was deceived to betray him, the powers of the Sirens, divine deception, and the use of words to charm and disarm people. Narrative and medicine are united in this quality by their association with the god Apollo, who can heal or deal out disease. Storytelling in early Greek poetry is something like wine, drugs, even love: it has the potential to relieve you, but it also has the ability to harm when misused.

Stories live *through* their telling too, and they bring people clear advantages: pleasure from a good narrative, useful lessons, an ability to develop a sense of belonging in space and time, and comfort that can come from all three. In the previous chapter, I focused on how narratives develop, emphasizing evolutionary models of convergence and parallelism to focus on the conditions that allowed heroic narrative to develop in the eastern Mediterranean in the way it did. Regardless of the exact process these developments took, human audiences lived with, through, and in the shadow of heroic narrative throughout their lives. In turning from *how* narratives developed over time, we need to consider more what they did in their environment. But stories develop in surprising ways and capitalize upon things that are outside their tellers' control. Like medicine, stories can have unintended consequences: they might develop for one purpose and end up being used for another. They carry on as if with plans of their own.

We need, then, to focus on narrative patterns from Greek heroism, particularly the rhetoric of fame inside and outside poetic narratives, to consider how well models of symbiosis can help us understand the relationship between stories and the people who tell them. The thematics of fame—and everlasting glory—are of particular import here because they provide a special case for understanding how narrative *lives* on human anxiety about death.

You Are What You Die For

One of the most important elements of early Greek heroic narrative is the invocation of *kleos,* "fame." Narratives of and around kleos resemble cells within a larger organism. As the larger narrative structures adapt to new circumstances, the specialized kleos function can adapt as well. The impact of these changes can be seen most clearly in dedicatory inscriptions. Sometime around 479 BCE an inscription was set up in the Athenian market (agora) announcing the imperishable fame of the men who had died fighting for the city:

> The fame [*kleos*] of the excellence of these men is
>   imperishable [*aphthiton*] forever
> As long as the gods foster the goodness of bravery.
> For they held on by foot and the swift ships
> So that Greece would not see a day of slavery.[6]

A cursory glance at the inscription suggests engagement with Homeric language, perhaps going as far as alluding to specific moments or invoking Homeric values. The combination *kleos aphthiton* (imperishable fame) has long been seen as an ancient formula, extending back through Homer and lyric song to Indo-European precedents: when these words appear together, they sing more loudly than others, asking audiences to consider the relationship between the words in the inscription and its antecedents.[7] Readers familiar with the *Iliad* may recall Achilles' thematic statement in book 9 about his choice:

> If I remain here, fighting around the Trojans' city,
> I lose my homecoming but receive aphthiton kleos.
> Yet if I go home again to my dear fatherland,
> I lose noble [*esthlon*] kleos, but my life will continue on
> For a while, and death's swift end will not overtake me
>   soon.[8]

Achilles' language articulates part of the heroic narrative we have been exploring, posing a choice between dying young with glory and living on without it. The earlier inscription leans on the former, celebrating the gift of freedom vouchsafed by the bravery of the dead. At a basic level, the core form of an idea—a narrative strand or cell—is shared by the two versions, but something is missing in each. The inscription lacks any notion of choice for the men who died; Achilles' passage bears no reflection on the consequences of his death (or his failure to face it). Much of the story of the *Iliad* after book 9 relies on that difference.

A typical approach to these passages is to imagine the epigraphic formulas as "adapted" or modified from Homer. If we think about how the content might engage with Homeric passages, the mental gymnastics become more difficult: *this* eternal kleos is not for a single person but for a group defending their city and all Greece against a foreign army. Adaptation seems, at best, a loose term for understanding the cultural moment that birthed the epigraph. But what if we think about the core elements of the inscription as expressions of a kind of narrative DNA, triggered or activated by a specific performance context, not beholden to our texts of Homer but instead sharing with Homeric narrative a deeper and less predictable genealogy? I do not mean to search for an original articulation of the rhetoric of fame; rather, I want to show how the biological frameworks can illuminate thematic differences in articulations of kleos as a more complex interplay between genetic antecedents and the ecosystem of performance and social context.

The rhetoric of eternal fame can have a life of its own, with unpredictable outcomes. But let's return to the importance of the narrative environment or ecosystem discussed in Chapter 2. Internal models of song and audience in the *Iliad* and *Odyssey* show that stories are shaped at the moment of performance by their environment. Consider the complex way in which Demodocus's story about Ares, Aphrodite, and Hephaistos reflects and reorders themes from the epic as a whole—marriage, fidelity, trickery—and the immediate context: the handsome but somewhat obtuse youths of Skheria compared with the physically compromised Odysseus.[9] The myth and its elements are adapted in a way that fits the interests of singer and audience alike. The performance context is an ecosystem in which certain aspects of a narrative structure are expressed in response to the environment and other organisms within it.

More complex examples include paradigmatic narratives that speakers use in the *Iliad* to persuade their audiences in which the relationship between the received narrative and the context yields surprises. Consider again Phoinix's tale of Meleager in book 9, which does not obtain the speaker's desired effect. Recall the model of reading from Sappho 16 in Chapter 2: stories take on their own life in the field of their reception. Homeric poetry is filled with characters misreading and intentionally rereading narratives. In similar examples, the relationship between the story as an entity and its environment seems unclear, even unmotivated, unless we understand each of the epic's "thinkers" as engaging with the story and modeling an interpretive blend between the narrative's details and their own experience. The ecosystem for this narrative, moreover, is not only the epic's internal audience but an external audience with entirely different relationships to the story from the one within.

So stories are indeed changed by their narrative environment—they adapt and other iterations evolve from one kind of a narrative to another, and yet in the cultural inheritance of a story tradition narrative details and patterns remain latent. This latency—whether we think of it as having vestigial or unexpressed meanings waiting for the right "epigenetic triggers" (external features that initiate a change in the operation of genes)—finds different actualizations among audiences. In its simple form, this evolving relationship is perhaps more akin to

a kind of symbiosis than one of specialized cell grouping. Biologically speaking, symbiosis describes a range of interdependent relationships that can change over time. As I will
explore to a greater extent in the next chapter, symbiotic relationships are often divided into beneficial or harmful extremes of mutualism and parasitism. Mutualism is when both
organisms in a biological relationship benefit; it is often depicted as cooperative. Parasitism is when one member of a
biological relationship derives benefit by harming the other.
Since biological relationships are by no means static and both
harm and benefit can be exhibited in different degrees, these
relationships are often matters of perspective subject to change.
If we consider the place of song at the beginning of epic tradition, for example, we can see a human tool that confers a considerable benefit, but we can also see that such a benefit is
vulnerable to destructive extremes.

Storytelling has been described as providing a species-
level advantage in our ability to communicate from one generation to another without everyone having to learn everything
the hard way.[10] But in the example to which I am about to return, I think we need to think in terms of potential disadvan-
tages as well and about how a narrative entity can cause both
benefit and harm.

The theme of fame (kleos) holds a special place in Greek
culture. Its meaning is expressed or activated differently in
changing contexts with somewhat different outcomes.

Back to Achilles' famous choice:

If I remain here, fighting around the Trojans' city,
I lose my homecoming but receive aphthiton kleos.
Yet if I go home again to my dear fatherland,
I lose noble [esthlon] kleos, but my life will continue on
For a while, and death's swift end would not overtake
    me soon.

My first observation from looking at this passage afresh is its compositional balance in antithesis, the near pithiness of the expression and its comparative simplicity in the context of Achilles' larger speech. It *feels* like an oft-spoken passage. But as is often the case, the details reveal far more than proverbial complexity. First, *kleos* is doubly qualified as *aphthiton* and *esthlon*. The adjectives' different meanings present a developed notion of kleos that invites different possible responses, but one that exists in contrast to a narrative line of *homecoming* and *life*. Without these contrasts, kleos seems simple and absolute. It is a narrative Achilles is working *with* or *against* that has the cultural force of encouraging him to risk his life despite the potential cost. As a kind of symbiote, this is a fully fleshed-out narrative structure, putting pressure on Achilles.

This version of kleos is clearly part of a larger discourse, based on its other uses. The word *kleos* appears throughout Homer to mean "story," "rumor," or "account," sometimes shading more into "memory," based on its etymological origin in verbal roots of hearing. *Kleos* can also be quite minor. In both epics, its referents can be comparatively insignificant: in the *Odyssey,* for example, it covers local rumors as well as the events of the ongoing story or the outcome of postdinner contests in Skheria.[11] In the short term, *kleos* can mean a shared memory, as indicated by Odysseus's use in *Iliad* 2. *Kleos,* in these examples, could be marked by the threat that it will fail, perish, or, perhaps, transform. The perishability of kleos is underscored by combinations like *asbestos* (unquenchable) *kleos.*[12] Unmodified, however, *kleos* has an immediacy or recency, waiting to be disambiguated, to be interpreted, speciated. In the plural, as many scholars, such as Gregory Nagy, have noted, *klea* becomes a record of the men of the past and may function as a gloss for what we would call a paradigm.[13]

Expressed in the right environment, kleos narrative has an impact on the world of its speakers, as is clear in the inscription above. A significant part of kleos's impact on its speakers and listeners comes in the activation of the language of praise and shame. Consider where the invocation of kleos is used to shame a single warrior into action or where it functions to rally groups, metonymically invoking a series of relationships and expectations. The effective rallying cry of *Iliad* 5 and 15 depends on prior knowledge and the existence of a kleos function:

> Friends, be men and retrieve your valorous hearts:
> Feel shame before each other through the strong battle
>   lines
> More men who feel shame are safe than die!
> And no kleos or valor arises for those who flee.[14]

Kleos thus clearly emerges within the *Iliad* as a social tool on the battlefield and off. Yet there is something uncertain about it. Even in famous passages, the promise of kleos is a prolepsis, an assertion about a future that no one alive can confirm. Hektor uses it in book 7 to motivate himself and a challenger, but its futurity masks an implicit anxiety. Kleos is never fully realized without a larger ecosystem.

Unmarked kleos—or inactivated by its context—is ambiguous but full of potential. We don't know how a person's memory will live after the individual's death nor what its content will be. Its story has a life cycle, and its ambiguity masks uncertainty about its duration and quality. The adjectives modifying Achilles' potential *kleos* address both these questions: his fame is noble, and it is imperishable. Kleos is a narrative *waiting* to be realized, but its reception is in doubt owing to the unclarity of its promises.

Choices, Changes

Living creatures can have outsized impacts on different environments. Invasive species like feral hogs and Asian carp have ruined ecosystems that are unprepared for them. I suspect that some narrative functions can have similar effects. There may be some hint of this behind *kleos*'s ambiguities. Being well known is a blessing so fraught that multiple ancient philosophers are credited with advising people to "live unknown" (*lathe biōsas*).[15] Achilles' choice could be framed as a philosophical one: there is no guarantee that fame will be positive, just as there is no guarantee that a long life will be good. Yet the narrative implications of some of the other examples help us to see that even this picture is too simple. Part of the problem in the *Iliad* is that Achilles does (or can) not see, understand, or acknowledge the transferability of kleos, its communal importance, or the greater glory secured by sacrificing oneself for others. If anything, this is part of the implicit dialogue between the characterizations of Achilles and Hektor: the latter clings to the idea of glory for defending his people, even though his people are doomed, while the former dooms his people by clinging to a kleos that can glorify only one.

There are two reasons why the rhetoric of fame fits well in a discussion of symbiosis. The first is that kleos narratives clearly seem to shift to fit their environment and to have a real impact on the people who tell and hear them. The second is that kleos appears to offer new life through the generation of new stories. Audience members who hear the stories of famous men receive the implicit and at times explicit promise that they too can join that number. Yet the promises are unclear and inexact. The *kleos* Achilles describes is perhaps as impermanent as the single life it is exchanged for. We know that Hektor and

Andromache are going to suffer and die in disappointment. When Hektor boasts that his fame will never perish or Andromache burns his clothes and imagines that his *kleos* will come from the Trojans, fame becomes unstable, perhaps inscrutable.[16] Indeed, the *Odyssey* continues an exploration of *kleos* as something that may be undesirable. When Telemachus compares his father's fate to Agamemnon's at the beginning of the *Odyssey,* he resets the scale:

> So all the Achaeans made him a burial
> And he left great *kleos* for his son after him.
> Now the winds have stolen him away without fame
>   [*akleiēs*]—
> He's gone, unsought, unlearned of, and he has left me
> Grief and mourning. But I have not yet lamented only
>   him, weeping
> Since the gods have crafted different evil pains for me
>   now.[17]

What does it mean to say that Odysseus is *akleiēs* in his own narrative, especially as Telemachus invokes language so characteristic of his and his father's stories? The *Odyssey* shows *kleos* shrinking in scale: its rumor and story fade as we move back to Ithaka, correlating first to the account of what is happening in Odysseus's home. By the end of the epic, *kleos* is something to be controlled, to be limited because its spread—encompassing by book 23 the slaughter of the suitors—represents significant danger to Odysseus and his family, potentially even imperiling his *nostos* (homecoming).

It is a typically Odyssean turn that the word *kleos* is not mentioned when Achilles appears in Odysseus's own narrative in book 11: Achilles tells Odysseus not to lie about death and proceeds to ask about his son and father. Later, in the second underworld scene in book 24, Agamemnon recounts Achilles'

funeral and games, however, and insists that "You did not lose
your name even though you died / But always your noble fame
[*kleos*] will exist among all men, Achilles."[18] This confirms the
first part of Achilles' exchange, but not the second. *Kleos* without a modifier is something like an empty signifier. Potential
anxiety about its durability, or susceptibility to decay, as well
as its quality is realized in part by its modifiers. In turning
back to Achilles' statement, his famous *kleos* must be imperishable, immune to decay, and it is also marked as *esthlos,* noble or good.

Looking at how *kleos* is used provides us with a good example both of how narrative shapes the way Homeric characters look at the world and also of how individual word choices
and adaptations act as indexes of thematic meanings. At the
beginning of the *Odyssey,* as part of a function similar to
that in the *Iliad, kleos* is offered as a promise to explain what
Telemachus is doing in a culturally recognizable way. But its
meaning is adjusted as it moves through the epic: Odysseus
tells Amphinomos that he has heard of the noble *kleos* of his
father—whether we see this as flattery, unverifiable framing,
or play, the phrase seems diminished in its instrumentaliza-
tion.[19] This noble *kleos* exists at a distance, claimed in the epic
only by Odysseus, a notorious rogue and mincer of words. The
Odyssey in its post-heroic way is interested in qualifying and
exploring kleos and situating the stories of the Trojan War
within its own frameworks. Its use of *kleos* acts in part as an
index of this process.

Both epics offer the dramatization of figures activating
conventional notions of kleos in a negotiation of its meaning
in their world. Just as the *Iliad* features particular concerns as
ill-famed or fameless, the *Odyssey* presents its own repeated if
rather bland formular connection for *kleos:* Penelope introduces the combination *kleos euru:* "The kind of person I long
for as I remember my husband / whose fame reaches wide

through Greece even to the center of Argos."[20] The "wide fame" combination is repeated in the epic five times, mostly with reference to Odysseus and his exploits. When he is disguised in book 19, however, Odysseus casts Penelope's fame in language that recalls that formula, positioned throughout the line, while also echoing his own language about his story from book 9. When Penelope responds, she returns to the combination and position she introduced at the beginning of the epic and expands it—the enjambed *pantas ep'anthropous* ("among all people") may recall the story of Orestes as posed in book 1, while her closing line qualifies his reputation among men as esthlon, that very quality hoped for but never realized for kleos in the *Iliad* and the *Odyssey*. Penelope seems to be integrating different images of kleos while focusing on the fact that its quality is decided by others. Speakers retain the generative force in telling stories, but audiences are critical in providing the environment to complete their meaning.

Each epic selects aspects of *kleos* to emphasize and shows its characters using different language and combinations to develop a meaning that contributes to their overall aims. As kleos narratives, moreover, each epic is both a form of kleos and an invitation to think about its meaning. While I framed this discussion with comments about life forms and symbiosis, I proceeded through the examples in a more or less conventional way. One of the things I want to emphasize is the sophisticated function of *kleos* within the epics that implies a complex life of narrative purpose outside the bounds of the poems. In each case, we find the variability of *kleos* to be an essential part of its nature. It carries a core range of meanings, activated or expressed by certain contexts whose fuller realizations are lost to us because we are not with ancient audiences. A vestigial meaning might change the experience of one person over another because the full complexity lies in the fact that kleos, as a living thing, is realized differently in different minds. It appears to console some and to torture others.

To return, only briefly, to symbiosis: kleos is a narrative pattern that has the positive effect of convincing young men to risk a finite thing (their lives) for something less finite (the lives of others and their cities) and for something ambiguously *in*finite, a metamorphosis into story itself. But since story itself can convey shame or praise, the value of its promise is unclear. This particular narrative can be mutually beneficial: the stories continue to have a life of their own and the societies that tell them continue amid challenges. Yet what is good for the superorganism (the state) is not necessarily good for the individuals who comprise it. Negative fame stalks and coerces people; even positive fame can ensure they are dead.

So far in this chapter I have alluded to kleos narratives as functioning like parasites, invasive species, or cell structures adapting or changing too quickly. While one available metaphor to model narrative harm might be the development of malignant cells in an otherwise healthy host, another one to think of is viral infection. Over the past decade, casual consumers of media have become more aware of viral growth rates, how viruses and viral analogues exhibit astonishing growth after seemingly slow starts. Viral growth—as is clear from the way memes develop and change online—also includes ample room for mutation and variation. Recent events have shown how much influence viral narratives can have on human action, as in the case of steadily diverging responses to the COVID-19 pandemic.[21]

When I look at the development of *kleos* motifs in Greece from the Archaic Age to the end of the Classical period, I see two hallmarks of growth: first is the explosion in references in the fifth century BCE, second is the variety of turns the themes take. And a third observation is the tenuous relationship kleos narratives have with their hosts. Viral growth is predictable only in its expansion, not necessarily in the form that the growth will take. Indeed, while there is some correlation between mutation rates and reproduction growth in viruses, other variables are at play as well.[22] Yet if a given idea is spread among separate but similar contexts, then that idea has the tendency to combine and change at higher rates. What we see in the evidence from early Greece is the testing, changing, and adapting of the story of *kleos* in many different settings. Any object that spreads on such an expanding growth curve must have some facilitating quality or context: a new environment may be free of obstacles; a novel idea or organism may have no competition; something *between* the creation and the context gives it an advantage.

Too often, I focus on the theoretical or literary side of ancient Greece without thinking about the material conditions that make kleos narratives attractive: hundreds—if not thousands—of small polities trying to maintain their political and material positions in and against one another and other entities as well. I suspect that the *Iliad* and *Odyssey* represent a record of reflections on the impact of kleos narratives rather than a final point. But they appear to exclude some approaches as well. Foremost among these are emphases on the city and the people.

Homeric epic clearly moves through various responses to kleos, but how these moves reflect potential benefit or harm is less clear without a little more discussion. Kleos has a kind of larger social principle of promising fame for daring and sacrifice, but a complexity is here enmeshed with concepts of shame and praise. Thus, kleos is a neutral strand, a potential thread, waiting to be combined with something else and explored for its emergent meanings. In this dance between shame and praise, we find the need to gloss good and bad fame.

Kleos's core neutrality receives support from its distribution as an alpha-privative (*a-kleiēs*, "fameless"); with the prefix *eu-*, meaning something like glorifying; and with the particularly Iliadic concern over *negative* fame, *dusklea*. These compounds give some sense of its flexibility and a range of associated anxiety. The alpha-privative compounds express a kind of social anxiety. As a corollary, being well-famed or glorified is offered as a positive motivation. The threat of having bad kleos appears explicitly only as *dusklea* in the *Iliad* (although it is echoed in tragedy), and it is attached, I think, to the specific reputation of a failed leader. In our explosion of evidence from the fifth century, tragedy and Epinician poetry (songs composed to commemorate an athletic victory) make explicit the intention of creating and perpetuating *good* kleos. Consider just a few lines from the fifth-century BCE Theban poets Pindar (A) and Bacchylides (B):

A. Come, Muse, send straight to that house
   A well-famed [*euklea*] wind of words [*epeōn*]
   For when men have passed away
   Songs and words convey their noble deeds.

B. I am easily persuaded to send
   A glorifying [*euklea*] word to Hiero, one [not
        outside] the path—
   For this is how the roots of good things grow full
   And may Zeus the greatest father safeguard them
   Immovable in peace.[23]

Song, from the perspective of victory poems, has a meta-narrative capacity to glorify, to convey not just kleos but kleos of a certain quality. The song becomes generative, perpetuating, yet still remains precarious, for the fame is contingent on

the song's success and divine benevolence as well as on the skill
of the poet and the implicit participation of the audience. So a
significant generic shift from epic to other genres is the claim
on the part of the singer to convey good fame. The epic narrator seems to complicate, even undermine fame even as the *Iliad* and the *Odyssey* claim for themselves the power to confer
it, while a praise poet like Pindar or Bacchylides makes his
money with something of an eternal-renown guarantee.
Among lyric poets like Simonides (A; sixth–fifth centuries
BCE) and Tyrtaeus (B; seventh century BCE) the sacrifices of
young men bring good fame to those who died and the people
they died for as well:

> A. Leonidas, the earth has covered here the well-famed
>   [*eukleas*] men
>   Who died there alongside you, king of wide-wayed
>   Sparta,
>   After they met face to face the strength of the most
>   bows
>   And swift-hooved horses and Persian men in war.

> B. Although he loses his dear life when he falls among
>   the first ranks,
>   He glorifies [*eukleisas*] his city, and people, and father,
>   Wounded much through the chest and embossed
>   shield,
>   And even through his breastplate in front.
>   The youth and the elderly mourn him equally
>   And the whole city grieves with a harsh longing—
>   His tomb and children along with his children's
>   children
>   And his family remain famous among people
>   afterward.[24]

Even in these positive examples, something of kleos is lacking: fame is not enough, it must be shared and combined with the promise of the sense of loss, perhaps itself generative of fame, as in Hektor's funeral in the *Iliad*. Tyrtaeus's fragment ends with something of the altruist's paradox: the grave and the family of the fallen live on, forever benefiting from the hero's sacrifice. A brief fragment from Mimnermus provides a taste of the complexity:

> We are all terribly good at envying a well-famed
>   (*eukleei)* man
> when he's alive, and praising him when he's dead.[25]

Bad fame—or shame—comes from the way people respond to us, our story, and the narratives that support them both as much as praise does. In Mimnermus's verse, the praise function of *kleos* is certain only when the story is complete, when someone is dead. Ongoing life has uncertainty, inviting envy and perhaps its dangers. In each of these cases the combination of the basic range of *kleos*'s meanings with the contexts and needs of the environment yields different shadings, different narrative outcomes. To what extent does the core load of potential meaning remain latent, heard or seen by some audiences but not others?

Recombinations from Myth and Contemporary Experience

Calling a given narrative motif "viral" is certainly hackneyed by this point. But pursuing the idea is useful insofar as it can provide models for the rapid popularity of an idea and its change in a short period of time.[26] The adaptation and use of kleos as I have explored it in this chapter demonstrates how a

narrative idea—or the range of ideas generated by a motif—
engages with audiences in ways that can bring both benefit and
harm at the same time. Something like the idea of fame derives its force from what we have called the human vulnerability to narrative. Such a phrasing, however, makes people
seem like narrative's victims. Instead, we are narrative's environment—we shape one another in turn. The relationship
between audience and narrative is a dynamic one. In some
ways, even this is too simplistic an account because it fails to
consider the interaction between kleos and other narrative
entities, such as *pothē,* "longing," so elegantly analyzed by Emily Austin and Rachel Lesser, or grief and lament, explored
by scholars like Margaret Alexiou and Casey Dué.[27] Still, I
want to close by looking at a few further examples of what
happens with *kleos* outside Homer to help us better conceptualize the growth and function of the kleos motif over time.

Writing as a technology existed in Greece in the Bronze
Age, but we do not really have literary or narrative evidence
until much later. We find a rapid growth in inscriptions during the Archaic Age. The corpora of Greek inscriptions are
filled with references to kleos, just as the remnants of Greek
lyric and elegiac poetry are. We find the notion of an object—
like Hektor's imagined monument in *Iliad* 7—as conveying
fame in an environment in symbiotic relationship with words
and an imagined audience from Rhodes at the turn of the seventh century BCE:

> Idameneus made this monument so that [he might
>   have] fame [*kleos*].
> May Zeus destroy whoever harms it.[28]

This inscription pretty much depends upon an already
extant understanding that kleos functions as a replacement for

life and adds an epigraphic wrinkle—namely, that the stone
sign is a means of preserving the words which will be reintro-
duced into the world of the living upon being read. (This adds
another variable to consider in the total narrative ecosystem,
that of the durability of physical monuments and their meaning to audiences who cannot decode them.) At the same time
that kleos migrates to the dormant possibility of renewal in inscriptions, it continues to develop in lyric poetry, where it re-
tains an association with myth. Note the different relationships
prefigured by the fragments of the sixth-century BCE poets
Ibycus of Samos (A) and Theognis of Megara (B):

A. Hyllis gave birth to him.
   The Trojans and the Greeks
   Compared Troilus to gold
   Three times refined to a rarer metal
   Considering him similar in his form's beauty.
   They also have a portion of beauty.
   And so you will have imperishable glory [kleos],
        Polycrates,
   Through my song and my glory

B. The gods grant happiness to many useless people,
   Which is nothing better for them or their friends
   Since it is meaningless. But the great fame [kleos] of
        excellence never dies.
   A warrior saves his land and his city.[29]

Ibycus joins Pindar and Bacchylides in noting the generative power of song that redounds on singer as well as addressee; Theognis can be seen as engaging in a traditional
debate about the kinds of deeds that convey kleos, emphasizing the importance of acting on behalf of others. Each channels

a different model of fame. Polycrates stands to gain, like Sappho's Anaktoria, from his relationship with a poet who tells a charming tale from the past, whereas Theognis's more elite poetry emphasizes the importance of warrior culture for the survival of the state. Where Sappho and Ibycus refer to narrative's power to persist, Theognis places the persistence of narrative on an individual's power to keep his people safe. Poetry and inscriptions from the fifth century follow the Theognidean strain but, I suggest, capitalize on other meanings as well: Simonides again demonstrates an adaptation in his epitaph, echoing the "dead but not dead" theme of Achilles' epitaph in the *Odyssey* as well as the repeated collocation of *kleos* and *aretē*:

> These men placed unquenchable fame [*kleos*] on their
>   country
> When they threw around themselves a dark cloud of
>   death.
> Although they died, they are not dead, since their
>   excellence [*aretē*]
> Glorifies them above and raises them again from
>   Hades' home.[30]

There is a public nature to Simonides' epigram, which functions both as a song and as an inscription to honor the courageous dead. Epigraphic evidence shows how kleos motifs move from the famous tales of the ancestors to the honoring of contemporary people, illustrating the influence of the discourse on the perception and presentation of their own experiences. Lyric poetry does similar work, but with a playful difference, perhaps imagining how lives worthy of repute are pursued outside martial contexts. If we look at another inscrip-

tion, more than a generation after these others, we see several
aspects of kleos narrative activated:

> These Athenians died at Poteidaia
> Immortal me, death . . .
> To indicate excellence . . .
> Along with the strength of their ancestor . . .
> When they died they earned victory in war as a
> monument.
>
> The sky welcomed their souls, while their bodies took
> this land.
> And they perished around the gates of Poteidaia.
> Some of their enemies have a tomb as their share, but
> those who fled
> Made their wall the most trusted hope for their lives.
>
> The city and the people of Erechtheus long for those
> Who died among the front lines at Poteidaia,
> These children of the Athenians—they set their lives on
> the balance,
> Earned their excellence, and brought glory to their
> country.[31]

The Athenian epigraph channels ideas found in Theognis, the *Iliad,* the *Odyssey,* and elsewhere in a dizzying array
of associations we could see as layers of allusion or symphonic
echoes. But we could also see this poem as a series of expressions of ideas latent in the language and culture of memorial
in ancient Greece. This poem attributes to its heroes that which
is promised to Achilles, and the language works in part because
of similar narrative environments: an existential battle against
an overwhelming enemy.

Rather than imagining the composers, commissioners, and viewers of this text as necessarily linking with any specific line of the *Iliad*, we can instead posit their presence as part of a larger narrative ecosystem that triggers or fosters certain aspects: addressing the potential decay of fame, noting divine sponsorship, and emphasizing collective action to prevent enslavement of all Greece. While this language sounds Homeric, its meaning is something different. Is it better understood as a response to Homer within a specific cultural moment or a recombination of ideas akin to the generation of a new specific example of a species? At some level, the frameworks are the same. Yet the former does not account for the fact that the inscription has different potential meanings for different audiences and could very well have been composed without knowledge of the lines from *Iliad* 9.

Panhellenism

A given narrative motif can expand in new environments and contexts beyond its original function, bringing at times new benefits or new harms. But what happens when external agents manipulate the conditions to achieve specific aims, as in the release of new species into ecosystems by individuals or institutions to shift the environmental balance in some way?

One of the major aspects of the spread of this language and imagery I have not discussed is the inclusion of Homeric language and motifs as part of the process of Panhellenization. I chose but a few epigraphic examples to show some of the repetitions of language and themes—similar inscriptions appear late into the fourth and fifth centuries CE. Homerists and others talk about Panhellenization a lot, but we probably do not pose it enough as a homogenizing, even coercive process. As I have described it elsewhere, Panhellenism encompasses both a reconstructed historical process and an interpretive frame we use for ancient culture. The process refers to a gradual integration of the separate, local cultures of the various peoples and cities of Greece into a larger cultural identity As a concept, it indicates the common characteristics shared by ancient Greek city-states as emblems of "Greekness."[32] The process of producing a shared cultural veneer was rooted in Greek rivalry, accelerated by conflicts with other cultures and changes in technology and its uses (writing), and given some of its Classical Age character through its connection with military and economic power. Some of the inscriptions and lyric responses to fame betray a simplicity or superficiality that I think is better explained by the pressures of cultural context than the genre.

To get an idea of how Panhellenism changed the narrative ecosystem of Greece—especially in reducing diversity—it can be useful to use a modern example. A conspiracy theory floating around online concerns a shift in American music that took place after the 2008 U.S. presidential election. The conspiracy goes like this: Bain Capital, the private-equity firm once led by Mitt Romney, bought up a majority stake in American Radio (Clear Channel/ iHeartRadio), and streaming music after 2008 was responsible for a shift in popular music to bands like Mumford and Sons, Imagine Dragons, and the Lumineers. This movement was largely white, Christian (Mumford and Sons) and culturally Mormon (Imagine Dragons). Combined with changes in listening trends toward headphones and streaming services that prize less dynamism and more of a certain kind of intimate positivity, the conspiracists claim that conservative forces were using capital to shift popular culture in a particular direction. This theory represents an attempt to tie together political conflict, economic power, and artistic popularity.

The details of this conspiracy are more than problematic. But I am fascinated by cultural trends that appear to strengthen it. One of the things I found dangerous about the stomp-clap music of that decade is that it was, as many noted, an attempt to erase black influence from popular white music. Along with others, these musicians drop the traditional instruments of R&B and double down on a kind of fantasy re-creation of rock and roll with folk instruments: banjos! Acoustic guitars! No drum kits! Forget the bass guitar! But this was part of a larger cultural aesthetic that gained in strength after the election of Barack Obama: from Brooklyn to Austin, Texas, bars and white subcultures turned to a Depression-era aesthetic that prized artisanal beverages and the construction of a beard-wearing, suspender-donning roleplay. And just as the music of this particular genre and subculture attempted to erase people of color from their albums, so too did this Depression-era fantasy function as a type of white cosplay. (The features are starker when we consider how popular hip hop and rap remained during the same period, pointing to a fragmentation in popular culture that was probably more felt in the genres than in the people who enjoyed them.) In my reading, this aesthetic was the white middle class's seemingly apolitical reaction to the election of 2008, the economic downturn, and a decade of war. It was not explicitly racist but instead a flight from the threatening present that was racist in structure, whose imprint can be seen in the style and accoutrement of white supremacists of a certain age today.

My point in this anecdote is not to support the conspiracy about Bain Capital and Mitt Romney but instead to illustrate how complex cultural moments can present with multiple causes and surprising correlations. The homogenization of American radio business emerged at a time when the monoculture for American corporate interests was moving toward a generic safety baseline. Similarly cultural anxieties that created the Tea Party—and entities that are now part of the alt-right—expressed themselves differently in other sociocultural groups. Bands like Mumford and Sons were already present before this cultural moment, but they were selected and featured as part of a complex cultural response. This selection of cultural elements that just happen to fit other cultural trends is analogous to evolutionary processes from a perspective that correctly understands evolution not as a certain progressive movement but as a series of changes over time that recondition the expression and selection of certain traits. This analysis shows how people can create a (somewhat) credible fantastic account; studies I cited in the Introduction help explain how vulnerable human communities can be to conspiratorial thinking.[33] Such a vulnerability also sets us up for manipulation by bad-faith actors: misinformation, propaganda, and "fake news" all rely on the same cultural and cognitive apparatus.

When I look at the final few passages in this chapter alongside dozens of other examples, I see an analogous explanation for the eminence of the *Iliad* and the *Odyssey* in the fifth century BCE. In later sources multiple legendary leaders introduce Homer into their cities, culminating in the narrative of the Peisistratid recension (the account in which the Homeric epics reach the forms we received them in through the intervention of the tyrants of Athens), which has some textual and historical reasons for being taken seriously. (To be clear, I mean taken seriously not as an actual event but as the kind of event in the right moment of time to more or less match up with what seems likely.) These foundational narratives echo elite sponsorship of the values espoused in the poems (to an extent) but more importantly reflect the social capital put in the espousal of these values and affiliation with a heroic past.

The conflict between Greek city-states and Persia made it easier to privilege and select a narrative tradition that united people from mainland Greece against people in Asia Minor (even if the parallels fall apart easily, cultural trends do not move according to strict logic); the rhetoric of war and sacrifice in which the Homeric epics shared was already a part of the language of memorialization in Greek city-states. The epics present a critical examination of these values, and I think they developed and encoded these ideas as their audiences were faced with the distance between the reality they experienced and the rhetoric of memorialization. One epic warns against aggressive warfare while acknowledging that fame consists of your city and people and those who sing for you when you die, while the other situates heroic fame even farther in the past, or at least outside the bounds of a city, at a remove where its persuasions harm other cities, not your own.

In a way, the epics reveal a fossil record of ideas about kleos, and the inscriptions show how language and concepts from the same family were expressed over time. Note that the agora inscription ("The fame of the excellence of these men is imperishable forever . . .") does not admit much anxiety about kleos's decline or doubt about the exchange. Rather than a corrective or response to Homer, this is an example of the expression of certain ideas in certain contexts. The rhetoric of glorious fame serves a cultural and political function in the inscription as multiple audiences use inherited language and concepts to provide interpretations of their own experiences. This is the model of what Achilles does with *paradeigmata* (stories from the past applied to persuade) in the *Iliad*. The inscription is a memorial, a consolation, an activation of social memory, but also propaganda. It is a beneficial symbiote here—but what happens when it operates in the service of empire in the words of a politician like the Athenian Pericles or an orator like the Athenian Isocrates?

Much of what I have suggested in this chapter is possible without using biological metaphors. An understanding of semantic ranges and sociolinguistics might get us to the same space. Similarly, studies in cognitive metaphor can support some of the same steps. Indeed, it should not be surprising that multiple metaphors apply when those I have mentioned all have flexibility, variation, and adaptability in common. Biological models may better reflect the complexity, uncertainty, and improbability of meaning-making in ancient Greek song culture, but we have to be open as well to how these models indicate narrative's harmful impacts as well.

5

Symbiosis and Paradigm
What Stories Do in the World

When I was an undergraduate, exploring ideas for a senior thesis, I became fascinated by Homeric similes, especially those comparing heroes to people doing everyday things, as when the sides of the battle in *Iliad* 12 are compared to two men arguing over a boundary marker in their fields.[1] I remember pouring out theories about how these comparisons were more sophisticated than animal similes only to be stopped by my adviser, Lenny Muellner, when I claimed it was obvious that complex similes arose out of simple ones. Lenny asked gently why it could not be the other way around, that simple similes—e.g., "Hektor was like a lion"—contained within them the potential of much longer ones. And, further, should not we distinguish between what an audience listening to the Homeric poems was likely to know and expect from similes and how they developed over time?

This conversation has remained with me for over twenty years. I take two essential lessons from it: first, not to forget the difference between the development of a thing (here a simile) and an audience's experience of it, and second, how the ecology of stories contains relationships and potentials far beyond what is immediately seen. To stay with similes for a moment, let's take an extended one from *Iliad* 12. As the battle between the Greeks and the Trojans rages around the wall protecting the Greek ships, two captains rally their troops:

> So those two yelled out to encourage the Greeks to fight
> And just as waves of snow fall thick on a winter's day
> When Zeus the master of all urges it to snow
> On human beings, showing them what his weapons
>   are like—
> And he reins in the winds to pour it constantly
> So that he covers the high mountains and the jutting
>   cliffs
> As well as the flowering meadows and men's rich fields,
> Snowing onto the harbors and the promontories of the
>   gray sea,
> Even as the wave resists it when it strikes. But everything else
> Is covered beneath it whenever Zeus's storm drives it on.
> That's how the stones fell thick from both sides,
> Some falling against the Trojans, others from the Trojans
> against the Greeks, and a great din overwhelmed the
>   whole wall.[2]

Here the weapons falling down from the Greek wall on the Trojan attackers are compared to snow. To a modern audience, a snowfall might seem peaceful or even romantic, but in Homeric poetry snow is dangerous. The comparison in this simile conveys a blanketing and overpowering blizzard of conflict, made clearer to us from a typological study of Homeric language. But contrast this with a shorter snow simile such as "Hektor went forward like a snowy mountain."[3] This simile creates a tension between what it says literally and the meaning it conveys based on associations unarticulated at this moment. It is not that Hektor moves like some abominable snowman or stands immobile like a wintry crag, but that the ferocity of his attacks is like a blizzard raging around a mountain. Ancient commentators add that Olympus, where the gods live, is snowy; and mountains are big, like Hektor, while snow is terrifying.

Whether the simile is an extended one or a compressed one, great potential exists within it for expanding upon what is given, for inferring meaning that is not obvious at first sight. And as discussed in Chapter 2, the framing of the simile invites audience members to integrate material from the outer narrative alongside their own lives. The compressed simile is in a way more interpretively complex: it demands an understanding of traditional meanings, of how they can be expanded and compressed, plus the inferential ability to see aggregate action over time. Thus, this poetic device provides a good opportunity to think about the biological metaphors explored in the earlier chapters. A compressed simile is in a way the core material of a story, a narrative waiting to find the right environment for growth and expansion. The history of a simile type—whether heroes as lions or weapons as snowfall—would record many expansions and compressions as the device adapted to different contexts and experienced success based on audience reception and replication. For audiences well versed in the art form, any given image draws on this history for meaning while also relying on its overall narrative ecology for support. In a fully realized simile about snow, certain narrative aspects are "expressed" while others are not, just as some genes find expression only in certain environments.

Muellner's response to my assumptions about similes contains a kernel of a theory of narrative, of the importance of metonymy and the crucial contribution audiences make to the creation of meaning. As discussed earlier, metonymy—a part for the whole relationship—is key to oral traditional poetry and, indeed, to language in general. It describes the relationship between a particular expression and its more general group. Just as a few lines of heroic poetry evoke and also rely on a vastly larger and more complex tradition, so too an individual human being is at once a single expression of the species and a representation of the potential of the whole.

The same kind of logic applies to proverbs and traditional narratives, how scant details in a pattern are suggestive of a larger inheritance, once we learn to see the manifestation of detail for what it is: engagement with specific environments and expectations. So in the simile pair we find material ready for comparison to the natural world: how a string of data expressed in one sample is compressed and latent in another, requiring a larger narrative ecology of minds to unpack, adapt, and develop them once more. As we read or hear these similes we open them up in our imagination and expand them, allowing them to combine with what we know or remember from other stories and our experiences to find their meanings. And just as living creatures change the environments they inhabit, so too do these narratives change us. We are hosts to replicating phenomena: we are part of their life cycles just as they are crucial to ours.

Stories in the Wild

What happens to us when we are hosts to stories? Are we merely their narrative hosts, the place where they expand and replicate, or do they change us along the way? A simple way to reframe these questions is to ask what stories do. Yet if we think of narrative not as a human creation but as a kind of living thing in its own right, we may also need to think about the problem from the perspective of stories themselves. Traditional narrative builds itself and replicates through structures that create ever expanding narrative worlds. These narrative worlds can outlast or even reshape their original contexts, adapting to different audiences with effects that can bring help as easily as harm.

This double-sidedness of narrative's gifts is also a false binary: one story can bring glory or shame depending on the time and the audience and then shift in either direction as the years pass. Story is not essentially either "good" or "evil"; to crib from Seneca the Younger's comments on life, narrative is where good and bad things happen.[4] But more to the point for this argument, if story is to be seen as a living thing, its motivations have no moral component. By this I do not mean that when someone tells a story the teller has no intentions with moral content but rather that once released into the world, stories do not necessarily replicate that particular content. Story exists in order to continue existing. And its effects—what narrative does in the world—depend on its ecology and its partners in space and time.

Modern disciplines have offered many reasons for the importance of stories to human development. As discussed in the Introduction, narrative's function has been analyzed as that of myth or discourse. Psychology and sociology have recognized how stories shape individual and group identities.[5] Individuals possess what psychologists call "narrative identities" that help them make sense of their world. Cognitive psychology from the past few generations has also credited narrative with our ability to negotiate who we are and even as the source of what we call consciousness.[6] Stories help us to

experiment with ideas and identities, while narrative also allows us to transmit information from one person to another
and from one generation to the next so that we can learn
from one another's mistakes and suffering without having to
have the same experiences ourselves.[7]

The evolutionary advantage of human language and narrative is certainly undeniable. As I discussed in Chapter 4,
moreover, the radical development of human culture at its
macro-level is connected to what we might see as a technology (story). But thinking of narrative as an entity on its own
that developed alongside and with humanity provides new
analogies for understanding their interrelationship.

There are many available models for conceptualizing
how living things develop symbiotic relationships. Indeed, we
are living in a period when our interdependent relationships
with the natural world are becoming increasingly clear. This
ecology of survival embraces animate and inanimate things:
from agriculture and the water cycle to weather systems and
climate change, we are facing ever more reminders of our
reliance on the nonhuman world and the precarity of our existence. At times such discussions can take on a mystical sheen,
as if we were discussing an unseen force that surrounds and
pervades all life. This mysticism, however, overlies obstacles
in human cognition: more or less, we experience things
as individuals with bodily wholeness and autonomy, and
although we benefit from the experiences and actions of
others, we tend to be rather poor judges of their impact in the
aggregate.

Just as we tend to underestimate the interdependence of
individual human beings on one another and the importance
of our minds functioning together, so too have we underesti-
mated the trans-species interdependence of the world in which
we evolved. As the science writer Carl Zimmer relates in the

introduction to *A Planet of Viruses,* only in the second half of
the twentieth century did we begin to understand the diversity of viral and bacterial life on earth.[8] And it took another
quarter-century for researchers to see how our bodies and our
species rely on these diverse and microscopic life-forms, from
the bacteria in our guts to viral contributions to our DNA. Our
sense of separateness from other forms of life is to a great degree fictive.

When we think about our relationships with viruses—
especially during a pandemic—we tend to think in terms of
danger and death, of an arms race that results in the enemy's
elimination or ours. This extreme view, however, belies the
reality of our physical reliance on viruses for various benefits.
One simple example is the norovirus: although human norovirus can cause severe digestive symptoms like vomiting and
diarrhea, in concert with certain bacteria it can also contribute to healthy digestion.[9] Symbiotic relationships between different organisms are often divided into beneficial or harmful
extremes of mutualism and parasitism. Both these models are
useful for thinking about our human relationship with narrative, but there is more to this particular story than a simple
opposition.

Symbiosis—literally, "living together" in Greek—describes
a range of interdependent relationships that can change over
time. The capacity of change and dynamism in such relationships can deeply enrich our analogies for the human species
and the narrative virus. As defined earlier, mutualism in biological terms is when both organisms in a symbiotic relationship benefit. From the animal world, a good example of
mutualism is cooperation across species, as when a pilot fish
cleans parasites and bacteria from a shark, receiving protec-
tion from other predators in the process. The very idea that
viruses can enter into mutualistic relationships with their

hosts was recently shocking enough to seem like the stuff of science fiction. But in recent years scientists have demonstrated that viruses have been essential to the development of many members of the animal kingdom. Most important for humans, endogenous retroviruses have been convincingly shown to have influenced mammalian evolution, making the development of placentation (the formation or development of the placenta) possible.[10] Our genome is riddled with retroviral DNA, and we have only begun to figure out the impact of some of it.

Part of what makes these relationships difficult to comprehend is that they develop by accident and convenience instead of by design. Yet since we stand at a particular point in the evolutionary narrative, our interpretation of the events can be influenced by teleological thinking: we know that human beings require placentas for gestation and birth, therefore a human being is, to our thinking, essentially a creature capable of producing and using placentas. Acknowledging that their development is somehow alien and perhaps even an accident of symbiosis alters our sense of who and what we are.

If we stick to the placental example for a moment, we can turn to parasitism in contrast. Parasitism is a symbiotic relationship in which one member derives benefit by causing harm to the host. This is, in essence, our popular notion of viruses: they exist to live off us. But successful parasitism does not necessarily result in host mortality. The more fast-spreading and contagious a virus, the more it needs to preserve the life of its hosts to sustain its own existence. Consider again a retrovirus concerned with human placentas: a purely parasitic lifeform might accidentally limit or end mammalian reproduction, thus foreclosing its own future. A "successful" parasite sustains itself by affording some form of life—and reproduction—to its host.[11]

From the perspective of a neutral observer, mutualism and parasitism are value judgments clear only at discrete points in time. In a wider ecological system, species exist as part of a system—just as the value of an individual member of a species may be immaterial to the whole class, any given species may have only relative value to the whole system. The impact of viruses and individuals on specific members of species varies greatly. But over time and generations, symbiotic relationships can change, yielding benefit as well as harm. The example of the influence of endogenous retroviruses above is useful here. When the DNAs of different life-forms become so entwined as to occur in individual development, it is called symbiogenesis.[12] In other cases, viral elements remain endogenous and mostly neutral until environmental factors like stress trigger a new expression (as proposed for the *banana streak virus,* a disease that can make banana plants necrotic and which has been shown to be part of the banana genome).[13] An example is the integration of avian leukosis into the genome of chickens and other fowl: a virus that once caused cancer became part of the avian reproductive process, thus beneficial, but leaving the chance open that under certain conditions it will produce tumors again.[14] And yet not all viral elements are sleeping dangers. Some can move from being harmful to bringing benefit. Drought conditions have shown plants to rely on parasites for survival in an abiotic environment (one hostile to life) that were previously destructive.[15]

Narrative for Good or Ill

At the beginning of the previous section, I asked what it means to consider human beings as hosts to narrative. Perhaps, given what we have learned in recent decades about viruses, it is more useful to think of us as inseparable from narrative. Indeed, the historian Yuval Noah Harari has argued in his *Sapiens* that it is our ability to cooperate in large numbers, to imagine and articulate order through language, that has helped us become the dominant species on our planet. But how does that help us understand our relationship with narrative?[16] This is difficult to answer if we have limited models for multidirectional relationships among independent things. My earlier simple division between beneficial (mutualistic) and harmful (parasitic) relationships breaks down in the messy details of life. Elements of the previous discussion are useful, however, if we take narrative seriously as an entity that develops and functions as a life-form in symbiosis with human beings. One theme that emerges from the comparison and resonates with the research of scholars like Michael Gazzaniga and Joseph LeDoux is the relationship between narrative and consciousness.[17] Indeed, just as certain viruses were crucial in human physical development, so too have language and narrative been instrumental in advancing our mental and cultural developments. Yet even with that model for human language and storytelling, we are still left to evaluate narrative's symbiotic status.

Narrative is, I suggest, more akin to the avian leukosis DNA than the placental retrovirus. It provides a significant species-level advantage but can have deleterious impacts on individuals. The replicability of story and its impact on its hosts is also central to some of the concerns of Greek epic. Before turning to narrative's most destructive potential, I would like to look at the *Iliad* and the *Odyssey* in brief, using some of the ideas discussed so far in this chapter.

Most readings of Homeric epic position the poems as authoritative narrative traditions, establishing mythic detail and cosmic relationships that became more or less standard for their audiences. Such an assumption projects our understanding of what Homer became in the ancient world onto what it had been. It is likelier, however, that the *Iliad* and *Odyssey* we have are variations on variations, expanding and adapting to appeal to their audiences in competition with other traditions.[18] In fact, rather than being authoritative narratives about the Trojan War, the *Iliad* and the *Odyssey* present highly critical depictions of how story operates. Such criticism comes through most clearly when participants of epic reflect on prior narratives and try to use them as precedents for their own experiences.

Characters *in* stories telling stories of their own provide something like a simulation of how story shapes audiences, a virtual experiment space. Ancient and modern scholars have called these instrumentalized narratives *paradeigmata;* its singular, *paradeigma*, gives us the English word *paradigm*, a pattern or precedent, something used to measure or judge something else or a model to be used in planning something new.[19] The implicit expectations for the impact of these stories on the world within epic probably reflect larger cultural expectations for narrative on the worlds outside the poems. What sets Homeric epic apart from simple retellings of tales, moreover, is that these expectations are in no small part disappointed.

The problem of paradigm use engages critically with the questions I pursue in this chapter. If we treat narrative as a kind of living thing that can have symbiotic relationships with its hosts—its audiences and tellers—then the tension between what people expect narrative to do and what it actually does informs our understanding of narrative's status in that particular context. Several basic assumptions about narrative surface in Homer: first is the often mistaken expectation that a precedent (or pattern) is prescriptive rather than descriptive. The epics provide a critical treatment of the naive proposition that stories are patterns to be followed in the world rather than the expression of a relationship between a narrative and its context. Second is the matter of symbiotic scale: many aspects of narrative can be harmful or beneficial depending on its expression in a given context. Third we find a notional symbiogenesis of narrative and participants/audience: an implicit understanding that story evolves as new generations contribute to it. And fourth, in turning to the *Odyssey* we find that destructive—perhaps parasitic—narrative traditions need to be eliminated to stop the spread of a dangerous contagion.[20]

Let's return to the paradigm for a moment. Homeric scholars have identified narratives instrumentalized by characters in epic as models to persuade audiences in some way.[21] The epic is filled with characters using narrative for this purpose, but the presentation of paradigms in the *Iliad* poses certain interpretative challenges because most of them are ineffective—they do not end up persuading their targeted audience to do as their speakers intended.[22] This disconnect between the intended use for a story and its function in the world may be a reflection on the incompleteness of narrative and how it needs to fit well into its environment to do its work. It may also convey that stories have complex DNA and carry messages and forces expressible in one context but not another.

The *Iliad* presents us with this problem in its first book. The epic begins with Agamemnon, a king and the leader of the expedition against Troy, falling out with Achilles, the epic's greatest warrior, who challenges Agamemnon when he fails to protect the army from a plague. (Apollo, here the wrathful god of health and disease, sent the plague to punish the Greeks for not returning the captive daughter of one of his priests.) Achilles promises to leave the Greek coalition, and Agamemnon threatens him in turn. Elderly Nestor—one of the leaders of the Greeks and a king who had lived to see three generations— steps in to try to persuade each man to put aside his anger and listen to Nestor's own advice.[23] He claims authority to advise them by telling them that when he was younger, better heroes than they called for him to join them and took his advice willingly. Nonetheless, neither Agamemnon nor Achilles heeds Nestor's advice or acknowledges the validity of his tale.

What can we make of this first paradigm in the *Iliad*? The story seems rather straightforward, and Nestor appears to have good reason to expect to be heeded. But its lack of efficacy points to the fact that stories engage with material outside themselves. A little more exploration shows that Nestor's story deals with when he went to fight *centaurs* in the mountains along with some heroes called the Lapiths. His claim to authority based on that experience finds little purchase in the *Iliad*'s world: a prolonged siege against a human enemy with a political conflict brewing in the Greek leadership. This story is simply not valid as an organism in the Iliadic context. We might even say the *Iliad* is ecologically hostile to Nestor's tale as one featuring a conflict with nonhumans, or irrelevant because it comes from a chatty old man. As audience members, we don't know why Agamemnon or Achilles ignores him or if they do so for similar reasons.

If narrative is in a symbiotic relationship with its "hosts," one might expect a story to have an impact, to receive a positive reception, and to be integrated into a cultural system to be told again. And to be fair, this one example alone might leave a modern reader with the impression that Nestor is just a garrulous old codger. A later passage in the epic illustrates how ancient audiences might have seen these paradigmatic narratives, which were expected to educate and advise.[24] Thematically, the limitations of narrative center around Achilles.

After Nestor's abortive intervention in book 1, Achilles withdraws from the Greek army and does not appear in the epic again until book 9, when Agamemnon sends the embassy to try to persuade him to return. When the embassy finds Achilles, recall, he is sitting near a fire playing a lyre and singing "the famous tales of men" (*klea andrōn*).[25] At first it is unclear what Achilles is doing and why it matters for the *Iliad*. But later in book 9, Phoinix, a member of the embassy and Achilles' own "tutor" of sorts, uses a similar phrase when he tries to correct Achilles' behavior: "This is how we have learned before in the famous deeds of men, the heroes, when raging anger overtakes someone—they are pliable to gifts and open to words."[26] In Greek epic's clearest articulation of the purpose of narrative, Phoinix positions stories as educational: they transmit information about how to behave effectively or properly. We can infer, then, that when Achilles was biding his time on the sidelines singing about the klea andrōn, he was looking for a paradigm to help frame or inform his own circumstances.

Phoinix's vision for narrative is not too far off from modern expectations either: stories communicate ideas and can help us understand our own circumstances and experiences when adduced properly. But just as Nestor's story in book 1 encounters a hostile reception, so too do Phoinix's words reveal a potential oversimplification. As discussed in Chapter 2, Phoinix tells Achilles the story of Meleager. According to Phoinix, Meleager was in a conflict between his city and his uncles over a dispute and refused to return to battle when offered recompense, only to fight at the end to stave off destruction. The lesson, Phoinix implies, is that if Achilles does not return to battle because of Agamemnon's offer, he will forfeit any reward when he does fight. Much to Phoinix's surprise, Achilles still refuses. He swears to stay by his ships until the Trojans threaten them directly.

This tale has been understood as infelicitous—that is, either Achilles does not properly hear Phoinix's tale or it was

somehow the wrong story. Instead, perhaps Achilles hears
Phoinix's story and takes his lesson to heart: he does not want
to accept Agamemnon's apology or his gifts. But he also does
not want to abandon the war entirely. So he takes Meleager as
a positive model instead of a negative one. He actively shapes
the meaning of the tale.[27] Here the *Iliad* demonstrates that narrative depends upon audiences for its shape and that a story
will transform into different things based on its interaction
with its environment. Indeed, this example shifts the metaphor
I introduced earlier a bit: in the symbiotic relationship between
audience and story, here story itself is being adapted by its
symbiote.

Iliadic paradigms consistently convey a tension between
what stories are expected to do and what they actually do in
the world, emphasizing their capacity to change and the importance of their context, their narrative ecology. Internal—
and, we may imagine, external—audience expectations are
frustrated by a mismatch between a prescriptive paradigm anticipating what should happen and a descriptive one conveying what has happened in the past. For this asymmetry alone
biological analogies are useful because they help us see how
much of narrative's function is epigenetic, or contextual. In the
examples we have discussed so far, however, we get little sense
of a symbiotic scale: the assumption on the part of the epic's
characters seems to be that narrative is simply beneficial and
that their problems arise from not following narrative paradigms closely enough. In the case of Nestor's self-referential
paradigmatic move or Achilles' search for a tale and reinter-
pretation of a conventional narrative, we find the sense that
narrative is not beneficial enough.

If Achilles' response to the embassy and Phoinix's story
in *Iliad* 9 explore how people use and reuse narrative, his actions later in the epic demonstrate how new narratives are gen-

erated in response to changing contexts. Between books 9 and 18, the death of Patroklos—who enters battle leading Achilles' troops in his place—spurs Achilles to return to the war. When he appears among the Greeks in book 19, he performs a public reconciliation with Agamemnon for the assembled troops. Among his first words he concedes that everything the two of them did was to their enemy's advantage and that "the Greeks will remember our strife for a long time."[28] To a modern reader, this statement may appear innocuous, but from the cultural perspective it is striking: the word for strife here, *eris*, has a "titling" function in early Greek poetry—it tends to point to narrative traditions. Just as poem's opening "rage of Achilles" is a short metonym for an entire range of associated stories and themes, so too does the "strife of Achilles and Agamemnon" become a marker for stories in its own right.[29] Here, then, we have Achilles acknowledging that he has already become a living paradigm with a less than beneficial impact. His story is a product of the experience and narrative witnessed together, a new entity.

The epic itself addresses any skepticism that the story of its first part has become an important entity on its own. Following the death of Hektor at Achilles' hands, the Greeks gather for funeral games in honor of Patroklos. As Patroklos's closest companion, Achilles runs the games and ends up intervening in conflicts between other heroes that lexically and thematically echo his conflict with Agamemnon in book 1.[30] The narrative tells us that strife (pointedly, *eris*) would have broken out between Ajax and Idomeneus if Achilles had not intervened by insisting that "you would both criticize any other person who did this kind of thing."[31] Again, to a reader of a modern translation, the resonance of these lines with the conflict from book 1 might be hard to detect, but in Homeric Greek they correspond, like a verse and a later reprise. The repetition of sounds, however, yields a different sequence and mood. Achilles shows how the narrativization of his own experience should influence the actions of later audiences. And in doing so, he gives a strong indication of how a narrative adapts and changes, especially in response to potential harm done to the people hearing the stories.

The *Iliad* offers us many different lessons on the role of stories in the world, but it emphasizes ultimately that paradigms should not act as inflexible models to emulate or avoid but instead should *furnish material for response* to audiences inside and outside the poem. Received narratives combine with their audiences and environments to create new things. Narrative lives through and with its audiences and generates new stories in response to and development of core characteristics. In the *Iliad,* the flexibility of narrative is crucial to its survival and to the vitality of the people who tell the tales. Even when they make mistakes, their stories become paradigms for future generations. In this cycle, stories evolve and adapt based on their contexts, combining and recombining as their situations demand.[32]

But if the *Iliad* demonstrates a productive symbiogenesis of narrative and audience, the *Odyssey* presses on its limits. As I explore in previous work on the *Odyssey* and psychology, the epic is deeply invested in narrative's power. It explores how stories can function as instruments of liberation and conquest or shackles for those in culturally marginalized positions. Central to this movement is how the epic's central figure, Odysseus, uses narrative to achieve his homecoming and manipulate those around him. The stories he tells to get a ride home from the Phaeacians or to test the loyalty of his people do not need to be demonstrably true to be effective. Instead, as I suggest, they need to cohere with people's expectations, to *seem* likely, and to appeal to what people want to be true. This is in part why Odysseus is praised as a singer who knows how to tell lies that sound like the truth.[33]

If our minds—and our sense of self—develop alongside narrative as interdependent organisms, what happens to us when we encounter environments or other narratives that are in some way incompatible? A narrative world develops based on the requirements for survival within a very specific context and then perpetuates itself regardless of the continued validity of those requirements and without concern for the rightness of its assumptions. Nearly every academic discipline can show examples of radical change that was initially resisted because new ideas challenged long-standing assumptions. This phenomenon is at the core of violent reactions to perspectives introduced by marginalized and minoritized peoples. Identity is a product of experience and narrative exposure—our minds develop in bodies that sense and process the world differently and receive different narrative input based on socialized categories of race, sex, gender, ability, and appearance.

The *Odyssey,* indeed, turns at its denouement on the problem of narrative obsolescence: that is, when a kind of story is either no longer applicable or is too damaging to continue without presenting a significant problem for its audiences. This turn, moreover, is anticipated by a pattern that starts in book 1 of the epic, asking its audience to consider a different story from the one being told as a parallel. It is a story of revenge and murder; it becomes a question of when a narrative becomes harmful—when a symbiotic relationship moves from being beneficial to being parasitic.

Appreciating this pattern—like isolating the separate genes of a particular virus—takes a few steps. The *Odyssey* starts on Olympus, where Zeus, the king of the gods, looks down on human events in exasperation. The story that angers him, however, is not the tale that becomes the *Odyssey* but the events that later came to be known as the *Oresteia*. Zeus complains that humans are always blaming the gods for their suffering when they make their fates worse than they need to be through their own recklessness.[34] He makes this generalization based on the case of Aegisthus, who ignored the gods' warning in marrying Klytemnestra and murdering her husband.[35]

Many a modern reader might stop after reading that last sentence, uncertain who these figures are, why Zeus should care about them, or what they have to do with the action of the *Odyssey*. For ancient audiences, however, these names resonated deeply as part of the cycle of tales that today are best known from the fifth-century BCE Athenian playwright Aeschylus's trilogy, the *Oresteia*. This narrative shares thematic space with the *Odyssey* in that both are concerned with heroes returning from the Trojan War, the wives they left behind, and the sons who succeeded them. Upon hearing the name "Aegisthus," ancient audiences would remember that Agamemnon, the brother of Menalaos, whose wife, Helen, was the cause of the whole war, sacrifices his daughter Iphigenia to appease the gods and secure safe passage for the Greeks to Troy. This act—among others—alienates his wife, Klytemnestra, who is unfaithful with Aegisthus (Agamemnon's cousin) during the war. When Agamemnon comes home, he is murdered. (The identity of his killer differs depending on the account.) The story does not end there, however. Agamemnon's son, Orestes, returns from exile, ordered by Apollo's oracle to avenge his father's death by killing Aegisthus and his mother, Klytemnestra. After he does this—reluctantly in some accounts—the earthbound goddesses of vengeance, the Furies, haunt him across the lands to avenge his mother's murder. In Aeschylus's play the *Eumenides* this conflict is resolved by the creation of trial by jury. The forces of vengeance are reintegrated into a system of justice.

The story of the *Oresteia* is offered by the *Odyssey*'s characters as a model to be emulated. But Zeus's warning that people make trouble for themselves through their own foolishness countermands a simple interpretation of any tale. The story of Aegisthus in the *Oresteia* has all the elements of a heroic return narrative: his father, Thyestes, suffered great harm at the hands of Agamemnon's father, Atreus, who served Thyestes' children to him in what purported to be a meal of reconciliation and who ultimately seized the throne, exiling his brother. And yet the homecoming revenge story cannot take root. Again, if we return to the idea of a story as a tree relying on a larger ecosystem, we can imagine the revenge story taking only partial root in the *Odyssey*, branching out into different shapes like trees at a high altitude or in briny soil.

For audiences to recognize this shape, however, requires more detail. Athena in book 1 and then later Menelaos and Nestor offer up Orestes to Odysseus's son Telemachus as a positive example of a young man claiming his place in the world. Frequently, comparisons are made that are less favorable to the narrative underlying the *Oresteia:* Odysseus's story is developed in response to that other homecoming tale as one of a hero who returns to a loyal wife and survives by killing all the men who abused them. In the narrative ecology of a homecoming tale, the *Odyssey* and *Oresteia* offer variant models for what can happen upon a king's return, giving different roles and outcomes to those who share lives with the hero. In a way, the *Odyssey* bears witness to how a given narrative develops variations in response to what it encounters: the *Oresteia,* stressed in one way through expansion or comparison, can be about a lonely wife or a forgotten son as much as it is about a returning hero.[36] Or consider the prominent place given to Orestes' sister Electra in the tragedies, in which her experiences are explored as part of the greater family narrative.

Yet the *Oresteia*'s central narrative provocation is not home-coming, infidelity, or how to become a man. Instead, it is the tension between vengeance and duty, between piety and fil-ial obligation. Orestes' story asks us to think about revenge: that the cycle of vengeance in killings can be essentially without end.

Even as the *Odyssey* tries to make the *Oresteia* theme about one thing—the heroic story of an avenging son—it con-stantly threatens to remind us of others: an unfaithful wife or the death of a husband upon his return home. In part, we wit-ness a demonstration of how stories can be used or how they adapt and develop depending on a context. But we also end up with a narrative about how stories shape their contexts. The *Odyssey* is in fact also an epic about revenge: Odysseus returns home in disguise, so he can see who is still loyal to him and punish those who have harmed his family. When he arrives at Ithaka, he finds 108 suitors in his home, vying for his wife's hand and control of the kingdom. He murders them all, along with the enslaved people in the household who served them. Late in the epic, then, we turn to the problem of cyclic violence. Odysseus has his servants clean up the bodies and pretend they are holding a wedding because he knows he is liable to blood vengeance at the hands of the suitors' families.

The final book of the *Odyssey* centers the question of ven-geance and how to resolve it. The people of Ithaka gather in book 24 to decide what to do about a king who has returned with none of the warriors he took to Troy and then killed un-armed men in his home. Eupeithes, a father of one of the suit-ors, complains that they will suffer shame and become objects of reproach if they do not punish Odysseus for what he has done. In this doublet of shame and reproach, Eupeithes artic-ulates concerns about how the Ithakans match up to prior tales (he anticipates shame because their models are different) and how they will be judged as a narrative on their own. The Ithakan people split their vote on the matter and half go to kill Odysseus only to be stopped by a divine intervention that ends the poem. Athena appears and declares an amnesty in which Odysseus's crimes will be forgotten and everyone remaining will live in peace and wealth.

What do we make of this ending? I argue elsewhere that this is like the end of an early Socratic dialogue: speakers debate a subject such as "What is friendship?" and then reach the end without a definition, needing to start over. In ancient Greek, this moment is called *aporia,* literally "pathlessness," as if the story had nowhere to go. Such moments prompt audiences to engage fully in the debate, to go back to the beginning and think through the problem again. They imply that the problem at hand may have no solution, or that we may be asking the wrong questions to begin with. For this moment in the *Odyssey,* the aporia tells us that the cycle of revenge has no natural resolution. That it will continue in perpetuity unless something changes.

The *Odyssey*'s closing complements the *Iliad* by taking a narrative through several environments and imagining what happens in different contexts and with different players. It makes clear that narrative elements require certain resources or environments to thrive, to make sense and be of use to their audiences. The narrative of vengeance, posed as widely spread and deeply influential, emerges as a destructive model, one that brings suffering to hero and people alike. As a narrative virus, it moves from being beneficial at the beginning of the *Odyssey* to being clearly parasitic at the end. When Eupeithes worries about his future fame and current shame, he is not thinking about the well-being of his living family, his city, or himself. He is serving the need of a story by adhering to its model. And the *Odyssey* puts us in a position to find our way out.

Homeric epic demonstrates that the stories we allow to shape our decisions can destroy us. In the *Iliad,* we witness a deep understanding of how narratives function paradigmatically alongside the development and exploration of the countermodel of the strife of Achilles. In the *Odyssey,* we see how a story mutates and recombines to appeal to different people and can eventually become parasitic to the point where the life of a story is a greater concern than of the people who live it. The worst-case scenario may be when a story ceases to confer any clear benefit to those who tell it.

The Last Heroic Tale

One of the basic differences between what we call myth and what we call literature is the self-consciousness of the latter. Reworkings of cultural narratives—integrating them into longer, more complex tellings—almost necessarily create opportunities for comparison and contrast, thereby increasing the likelihood of metanarrative reflection. While the very term "literary" is fraught (for good reason), the structural and conceptual difference between Homeric poetry and less structured, "simple" storytelling like a fairy tale—if such a thing as a simple story ever existed—is similar. The *Iliad* and the *Odyssey* are synoptic and synthetic re-presentations of earlier tales, expanding some aspects, compressing others, and forcing their audiences to think about their meaning and impact. I suspect that part of the reason the poems do this so pressingly is that the values espoused in those transmitted tales may ill fit their audiences' worlds. In an ecological context, we see a shift in the sustainable relationship between environment and species: there is a potential imbalance that threatens both parties. The Homeric epics provide a record of such shifts in the way they handle the stories they present as preceding them. The *Iliad* and *Odyssey* offer resounding critiques of heroic behavior, if audiences are willing to hear them. The *Iliad* begins by declaring that Achilles caused the death of countless Greeks and the subsequent narrative shows him praying to Zeus for his own people to suffer. The *Odyssey* starts not by singing the successes of its hero but acknowledging his failure: he tried *really hard*—according to the opening— to bring his people home from Troy, but he failed. The rest of the epic details how much harder Odysseus has to work to get home, where he kills even more of his people.[37]

As a sophisticated reception of narrative, Homeric epic attempts to provide what we might see as a vaccinating effect. It exposes its audiences to heroic myth, attempts to provide a critique to induce a response against it, and sets up frameworks for surviving the story and developing alternatives. Two problems confront such a strategy of inoculation: not enough audience members absorb and re-create the critique, and epic narrative continues to replicate the basic elements of the very narrative it tries to change.

Indeed, the structures of heroic myth continued centuries after the *Iliad* and the *Odyssey* reached the form we have today. Let me return to the story with which I began the Introduction, the tale of a boxer named Kleomēdēs, who killed an opponent during a match but was stripped of his victory for cheating and returned home in rage. As the travel writer Pausanias describes it:

> In the Olympiad before that one they say that Kleomēdēs the Astupalaian killed the Epidaurian Hippos while boxing him. When he was charged by the referees with cheating and was deprived of the victory, he went out of his mind with grief and returned to Astupalaia.

There he attacked a school which held as many as sixty children and knocked down the pillar that supported the roof. After the roof fell on the children, the citizens threw stones at Kleomēdēs, and he fled into the temple of Athena. He climbed into a chest and closed the lid over him.

The Astupalaians wore themselves out trying to open or break the chest. When they finally broke open the chest and did not find Kleomēdēs there dead or alive, they sent representatives to Delphi to ask what kind of thing had happened with Kleomēdēs. The Pythia [oracle] is said to have given the oracle that

> Kleomēdēs the Astupalaian was the last of
>   the heroes—
> Honor him with sacrifices since he is no longer
>   mortal.

For this reason, the Astupalaians have honored Kleomēdēs as a hero since that time.[38]

Another version of the story appears in Plutarch's *Life of Romulus* with some minor differences:

This is, then, similar to those stories told by the Greeks about Aristeas of Prokonnesos and Kleomēdēs of Astupalaia. For they claim that Aristeas died in a fuller's shop and his body disappeared when his friends came to get it. Soon afterward, people who were returning from abroad said that they met Aristeas traveling toward Kroton.

Then there was Kleomēdēs, who had extreme strength and size but was easily enraged and like a crazy person. They claim he did many violent things and then finally went into a school for children and punched the pillar which supported the roof and broke it in the middle, which made the roof collapse. Because the children were killed, he was pursued, and he hid in a giant chest. He closed the lid and held himself inside so that many people struggling together were not able to lift it. After they broke the chest apart they found no one alive or dead inside. In their shock, they sent people to consult the Delphic oracle. The Pythia responded: "Kleomēdēs the Astupalaian is the last of the heroes."[39]

Whether you encounter this story with a significant background in heroic myth or none at all, it presents several points of confusion. What is the meaning of the sequence of events? Why does the Delphic oracle call Kleomēdēs a hero? Why does Kleomēdēs kill schoolchildren?

The sequence of events is probably the easiest to explain. Kleomēdēs withdraws and returns to his community, angry about the slight to his expected honor and place in that community, just as Achilles does in the *Iliad*. So we can imagine the narrative pattern explored in the *Iliad* persisting into the real world, the lives of the people of Astupalaia, to disastrous effect. But why does the oracle command them to honor him? What about the death of the children?

It is nearly impossible for me to reread this story now without thinking about school shootings in the United States, not to mention other mass shootings motivated by prejudice and hatred like those at the Emanuel African American

Methodist Episcopal Church (2015), the Pulse nightclub (2016),
and the Tree of Life Synagogue (2018). If I am a host for narrative myself, the resonances among these narratives—the
recombination of tales that put them in dialogue in my mind—
may have more to do with my particular circumstances than
with any causal or genetic relationship. Nevertheless, the core
narrative of a disaffected man killing children is hard to ignore. How is it possible for a champion of a community to kill
his own people? As the *Iliad* and the *Odyssey* make clear,
bringing harm to one's own people is an essential part of the
DNA of a heroic narrative. But what are the environmental
features that make it expressible?

As an undergraduate, I watched the Columbine shootings unfold on the news in a deli near my school. Nearly two
decades later, I left my office in San Antonio as a faculty member during the Newtown shootings, unable to respond to an
administrator's claims that those children would have survived
if their teachers had been armed.[40] In the twenty years since
Columbine, the United States has been home to a dozen school
massacres among nearly two thousand multiple fatal shooting
incidents. Our failure to prevent additional slaughters has been
matched by a proliferation in armed citizens and militarized
police. Violence, simply put, has begotten violence. And each
of the decisions made in the wake of catastrophe is essentially
a turn in a larger narrative of the interdependence between the
self and the community.

Let's think about the environment of our school shootings for a moment before returning to Kleomēdēs the Astupalaian. Repeated cultural events follow a basic pattern. In the
case of mass school shootings, the perpetrators fit a type:
almost exclusively white and male, ranging in age from late
adolescence to early thirties. This is our "heroic" antagonist.
There are also social discourses of alienation involved: We

know that the discourses that perpetuate structural racism and misogyny produce "white rage" and what some call toxic masculinity. Yet our public conversations seem incapable of generating answers. How would our responses change if we saw these narrative patterns themselves as having agency, if we viewed school shootings as a result of a complex process involving overlapping narratives?

Heroic narratives, like the specific tales we are discussing and the narrative pattern discussed in Chapter 3, follow what some have called a cultural script or a master narrative of a social group. Such master narratives speak to particular identities within a community to convey a historically authorized kind of identity: it is steeped in ideology and typically in support of a kind of political or economic status quo.[41] These master narratives, according to the psychologists Kate McLean and Moin Syed, provide guidelines for living, are everywhere, are often invisible, and possess a compulsory force marked by a kind of structural rigidity. To challenge the essential framework of such a narrative is to threaten both individual identity and faith in a world that provides that identity with meaning and belonging. For those most fully invested in a dominant worldview, the challenging of master narratives is tantamount to pulling apart the fabric of reality itself. Master narratives include the "scripts" or patterns that dictate how people are conditioned to expect to live their lives based on their socially constructed identities. Consider for example the traditional expectations for women to be bearers and caregivers of children. Such frameworks shape the way we dress, educate, and legislate the lives of people *we* identify as women.

When it comes to Greek masculinity and the "hero" Kleomēdēs, there are several interesting differences between the accounts of Plutarch and Pausanias. One that is striking is in the language attributed to the Delphic oracle. In Pausanias's account, the oracle calls Kleomēdēs the "last-est of the heroes" (*hustatos*) while Plutarch's account labels him "the *farthest* of the heroes" (*eskhatos*). Both adjectives are superlative, but *hustatos* is about immediacy, recency, and perhaps finality, while *eskhatos* is about distance and, perhaps, extremity (consider our word *eschatological*, which refers to death and the afterlife). While both versions appear to signal that Kleomēdēs comes at the end, the former makes him last (as in the end of a series) and the latter renders him *extreme*, perhaps to the extent of transgression.

What do these differences mean? As Pausanias's version of the story goes, although he killed his opponent, Kleomēdēs was denied honor, and his disappointed rage led him to return home, tear down a local school, and kill over sixty children. After he mysteriously disappeared from Athena's temple, where the townspeople had chased him, the Delphic oracle declared, "Kleomēdēs the Astupalaian was the last of the heroes—/ Honor him with sacrifices since he is no longer mortal." One easy mistake would be to think that the "hero" Kleomēdēs is exceptional when he rages against his community to gain vengeance for perceived suffering. But this is *the* traditional heroic narrative. As classicists like Erwin Cook have argued, the capacity to suffer or cause suffering is central to Greek heroes: Herakles, among other acts, murders his own wife and children.[42] As we have already noted, both Achilles and Odysseus are responsible for countless deaths, and they seem to move through the world with little remorse, expressing sorrow only when the deaths in some way inconvenience them or deprive them of something they value. When Kleomēdēs is called a *hero*, it is neither ironic nor transgressive. The ancient word *herōs* has little to do with virtue: it indicates a member of a generation of mortals before our own or a person in the full bloom of youthful strength. But on a grander scale, *hero* implies character traits. Overwhelming heroic power is matched by an overweening sense of entitlement and rage at the denial of an expected reward.

As discussed in Chapter 4, these narrative elements emphasize the individual over the community and increase the value of reputation among all else. In a way, the risk that a community takes in order to afford such rarefied value to a few is proportionate to fame's worth. A casual reader of myth or fan of the Marvel Cinematic Universe might miss the conventional nature of Kleomēdēs' heroism because we lionize and idolize heroes by conflating the concepts of hero and savior, owing to narrative influences from other traditions, such as religion. Again, as discussed earlier, even the self-sacrifice and savior narratives that evolved over time emphasize the glory and honor of the individual over all else. People who tell stories of heroes are shaped by those narratives in a symbiotic relationship: they internalize the roles and cast themselves now as hero, now as the saved, now as all the other helpers and bystanders to the major narrative. These narratives mutate when exposed to other stories and pressures, crusader and settler patterns combining with the discourse of exceptionalism to justify violence.

There are benefits to this if we think of the narrative in terms of symbiosis: the heroic tale encourages young men to take risks to protect their community, but when the narrative context prevents their performing that role, what is left is the expectation that a man who commits great deeds will receive certain portions of honor in the community during his lifetime, along with glory to extend his life beyond its mortal bounds. Kleomēdēs is a malignant variation of the heroic tale. The lack of a proper context deprives him of his expected reward, and so he turns his strength upon the community he was supposed to protect. At a symbolic level, he attacks the children because they have what he wants: a renewal of life, the potential of futures unlived, the undivided attention of witnesses to his greatness.

We can imagine the Delphic oracle calling for the Astupalaians to honor a mass murderer as a response to the last hero's perspective. If we imagine Kleomēdēs as a real person, he imitates and performs the roles he has absorbed to their extreme ends; as a ritualized narrative, then, he provides a different kind of opportunity for metanarrative intervention. Ancient Greek communities understood that myths shape lives. If the myths' environments are not receptive to them or present entirely different narrative options, then the composite entity—the story and the person—cannot thrive. When there is a mismatch between expectations and experiences, we feel a deep grief, a crisis of belonging, even existential angst.

I want to make explicit the implicit comparison between an unfulfilled narrative and a failed organism. What we see here is perhaps more akin to a narrative species adapting to a changing context, evolving to fit better in a different ecological balance. Stories constantly change as a response to what happens in the world. In truth, most of us will face disappointment about how some part of our life turns out. Many will fantasize about acting out, breaking with convention. This is central to heroic narratives, in fact: the possibility that we are all foundling royalty, waiting to be told of our noble origins and the secret prophecies that govern our lives. Such a narrative element is a kind of release valve, a fantasy. The tale of Kleomēdēs does not turn on that part of heroic narrative: it exemplifies the story pattern's extreme narcissism and the expectation of greatness: if you cannot be the avenging hero or the savior, you can still be a tragic king.

It puts a lot of responsibility on narrative itself to claim that it causes people to commit mass murder. Whether or not we conceive of stories as living things, claiming that they are causal factors in human actions deprives individuals of autonomy. And yet there is a long history to thinking this way. In the *Republic,* Plato certainly worried about the impact of epic when he has Socrates suggest that it is dangerous for people to know the story of the *Iliad* because they might believe that it is acceptable to be insubordinate to a commanding officer, the way Achilles is to Agamemnon. This reading of epic flattens it and limits its meaning, but Plato may also be conveying here how stories become flattened in their reception. Alexander the Great allegedly saw in Achilles a model of bravery and glory; Simone Weil, writing during the Nazi occupation of France, saw a brutal hymn to violence and destruction in Homer's *Iliad.*[43]

Indeed, after the Columbine shooting, politicians and journalists speculated that the killers had been influenced by violent, edgy music like that of Marilyn Manson. Second Lady Tipper Gore and others held the video game industry responsible for encouraging violence, in that it facilitated the subjective fantasy of murder and mayhem. Just five years before Columbine, the U.S. House of Representatives held hearings on whether or not "gangsta rap" was inciting crime and violence. These hearings, of course, were racially motivated, focusing on Black music and violence in communities of color. At issue in both cases is the relationship between representations of experiences and events and their causes. As one of the House representatives for the Los Angeles district, Maxine Waters, an African American, responded in an interview for the *Los Angeles Times,* "It would be a foolhardy mistake to single out poets as the cause of America's problems": "These are our children and they've invented a new art form to describe their pains, fears and frustrations with us as adults."[44] Stories emerge out of their environment according to Waters's perspective.

But what happens when these stories are free in the world? The years following Columbine saw an increase in school shootings despite efforts (which did not include more extensive gun control) to stop them. In thinking through the relationship between coverage of shootings and their proliferation, the essayist Malcolm Gladwell has applied the sociologist Mark Granovetter's work on "behavior thresholds" to the influence of popular narrative on violence.[45] As Gladwell notes, many subsequent shooters and would-be killers became obsessed with the Columbine shootings, lionizing their perpetrators and engaging in online communities dedicated to discussing them and plans of mass violence. He suggests that tales of school shootings are akin to mob violence, that our limit or "threshold" for behaving extremely is lowered when we are surrounded by examples of extreme behavior. The explanatory power of this idea is attractive because it avoids pathologizing individuals and foregrounds aggregate individual choices as a function of collective identity.[46] In essence, it is a statistical argument about the narrative conditions that increase the likelihood of marginalized individuals engaging in antisocial behavior.[47]

Rather than focus on the content of violent songs or specific expression of their harm in the world, I want to look at the particular form of the narrative. In popular culture, the term "toxic masculinity" has emerged to describe, among other things, a sense of male entitlement to certain social goods. And like "white fragility," its ability to frame observable phenomena is countered by the nearly violent response it elicits from the people who best exhibit its traits. But how else can we understand the essential lack of empathy that characterizes a lifetime spent abusing and using others or the choice to kill peers and children? Toxicity and fragility are disruptive responses that ensue when the assumed place of honor granted to an individual or group is threatened by new social realities. The dislocation they describe contributes to the puzzle of mass killings, one formed by the interaction between who we are and the stories we tell.

The DNA of the stories we tell prizes individual achievement and reward over all else. This sense of entitlement is connected to a cultural narrative of selfhood. The basic notional narrative structure has spread and recombined in our social and psychological discourses. We possess a general belief in intrinsic, individual identities which remain largely unchanged through life. Even if this belief falls apart when tested, it is reflected—and projected—in our political/economic focus on individual responsibility and our judicial focus on punishment and incarceration over rehabilitation. Cognitive science and psychotherapy demonstrate that such beliefs limit our sense of agency in the world in assuming that a specific and mostly unchanging set of characteristics lock us into courses of action. This framework—what the psychologist Jerome Bruner and the psychotherapist Michael White following him call "internal state psychology"—is a type of psychological determinism, the belief that characters cannot truly change.[48] The patterns of the stories we tell, when understood too simply, generate a savagely simple choose-your-own-adventure tale: A hero must have honor gained through extreme behavior. If the honor is not received, paradigmatic violence both performs this determinism and gives the actor the illusion of breaking with the system.

The concept of "internal state" psychology also demonstrates how a static identity, dependent on external markers of esteem, is strong up until the moment it crumbles. To return to an earlier question: Kleomēdēs destroys his community because it does not offer him the social position he believed was his right. Modern paroxysms of misogyny and racism follow the same terrible logic. If we imagine Kleomēdēs as a real person—or at least as representing the real enough to be credible to ancient audiences—he is a composite being, a symbiote produced by his own experiences and the narratives that shaped him. A part of his narrative self was ill fitted to his environment and went from being potentially beneficial to his community to being positively harmful, parasitic.

The final part of Pausanias's tale, the treatment of Kleomēdēs after his death, may stand as a recommendation for how a community comes to terms with a pathological narrative. The cultic rites the Astupalaians provide Kleomēdēs preserve the social memories of the damage that heroes can do while also marking him out as the last one. The "hero" in this final case is clearly opposed to the community structurally (he fights them) and symbolically (he kills the future). There are several critical metanarrative steps here: first the community identifies a story as dangerous and commemorates the damage done, isolating and naming the variation for what it is. Second the members mark the heroic tale itself as taboo by declaring Kleomēdēs the final hero. Third they establish a ritual practice to strengthen the transmission of this particular story. In a way, the combination of social practice and narrative echoes the complex function of the *Iliad* and the *Odyssey* with far less ambiguity left for interpretation.

Living myth and ritual offer such opportunities where passive entertainment may not. If we accept that the problem of mass violence is not simply one of individual mental health but also part of a deficiency in our social order, in the long term we need to change the stories we tell about ourselves and each other; we need to educate our community about how narratives condition us; and we need to consider whether our social organization allows people to live lives of meaning.

As discussed in Chapter 3, heroic narratives leave little room for the mundane challenges of life, for navigating the world when we are not the strongest or fastest, for aging, raising children, or living alongside imperfect others. When I think about the stories my children read and view today—and the world they may read as a story—I see the limits they impose on both my daughters and my son as hero, villain, helper, or prey. And to tell the truth, I despair—how much of their freedom to determine *their selves* was already curtailed before they started elementary school? Is there anything I can do to ensure they will not lash out at others or, among my greatest fears, lie dead before their time as victims?

I started this chapter thinking about similes. They remain important not because of their status as literary devices but because their invitation to compare and interpret and their openness to change and adaptation provide a small-scale view into how stories work to, with, and through us. Indeed, this chapter's main title, "Symbiosis and Paradigm," could be phrased as a binary. We treat stories as paradigmatic when they are so much more than that. Yet even if stories live with us, they are still put to paradigmatic uses because we misunderstand them or, more dangerously, understand them too well.

In turning to the conclusion of this book, I want to close by emphasizing a few things from this chapter. First, I ask readers to consider with seriousness the notion that stories act according to the rules of living things, that they grow, change, and combine, and function on what I have described as a symbiotic scale. Stories are rarely intrinsically good or bad, but depending on their ecological context, they can have beneficial or harmful effects on those who tell and hear them. The main question that emerges from this argument, then, is What do we do about stories in our world if this is their nature? Just as our vulnerability to a virus is mitigated by vaccines and survival, so too is our weakness to narrative relieved in part by narratives we shape and apply together. "Metanarrative" is a term rarely used outside literary theory and the academy— beyond the shortened "meta" used for genre-reflective commentary across popular arts—but the collaborative and reflective reception of narrative modeled in Greek epic and the ritual behavior recorded by Pausanias provide us with a first step in pursuing "narrative vaccines."

Conclusion
Inoculation and the Limits of Analogy

In this book I have used examples of language and narrative from Homeric epic and Archaic Greek poetry to argue that we should think of stories as living things. I have focused on Greek poetry—and epic in particular—both because of my training as a Hellenist and because these bodies of narrative sit at the boundary of what we know as history and are simultaneously familiar but also strange enough that we can look at them differently from art in our own time. I have also framed this discussion by arguing that, given its development in performance contexts over time, Homeric poetry especially reveals organic or natural structures in narrative that make it easier to understand story as a living, adaptive thing.

This analogy is multilayered, scaffolding up from the argument that words and phrases engage with their communicative ecosystems in ways that are similar to the recombination of DNA. Phrases and ideas grow into larger structures through rings, doublets and triplets, and repetition in an analogy to multicellular organisms scaling up from simple cells to corporate structures. These structures function like symbiotic life-forms, requiring human communities for their replication and spread, showing both beneficial and harmful effects for their hosts.

Understanding narrative as being *like* a living thing can help us better conceptualize our relationship with it. But imagining that narrative *is* alive puts us in a position to be better stewards of the lives we live alongside it.

As mentioned earlier in the book, viruses are not considered to be alive in the same way as a koala or jellyfish because they cannot reproduce on their own and rely on hosts for material, energy, and everything else required for their ability to spread. Narrative similarly fails certain tests for vitality: it certainly cannot live without human hosts. Yet I would press for a redefinition of both virus and story, since they evince that most essential quality of something that exists, that in some way lives: they persist and possess essential qualities aimed at continuing to do so. Debating to what extent they are alive distracts us from more immediate questions. How do *we* persist while knowing they have developed to exist with and within us? Is story an essential part of us, or is it in some meaningful way *apart* from us?

To insist that story exists beyond us would challenge even the most metaphysically credulous. To return to a biological contrast, I think it is a matter of the difference between a fungus like the *Ophiocordyceps unilateralis* and a retrovirus like those that helped shape mammalian placentation. *Orphiocordyceps* is a fungus that takes over certain species of ants and drives them to their individual destruction for its own survival and spread (*Cordyceps* is the fungus made famous by the video game and television series *The Last of Us*); the retrovirus did not necessarily have to destroy its hosts to survive, and over time became an essential part of our own evolution. Narrative is, to the best I can imagine, like this: it needs humanity and we need it. But sometimes—and perhaps lately, too often—this relationship's damages are more apparent than its advantages.

If we linger just a bit longer on the virus analogy for a moment: Viruses are "intracellular parasites" that require their hosts to reproduce and spread. Part of the reason they spread so quickly is that their replication is "error-prone"— they mutate and change quickly, becoming obsolete or extremely dangerous on sudden turns.[1] Public health responses to viruses—including vaccine development—require a knowledge of how the viruses function and often use the viruses themselves to provide treatment and inoculation. But there are other biological models as well: researchers have identified glioma—a kind of brain tumor—as parasitic in that it relies on brain activity to fuel tumor growth.[2] This parasitic relationship does not threaten the host's life, but it does change the person's behavior and personality, especially when it comes to aggression and loss of control.[3] Brain lesions can cause hallucinations and transgressive behavior, sometimes to the extreme, as in the case of the mass shooter Charles Whitman or the anonymous man whose brain tumor prompted a previously unknown obsession with pedophilia.[4] If, as discussed in Chapter 5, discourse can shape murderers, to what extent can we consider narrative different from other kinds of invasive, parasitic changes?

Even if comparing narrative to a malignant tumor is unhelpfully extreme, it is still necessary to consider how stories change us. We need to understand *and use* stories in order to stave off their worst effects. Another analogy I offered briefly in this book draws on physics: I compare the dynamic relationship between prior narratives, authors, and audiences to the spatial three-body problem. In classical mechanics, the three-body problem is the difficulty of predicting the motion of three bodies in space according to Newtonian laws of motion and gravitation, provided we know their initial positions and motion. (In literature, it is a challenging and fascinating science fiction novel by Liu Cixin.) As each of these bodies moves in space, they exert force on one another, turning and orbiting in a pattern that is explicable but fantastically difficult to predict. This analogy is attractive to me because it re-centers audience and tradition in prompting us to think about what narrative does in the world, but it does not account for what story wants or for multiplicities of movement and change in the bodies themselves. Imagine if those Newtonian laws had intention or desire and could change; imagine as well that the mass and motion of those three bodies appeared unstable, surging and relenting over time.

The sheer complexity and unpredictability of these relationships points to one reason that AI art and literature are not likely to replace human production. They will imitate, they will replicate, but they will probably not achieve the dynamic change and interdependence critical to human minds and stories. (Nevertheless, market forces will probably constrain human creative input in service of the faster and "cheaper" work of AI applications, limiting *who* gets to contribute to narrative's evolution and endangering our brief flowering of multiculturalism.) Indeed, in most of this book I have downplayed that complexity by eliding between very different levels of narrative, between what we consider myth or discourse and the creative storytelling enacted by individuals (and groups) drawing on narrative's greater store. As I suggested earlier, individual creations on the back of narrative in general are less significant than the body as a whole, but by treating the two as identical, I have left less room to consider story's own agency.

But I don't think that making this elision is a mistake—as the literary critic Florian Fuchs argues in his recent book, storytelling now includes journalism, videos, video games, and the myriad forms of narrative that have exploded with the rise of the internet.[5] One of the problems, as Fuchs sees it, is that modern "short forms" blend fact and fiction in subordination to an essayist stance, with far more emphasis on the subjective self than on a shared reality. But the tension here is not as simple as it might seem: Fuchs suggests that micronarratives and individual stories can bear witness to climate change and help produce a "device of collective intelligence" against more destructive, insidious, top-down narrative models.[6]

The tension between larger social discourse—or traditional narratives—and individual stories strikes me as echoing in some way the dynamic relationship between individuals and their cultural groups. The larger body of story exerts certain expectations and formal/thematic pressures on individual stories just as larger human groups use narrative to shape individuals within them. Pointing out these tensions can sometimes be off-putting, but the past few generations have seen an upswing in targeting discourse as a rhetorical ploy, a tool of discourse itself. Consider in recent years the bugbear of "cancel culture" or the specter raised by luminaries like Elon Musk of the "woke mind virus" that is destroying us. (Note that the groups most loudly decrying indoctrination are the ones most deeply invested in traditional forms of indoctrination.) As discussed in Chapter 5, "master narratives" are a potentially dangerous part of human culture, insofar as they enforce and support a kind of status quo and contribute to harming individuals. When these dominant scripts are challenged, culture can erupt, sometimes into violence, often with more rigid and damaging structures. The return of thinly veiled white supremacy and its retinue of hatreds over the past decade is not happenstance: it is a paroxysm in response to marginalized groups taking control of narrative themselves, and modern technology allowing those who have been taught to see themselves at the center of the world to know about it. These stories—our stories—have reached a point where they are doing demonstrable harm. Is there anything we can do about it?

Stories Make Us, Stories Break Us

The ancient Greek word that gives us *poet—poiētēs*—is an agent noun from a verb that can mean "make, create, do" (*poieō*). *Poem,* formed from the same root, adds a material suffix *-ma* to mean a "made thing" or a "creation." These terms can be translated appropriately in literary senses as "composer" and "composition," but the side of me that leans toward the mystical also likes thinking of a poet as a maker and poems as worlds, stories as universes waiting for their unveiling.

While I have returned repeatedly to ancient commentary, it is worth acknowledging that modernity has produced a deeply varied body of work about narrative as well. Sometimes it is difficult to put it all together because of the separation I mentioned earlier between approaches to discourse from disciplines like sociology and psychology and treatments of narrative as an art form in philosophy and literary theory. (Folklore and myth exist tenuously in between these poles, to my mind.) But asking what stories do in the world invites a wide array of answers that need to be understood as working together, in some sense, to provide pieces of a larger, shifting, growing, and deceptive puzzle. I have discussed several models throughout this book, emphasizing cognitive, psychological, and theoretical approaches, but in closing, I'd like to focus a bit on the narrative threads strung between disciplines, on that tightrope between narrative's advantages and its perils.

One of my favorite approaches to narrative centers the value of what it has given us. Evolutionary psychology, for example, often emphasizes that storytelling allows the transfer of knowledge from one generation to the next, and that it provides individuals with the capacity to contextualize their lives and give them meaning. Indeed, in *Sapiens,* Yuval Noah Harari proposes that language and narrative were essential parts of human development that helped us become the dominant species on the planet. He specifically credits our capacity to imagine and engage in fiction collectively as the "secret" that helped make cooperation in large groups possible.[7] And this secret can help predict or at least explain our behavior: as the biologist E. O. Wilson suggests, human beings demonstrate a need to believe in sacred narratives.[8] The literary scholar Brian Boyd traces the advantages of the development of art well in his *On the Origin of Stories,* but he is rather prolix on how stories can go wrong.[9] Of course, narrative itself has no innate moral content. Even stories that seem frightening or harmful can have positive impacts, as John Jeffries Martin argues in *A Beautiful Ending:* according to Martin, stories about the end of the world (his "apocalyptic imagination") are a particular feature of the modern world, in part because they offer a sense of agency through providence. This kind of optimism pervades books like Angus Fletcher's *Wonderworks* that catalogue and credit stories over time for significant human innovations, for narrative's ability to entertain but also to educate and by doing so to liberate. Among a certain subset of popular academics, it is common to emphasize story's potential to increase empathy or connect us, even though they can sometimes have the opposite effects. As with many other technologies, we tend to focus on advantages to a deleterious effect.[10]

Yet for every paean to narrative's positive power, we must also acknowledge that what is positive or liberating is also a feature of narrative conditioning, and what is available to some may be denied to many. Too many of us who sing narrative's praises are those who are "winners" from the perspective of cultural scripts or master narratives. We see the advantages of story more clearly because it has not disadvantaged us.

One of the things I have long taught students in my myth courses when they express concern about comments on human belief and religion is that observations about the impact of an idea *as a narrative* say little about its veracity and everything about its impact. (It should be a truism that "fake news" has had an equal if not greater effect on human history than the truth.) But the effects of belief can be tallied just as easily in the secular realm, as Robert Shiller does well in his *Narrative Economics,* where he surveys the myriad ways that profit and loss are driven by stories. It should be no surprise that he argues that irrational behavior (such as speculative bubbles) can appear perfectly rational, or at least sensible, given the information people receive within a certain narrative mindset, for example, the *belief* that property values will always increase, or the assumption that a particular credit rating has reliable and transferable value. Indeed, authors like Jonathan Gottschall who have identified the essentiality of story to human identity note the danger of this essence: in *The Story Paradox* he starts by telling readers never to trust a storyteller and moves through the twentieth century to our current fragmented narrative environment.[11] Not only do we exist in often separate and contrary narrative ecosystems, but we are also entering a golden age (my term) of fictiveness: deep fake videos and audio combined with the confabulating interventions of artificial intelligence and the willful interference of bad-faith cultural actors.

Worrying about this extreme can distract us from the immanent problem. As Peter Brooks argues in his recent

Seduced by Story, "the weight of the unanalyzed stories, those that are propagated as true and necessary myths, may kill us."[12] But Brooks suggests that the study of literature should provide "tools of resistance" to "dismantle the myths of our time." Narrative on a broader level serves both its own purpose (for narrative to survive) and, as a secondary impact, to preserve the structures that facilitate its survival. Our dominant cultural scripts support and advance white supremacy; but the same patterns of essentialism can be found to shape studies and policies that are intended to address the structures of hate, as Zakiyyah Iman Jackson so disarmingly argues in the conclusion of her *Becoming Human.* Indeed, one of the most alarming and potentially harmful developments of the industrial world is the assumption that the sciences are somehow free of narrative, that truth is available to one but not the other. Such a social discourse serves our economic and political orders by marginalizing the very fields of study that attempt to help us understand that all disciplines are shaped by discourse: story shapes what we call science, how we value it, and what we think it does in the world. Benjamin Labatut's *When We Cease to Understand the World* is an eloquent and understated exploration of the relationship between scientific endeavors and the lives led by the people who drive those endeavors: we are all shaped by our experiences, and all these experiences were shaped by the stories we know and those right beneath the surface.

Perhaps narrative has so thoroughly overcome us that we imagine its dominance in a way that ensures its continuance. The philosopher Galen Strawson in his essay "Against Narrativity" argues against approaches like those of Jerome Bruner and Daniel Dennett that claim empirically that narrative is central to human experience, or ethically that we should be living our life as if it were. Strawson suggests instead that life is episodic and disjointed and does not work as "a normative claim about what good or authentic human life must be like."[13] He offers as a counterproposal the model of Michel de Montaigne and modernists who challenge or escape memory. Indeed, another feature of twentieth-century art is the artists' attempt to undermine stories and tell new ones, to escape the bounds of history and live *in* a time instead of through it. But this is not necessarily a new approach: as I argue in *The Many-Minded Man,* part of the point of the prophet Tiresias's prophecy that Odysseus will go a-traveling again until he comes to a land where people mistake an oar for a winnowing fan is that to escape the limits of traditional storytelling, we must endeavor to enter a world free of its language, beyond its precedents.

But how is that possible for minds shaped by story? While I find Strawson's arguments attractive, they assume a rational mind existing on its own, able to choose action and thought free of the influence of narrative. Nothing I have read in developmental or cognitive psychology makes this seem plausible. Strawson's conclusion that "narrativity . . . is in the sphere of ethics more of an affliction or a bad habit than a prerequisite of a good life" provides some promise of peace but also resonates with the words of the philosopher E. M. Cioran in "The Decor of Knowledge":

> That History has no meaning is what should delight our hearts. Should we be tormenting ourselves for a happy solution to process, for a final festival paid for by nothing but our sweat, our disasters? For future idiots exulting over our labors, frolicking on our ashes? The vision of a paradisiac conclusion transcends, in its absurdity, the worst divagations of hope. All we can offer in excuse for Time is that in it we find some moments more profitable than others, accidents without consequence in an intol-

erable monotony of perplexities. The universe begins and ends with each individual, whether he be
Shakespeare or Hodge; for each individual experiences his merit or his nullity *in the absolute*. [14]

In each case, the world and its stories seem to be judged
from the point of the one, of the singular life and the singular
individual examining it. A whiff of nihilism clings to this, even
if it also leans toward a carpe diem–ing across the page. Perhaps I am too obtuse or mutilated by narrative to even imagine the lives Strawson and Cioran see, but human beings do
not exist alone: we are part of communities, of corporate bodies, of bodies politic. Language connects us to one another;
story translates us through time.

Facing Up to Story

When I presented some of this work at an academic confer-
ence, a few of the participants asked me a simple question:
What about pleasure? Indeed, academic literary criticism, as
Brian Boyd notes, tends to jump to "meaning" in a rather narrow way without first considering how "works of art need to
attract and arouse audiences before they 'mean.'"[15] To deny
that stories matter to us, that they bring us pleasure as well as
pain, and that they can be part of a meaningful life is to deny
that storytelling is very much a part of what makes us human.
Positing that the pleasure from stories is somehow merely incidental may be an even worse step. Consider other bodily
pleasures—sex, eating; from some perspectives these acts do
have purposes separate from their effects: eating keeps us alive,
but can also make us feel (and be) content; sex and intimacy
may be incentives to help drive procreation, but to consider
these things incidental is to so thoroughly narrow what it

means to be human and lead lives in these bodies as to double down on a naive view of the mind/body split. Proposing a wholescale resistance to stories is practically impossible given how crucial narrative is to our identities and the communities we build together. In a way, I think advocating for a hardline resistance to narrative is akin to insisting on abstinence-only sex education: both deny us the rare pleasures that nature affords; both approaches try to make us into something we are not, and perhaps should not want to be.

A few decades ago, researchers into mirror neurons made something of a splash by showing that our neurobiological responses to fiction are essentially the same as those from real experiences—when we laugh or cry over the experiences of imagined others, our bodies laugh and cry, we feel and we live vicariously through them.[16] Story is not essential merely because it allows us to learn from the mistakes of others; narrative is not needed simply because it allows us to explore different options and worlds without harming others or ourselves—storytelling allows us to live countless lives from the finitude of our own, to commune with the ancients, to journey into the future, to develop understanding of and empathy for others, to expand our very notion of what it means to exist by learning that other bodies and minds experience the world differently, but are nonetheless vitally alive and undeniably real.[17]

Other solutions offer some points to consider: the hope that narrative loses its power over time the way viruses attenuate during an epidemic is well placed, but downplays the speed of mutation and recombination of each. To refuse narrativity, as Galen Strawson insists, is to embrace self-determination and imagine ourselves as wholly separate from others. Can we truly unplug? Can we take the now half-century-old advice of John Prine and throw our televisions away and move to a farm? But to follow the metaphor of Plato's cave and insist that we must liberate ourselves from narrative and embrace only the real ignores the blood-and-flesh truth of the human relationship with stories: the shadows on Plato's wall might not be real, but they make us think and feel, and provide us with the practice to begin to define reality for ourselves.[18]

It may come as no surprise that a humanist uses so many thousands of words to suggest that the cure for the dangers of story, the vaccine for this narrative virus, is engaging with story itself.[19] Our vulnerability to narrative is increased when we do not learn about its power, when we are not taught how to engage with it directly. We need to be taught to develop the tools to engage with story intentionally rather than passively allowing it to shape us.[20] From primary school education on, we need to emphasize rich and complex engagement with narrative. This means focusing less on standardized testing and more on reading and discussing stories together. (And "story" here is inclusive of narrative in all its forms, visual, aural, moving, and static.) This means emphasizing media literacy alongside the history of ideas. This means teaching about cognition, psychology, and evolution much earlier in education and framing STEM fields as subject to discourse too, not just as instruments to make us better partners for computers or more effective gears in production machines.

This also means making judgments about the kinds of narratives that are more conducive to improving our collective relationship with stories: they need to be complex, ambiguous, multicultural, and diverse. We must challenge received canons, but also acknowledge when older stories still have something to contribute. Narratives with open ends that challenge how we see the world and provide problems instead of paradigms should be central. Yes, it is also no surprise that a Homerist points to the Homeric epics as examples of how to do this: but, as if in creating an actual vaccine, these poems take the essential features of narrative and reweave them into sophisticated ruminations on narrative's power and "problem sets" about how it works in the world.[21] They are examples, I believe, of how one people developed a way of managing narrative and of transmitting this management from one generation to the next.

The speed of how we transmit narrative has accelerated the pace of change. Whether we are talking about conspiracy theories or streaming entertainment, we encounter a greater intensity and frequency of story than at any time in human history. Teaching people how their brains respond to narrative, how they rely on it, and the good and ill it can do is as important as ensuring they know their multiplication tables and how to spell. One of the main ideas of the liberal arts as traditionally posed is that they are the disciplines *worthy* of free people. But I deeply believe that in education they should be the practices that help us *become free*. In my own imaginary university, *the* core course is "The Handbook to the Human Mind": an interdisciplinary mix of biology, psychology, literature, and the history of ideas, a course to help us all understand how we make a story of the world and what stories do to us in turn. Education should empower us to control our own stories, to self-determine the patterns we will take, to escape the circularity of essentialism, and to create our own meaning in the world.

And then? What tears us apart can bring us together again. We should read, view, and interpret together. Education should be based in learning how to respond to narrative and art and then reconciling our responses with others and by doing so building communities around the story of making sense of stories, of making meaning in the world together. To do any less reduces us all to fading marks on a forgotten page.

Suggestions for Further Reading

Introduction

For recent work on the formulaic nature of human language and activity in general, see the collection *Weathered Words: Formulaic Language and Verbal Art,* edited by Frog and William Lamb. The canonical readings on this topic include Milman Parry's *The Making of Homeric Verse,* Albert Lord's *The Singer of Tales,* and John Miles Foley's *How to Read an Oral Poem.* See also Robert Kanigel's recent biography of Parry, *Hearing Homer's Song.*

For work on authorship in literary criticism, the most famous text from the twentieth century may be Roland Barthes's "The Death of the Author," anticipated in part by the earlier concept of the intentional fallacy, introduced by W. K. Wimsatt and Monroe Beardsley in *The Verbal Icon:* the idea that a text once separated from its author owes more to the audiences than to its creator. For an extended discussion of this concept in postmodern literary theory, see Seán Burke, *The Death and Return of the Author.* Other literary theoretical approaches emerged subsequently that de-centered the author in more practical ways, such as reader response theory—see Wolfgang Iser's *The Implied Reader* or, for an emphasis on community, Stanley Fish's *Is There a Text in This Class?* For a cognitive approach that focuses on how readers create a "blend" between narratives and their own experiences, see Mark Turner, *The Literary Mind* and the broader considerations in Terence Cave's *Thinking with Literature.*

Chapter 1. Scripts for Life

In addition to the work by and on Parry and Lord and John Miles Foley's *How to Read an Oral Poem* mentioned above, see Walter Ong's *Orality and Literacy* and Ruth Finnegan's *Oral Poetry.* Eric Havelock, in *The Muse Learns to Write,* provides a critical, if now dated, overview of the transition from performance to writing in antiquity. The work of Gregory Nagy (especially *The Best of the Achaeans*) and Egbert Bakker's *Poetry in Speech* also represent good examples of how classicists have built on the Parry-Lord approaches. Parry's work built on theories of linguistics found in Ferdinand de Saussure's *Course in General Linguistics.*

Chapter 2. Recombinations and Change

For a discussion of ring structures in literature see Mary Douglas's fine essay *Thinking in Circles.* The meaning of ring structures is still somewhat at play in responses to oral or oral-derived poetry. Inspired in part by work like that of W. A. A. van Otterlo on ring compositions (*Untersuchungen über Begriff, Anwendung und Entstehung der griechische Ringcomposition*), Cedric Whitman has probably provided the most exhaustive study of these structures in Homer in his *Homer and the Heroic Tradition,* although he focuses more on themes and content than on formal features. Dieter Lohmann's *Die*

Komposition der Reden in der "Ilias" demonstrates how important ring structures are to Homeric speeches. Keith Stanley's
The Shield of Homer offers a more global view of the function
of ring composition in small scale (Achilles' shield) and
throughout the whole poem, if he also ends up concluding too
much on the side of textualist approaches. For a study of the
design of the *Iliad* based on performance and the epic's tri-
partite structure, see Bruce Heiden's *Homer's Cosmic Fabrication.* Erwin Cook's essay "Structure as Interpretation in the
Homeric *Odyssey*" makes essential progress in moving between the generative and interpretive approaches to ring composition. Brian Boyd's *On the Origin of Stories* has some fine
chapters on how Homeric epic fits into the development of
human narrative.

Chapter 3. Crabs and the Monomyth

For a broad overview of the history of the science of evolution,
see Donald Prothero's *Evolution;* for a more polemic approach
to the issue of evolution and design, see Richard Dawkins, *The
Blind Watchmaker.* Jonathan Weiner's *The Beak of the Finch*
and Stephen Jay Gould's *Ever Since Darwin* both provide read-
able overviews of the current debates. For human evolution,
see the narrative provided by Alice Roberts in *The Incredible
Unlikeliness of Being.* For human impact on natural evolution,
see Elizabeth Kolbert's *The Sixth Extinction.* Augustín Fuentes's *Why We Believe* can add to this conversation human culture and our need to believe ideas and narratives—while
Fuentes focuses on "culture," I would argue that narrative is
central to culture from the level of discourse at least. For a
powerful critique of our modern discourse of epigenetics (in
particular how it reinforces racist biological essentialism), see
Zakiyyah Iman Jackson's "Conclusion" in *Becoming Human.*

For discussions of the heroic pattern and the monomyth, see in brief my essay with Sarah Bond ("The Man Behind the Myth"). Joseph Campbell's *The Hero with a Thousand Faces* is probably the most popular book on the topic, but interested readers should also consult Vladimir Propp's *Morphology of the Folktale* and some of Carl Jung's work on archetypes, such as *The Archetypes and the Collective Unconscious,* and Otto Rank's *The Myth of the Birth of the Hero* for how this idea presages many later ideas. For Greek heroes, Gregory Nagy's *The Best of the Achaeans* remains a mainstay, although his *The Ancient Greek Hero in 24 Hours* is more accessible for those who do not know ancient Greek. For a theoretical overview of myth, see Eric Csapo, *Theories of Mythology;* for an approach that parallels mine, see Sarah Iles Johnston, *The Story of Myth.*

For a recent translation of the Gilgamesh poems, see Sophus Helle, *Gilgamesh* (which includes several useful interpretive essays); for a series of discussions about Mesopotamian literature, see Martin Worthington, *Ea's Duplicity in the Gilgamesh Flood Story;* Gina Konstantopoulos and Sophus Helle, *The Shape of Stories;* and the overview provided in Sophus Helle, *Enheduana.* For themes and motifs in the Gilgamesh poems, see Tzvi Abusch, *Male and Female in the Epic of Gilgamesh,* and Louise Pryke, *Gilgamesh.* For a classic investigation of the development of the Gilgamesh poems, see Jeffrey Tigay, *The Evolution of the Gilgamesh Epic,* and Tzvi Abusch, "The Development and Meaning of the Epic of Gilgamesh."

Chapter 4. Going Viral

For a discussion of the dangers of narrative in Greek myth, see especially Ann Bergren's collected essays in *Weaving Truth* and the discussions in Pietro Pucci's *Song of the Sirens.* Michael

White discusses the impact of harmful narratives and how to address them in his work on narrative therapy (starting with *Maps of Narrative Practice,* which I draw on extensively in *The Many-Minded Man;* see Stephen Madigan's overview in *Narrative Therapy*). Modern work like that of Angus Fletcher in *Wonderworks* rightly focuses on how much narrative does for us, but it overlooks how much damage narrative can do. For other perspectives on narrative's harm, see Jonathan Gottschall's *The Story Paradox* and Peter Brooks's *Seduced by Story.*

A good overview of the relationship between poetic traditions assigned to Homer and Hesiod is Barbara Graziosi and Johannes Haubold, *Homer: The Resonance of Epic.* Jenny Strauss Clay's *Hesiod's Cosmos* also provides a lot of comparative treatment of the traditions. Zoe Stamatopoulou's *Hesiod and Classical Greek Poetry* provides another fine recent overview. A good deal of Hesiodic poetry is only fragmentary; see Kirk Ormand, *The Hesiodic Catalogue of Women and Archaic Greece,* for this larger body of lost work as well as Richard Hunter's edited volume *The Hesiodic Catalogue of Women, Constructions and Reconstructions.*

Chapter 5. Symbiosis and Paradigm

For additional information on Homeric similes, see William C. Scott, *The Artistry of the Homeric Simile,* which provides a fine overview of typology and functions, and Jonathan Ready, *Character, Narrator and Simile in the "Iliad,"* for a sustained analysis of how similes are used by Homeric speakers. Ready's *The Homeric Simile in Comparative Perspectives* provides a good overview of other traditions and orality. I. A. Richards's treatment of simile as a subset of metaphor in *The Philosophy of Rhetoric* has long influenced my thinking. For an in-depth

exploration of a single Homeric simile that examines its metonymic and thematic effectiveness, see Leonard Muellner, "The
Simile of the Cranes and Pygmies."

The first cognitive approach to literature that changed the
way I read was Mark Turner's *The Literary Mind*. Brian Boyd's
On the Origin of Stories approaches the issue from a cognitive
perspective, with some criticism for Turner's theory. Terence
Cave's *Thinking with Literature: Towards a Cognitive Criticism*
provides a short yet detailed overview of cognitive approaches
with some applications. Paul Armstrong's *Stories and the Brain*
is an excellent addition to this growing bibliography, which
should also include Michael Tomasello's *The Cultural Origins
of Human Cognition*. Work centered less in cognitive science
and more in cognitive psychology is helpful as well. Jerome
Bruner's *Actual Minds, Possible Worlds* is a classic, critiqued
in part by Galen Strawson in "Against Narrativity." But Bruner's approach was influential on Michael White's work narrative therapy, which has influenced my thinking a great deal.
See White's *Maps of Narrative Practice* and Stephen Madigan's
Narrative Therapy. Dan McAdams's "'First We Invented Stories, Then They Changed Us'" provides a good blend of varied
approaches.

Notes

For the benefit of readers, I have included currently available translations of classical works in the Further Reading section, but unless otherwise indicated, all translations of classical works are my own. The notes in this book have been kept intentionally short; for fuller discussions see the Suggestions for Further Reading, which are keyed to each chapter.

Introduction

1. In this book, Greek names are usually transliterated letter by letter, with macrons used to distinguish the long vowels *eta* and *omega*, and *kappa* transliterated as "k," not "c," except in cases where the "k" could be confusing (e.g., "Kirke" for "Circe") or in names that have entered the language with the "c" transliteration (e.g., "Socrates," "Achilles").

2. See the Further Reading section for more on authorship and models of reading. For a late-twentieth-century overview of Homeric studies and literary theory, see Lynn-George's 1994 review article.

3. Hesiod, *Theogony* 27–29. See Scodel 2001 for a discussion of this passage; for these lines and the memory forces of correspondence and coherence, see Christensen 2020, 120–23.

4. Plato, *Ion* 533d–534e. For the performance of Homeric poetry, see González 2013; cf. Nagy 2008.

5. Consider how the historians David Graeber and David Wengrow position heroic literature cross-culturally in the tension between growing urban civilizations and the rejection of the principles of those civilizations (2021, 311–12).

6. For a narrative discussion of studies in memory, see Fernyhough 2012.

7. See Christensen 2020, especially chapter 1, influenced by Bruner 1986 and Turner 1996.

8. See Matute et al. 2015 for causality bias and van Prooijen and Douglas 2018 for a vulnerability to conspiracy theories.

9. For teleological mindsets as essentially human, see Schacner, Zhu, and Kelemen 2017; For intuitive concepts of agency and design in child development, see Keleman 2004; see Mermelstein and German 2021 for how this translates into acceptance of pseudoscience, Preston and Shin 2021 for anthropocentric bias in our approach to nature, and Reiss 2005 for comments on the impact of teleological thinking in biological arguments.

10. See, for example, Gopinath, Hagan, Marchetti, and Baskaran 2012 and McCandlish, Baskaran, and Hagan 2012.

11. This answer was generated by OpenAI's ChatCPT program when queried "How do you work?" on February 5, 2023.

12. See, for example, Dennett 2017.

13. See Yuval Noah Harari's argument (2015) that true AI would be an intelligence wholly unlike our own, to the point of being *alien*. My thanks to an anonymous referee for this point.

14. See Augustine, *Confessions* 6.3.3.

15. Cave 2016, 5.

16. See Brian Boyd's view of the "biocultural approach to literature" (2009, 253).

17. Sperber 1994; see also Sperber 1996.

Chapter 1. Scripts for Life

1. For somewhat contrasting overviews of the history of textual problems with Homer, see West 2001 and Nagy 2004. Where West emphasizes a fairly traditional author-writing model for the generation of the texts of each epic, Nagy explores an evolutionary/staged development. For more on a multitextual approach to epic "texts," see Dué 2019.

2. For an overview of epic verse, see the introductory chapter in Barker and Christensen 2013.

3. For a detailed examination of the multiform in oral poetry as corresponding to variations within populations on an evolutionary level, see Drout 2011.

4. For a longer discussion of parallel and convergent evolution see Chapter 2.

5. Here is a transcription of the Greek with the digammas restored:

Mēnin aeide Thea Pēlēiadeō Akhilēos
Oulomenēn hē muri Akhaiois alge' ethēke
Pollas d'iphthimous psukhas Aϝidi proiapsen
Hērōōn autous de ϝelōria teukhe kunessin
Oiōnoisi te pasi Dios d'eteleieto boulē
Eks hou dē ta prōta diastētēn erisante
Atreidēs te ϝanaks andrōn kai dios Akhilleus.

6. There are some political controversies about such claims, but emerging research supports them. See for example Scorza et al. 2019; for poverty and infectious diseases Bonds et al. 2010; for the epigenetic effect of famine, see Heijmans et al. 2008; for epigenetic impact of childhood stress, see Jiang et al. 2019; and Cohen et al. 2006 for stress and socioeconomic pressures. For a critique of the way some of these studies are set up, see Jackson 2020, "Coda."

7. See Muellner 1996.

8. Tomasello 1999. See Harari 2015, chap. 1, for language's importance to the supremacy of *Homo sapiens*.

9. This kind of analogy has the danger of falling into a naive Sapir-Whorf framing. "Sapir-Whorf" refers to a hypothesis of linguistic relativity, arguing that the language people speak structures how they think and see the world.

10. *Iliad* 1.58.

11. *Iliad* 1.488–92.

12. For a discussion of this epithet in particular, see Barker and Christensen 2019, 50–60.

13. Xenophanes fr. 2, 16–19 = Athenaeus X 413f–414c.

14. Alcman fr. 1.

15. *Odyssey* 13.259–62.

16. *Iliad* 9.168–98.

17. For the most recent bibliography, see Lesser 2022, 139–40. For other overviews, see Griffin 1995, 51–53. Scodel 2002, 160–71. See also Nagy 1979, 49–55, and Martin 1989, 236–37.

18. For Achilles' excluding Odysseus, see Nagy 1979; for Phoinix and Ajax, see Martin 1989.

19. This is found in the marginal notes of medieval manuscripts to Homer called "scholia" for line 9.182 of the *Iliad*: Schol. T In Hom. ad. *Il.* 9.182.

Chapter 2. Recombinations and Change

1. Combellack 1960, 159, 166.

2. Donna Wilson (2002) offers the model of "refraction" instead of reflection for thinking about how themes and plots echo each other from one iteration to another in narrative myth.

3. See especially Alberts et al. 2002, chapter 21.

4. Arend (1933) presents a classic overview; for composition by theme, see Lord 2000 (originally published in 1960), 120. Fenik 1968 is a groundbreaking study on aesthetics and type-scenes (focusing on battle scenes). More recent full-length examples include Reece 1993 (hospitality scenes) and Hitch 2009 (sacrifice). For conversation as type-scene, see Beck 2005.

5. For composition by theme, see Lord 2000, 120, and Martin 1989, 206–30, and more generally Nagy 1979 on the interplay between meter, diction, and theme.

6. See Hitch 2009, following Bakker 1997.

7. For vocabulary in arming scenes, see Fenik 1968; for sacrifices, see Hitch 2009.

8. See Christensen 2020, 80–82.

9. For the importance of Odysseus's deliberation in *Odyssey* 5 as "personified interchange" of an internalized mental process, see Russo and Simon 1968, 488; cf. Gill 1996, 59, 86–87.

10. Otherwise, as Becca Frankel suggested to me, "Odysseus would be like a Ken doll, no choices, just an accessory."

11. See Saussy 1996 for a similar argument about the *Odyssey*'s entire structure being built from repetitions.

12. *Iliad* 11.407–10; 17.90–105. For the phrase *autar ho mermērikse polutlas dios* indicating an Odysseus type-scene of pondering options, see Dué and Ebbott 2009, 366.

13. The first two lines occur at *Odyssey* 5.354–35; for a fuller discussion of this scene, see Christensen 2020, 80–82.

14. See Hitch 2009, 8–13, for a fine discussion of repetition and variation in type-scenes.

15. The Trans-Canadian Research and Environmental Education (TREE) program website is a great educational resource: https://tree.lightsource.ca/home.

16. In literary theory in general, *synecdoche* often indicates a part-for-whole relationship where one word is replaced by a related part of another. Synecdoche is a subset of a metonymy. I follow Leonard Muellner (2019) and Gregory Nagy (2016) in the use of metonymy for Homeric meaning making. Muellner writes: "Metonymy is the establishment of a relationship between

tenor and vehicle that is based on attachment or connection, either physical or psychological" (2019, 141). For "tenor" and "vehicle" see Richards 1965.

17. Cited in Douglas 2007, 6.

18. See Douglas 2007 for an overview of the history of interpreting ring composition in literature.

19. Minchin 2001, 23–28, 181–202; cf. Arft 2017, 8–11. See Cook 2014 for how ring composition may guide interpretation.

20. *Iliad* 9.97–98.

21. *Iliad* 9.102.

22. The proem to Hesiod's *Theogony*, for example, begins with the declaration that the narrator "begins" with the Muses (1)—a nice parallel for my argument is that the proem also "ends" with the Muses (114) and, there is yet another ending at 1022, which may be, importantly, also the beginning of the Catalogue of Women. Cf. Collins 2004, 148n4.

23. See Douglas 2007, 7.

24. See Douglas 2007, 101–24.

25. See Kwapisz 2014 for the so-called Behaghel's law for the "tricolon ascendo."

26. *Iliad* 2.173.

27. *Iliad* 1.145.

28. Kakridis 1949, 43–49; see also Fenik 1974, 142–207; Sammons 2014, 302–10.

29. *Iliad* 6.450–55. On this passage, see Warwick 2019.

30. *Iliad* 2.378; 22.237. For more on doublets in the *Odyssey*, see O'Nolan 1978.

31. Fenik 1974, 142–207; cf. Sammons 2013 for an overview of doublet structures in the so-called epic cycle.

32. Hesiod, *Works and Days* 223–32; Barker and Christensen 2019, 560–65.

33. Hesiod, *Works and Days* 161–65; Barker and Christensen 2019, 108–11.

34. For how chiastic structure facilitates the development of meaning in ring structures, see Arft 2022, 136.

35. Turner 1996; Armstrong 2020, 6.

36. Armstrong again: "To follow a story is to engage in a two-way, back-and-forth interaction between the configured patterns of action emplotted in the narrative and the figures through which the recipient experiences the push and pull of the world" (2020, 178).

37. This translation is my own. The most engaging translation of Sappho's poetry in English remains Anne Carson's *If Not, Winter* (2002). For an introduction to the background and interpretative issues in the fragments attributed to her, see the recent *Cambridge Companion to Sappho* edited by P. J. Finglass (2021).

38. *Iliad* 9.525–26.

39. *Iliad* 9.189.

40. *Iliad* 9.600–605.

Chapter 3. Crabs and the Monomyth

1. See Brett Rogers's 2011 essay for a longer critique of the application of the hero's journey pattern to superhero narratives.

2. I thank Becca Frankel for this analogy.

3. See Christensen 2008.

4. See the technical discussion in Wolfe, Luque, and Bracken-Grissom 2021; for a simpler overview, see Willis 2022.

5. *Odyssey* 1.215–16.

6. For definitions of myth and narrative, see Csapo 2005 and Johnston 2018.

7. See Sophus Helle's recent work on Enheduana (2023).

8. Aelian, *On the Nature of Animals* 12.21.

9. *Iliad* 19.63–64.

10. Abusch 2001, 614.

11. See the discussion in George 2007.

12. George 2003, 103.

13. See George 2007, 23–24; cf. Foster 1993, 43.

14. On the question of transmission, see Bachvarova 2016 and the discussion in West 1997, 586–630.

15. See Sanders 2015 and Bachvarova 2016, 76, especially for indications of bilingual oral traditions.

16. See Christensen 2008.

17. *Iliad* 24.128–32.

18. See Pryke 2019, 156–57, for a discussion of the Old Babylonian version and its differences from the more standard one.

19. See Tigay 1982, Abusch 2001, and the essay in Helle 2021 for discussions of this specific difference between the Old Babylonian and Standard Babylonian texts.

20. Sippar Tablet III 6–13, trans. George 1999, 124. Both Sasson (1972, 274) and Beye (1984, 17) see this advice as traditional.

21. My translation from the epigram preserved in Athenaeus's *Deipnosophistae* 8.14.

22. This pattern caused M. L. West to compare Shiduri to Circe; see West 1997, 404–10.

23. See Bachvarova 2016, 190.

24. "Spanish Pipedream," words and music by John Prine and Jeff Kent, 1971.

25. See Abusch 2015, 5.

26. See the overview discussion in Grant 2012 and Chirigati 2022 and the critique in Heyes 2010.

Chapter 4. Going Viral

1. Hesiod, *Theogony* 93–102. Previously, 66–93 summarized.

2. See Christensen 2020, 36–38.

3. *Odyssey* 12.39–44.

4. For the connection between drugs and poetry in the *Odyssey,* and in this episode in particular, see Bergren 2008, chap. 5, "Helen's 'Good Drug.'" Cf. the afterword in Stewart 1976 and the discussion in Clay 1994.

5. For homecoming as a return to life and light, see Frame 1978; cf. Bonifazi 2009 for homecoming as salvation.

6. SEG 40:28, AI[2].

7. For this formula, see Nagy 1979.

8. *Iliad* 9.412–16.

9. *Odyssey* 8.256–369. For an overview of the correspondences between the song of Ares, Aphrodite, and Hephaistos and the larger *Odyssey,* see Burkert 1997; see Alden 2017, 211–16, for an extended bibliography.

10. See Zipes, 2023, 6: "Fairy tales are relevant because they pass on information vital for human adaptation to changing environments." For a recent overview of the dangers of narrative, see Brooks 2022.

11. See *Odyssey* 4.584 and 7.333.

12. See *Iliad* 16.461 and 23.137–40.

13. See, e.g., Nagy 1996, 71–81.

14. *Iliad* 5.529–32; see also 15.487–91.

15. The Suda, a Byzantine Greek encyclopedia, attributes the saying "live unknown" to Epicurus's brother Neoklēs, although it was proverbially credited to the former. Stoic philosophers argued in contrast that living publicly was the only way to guarantee virtue. See Seneca's *Moral Epistle* 10.5 or Plutarch's essay in the *Moralia* "On Whether Living Unknown Is a Wise Precept."

16. *Iliad* 7.89–91 and 22.512–14.

17. *Odyssey* 1.239–44.

18. *Odyssey* 24.93–94.

19. See *Odyssey* 18.126.

20. *Odyssey* 1.343–44.

21. See especially the studies performed by Guo et al. (2021) in the early part of the epidemic.

22. For viral growth and epidemiological models applied to economic narratives, see appendix A in Shiller 2019. See also see, for example, Lauring and Peck 2018.

23. A = Pindar, *Nemean* 6.28–30; B = Bacchylides, Ode 5.195–97.

24. A = Simonides, *Greek Anthology* 7.301; B = Tyrtaeus fr. 12.24–28.

25. Mimnermus fr. 25=Stobaeus 4.57.11.

26. For "recurrence and mutation" in economic narratives, see Shiller 2019, 107–14.

27. See Austin 2021 and Lesser 2022 on the impact of desire and longing in the *Iliad* in contrast, but also complement, to the rage emphasized by Muellner 1996. For lament and Greek epic, see Alexiou 2002 and Dué 2002.

28. IG XII, 1 737, Rhodes, ca. 600–575 BCE.

29. A =Ibycus, fr. 282(a) 41–48 [= P.Oxy. 1790]; B =Theognis, 865–68.

30. Simonides, *Greek Anthology* 7.251.

31. IG I^3 1179, ca. 432 BCE.

32. See the discussion in Barker and Christensen 2019, 270–73; Snodgrass 1971, 55–57; and Mitchell 2007.

33. See Matute et al. 2015; van Prooijen and Douglas 2018, especially.

Chapter 5. Symbiosis and Paradigm

1. *Iliad* 12.421–26.

2. *Iliad* 12.277–89.

3. *Iliad* 13.754.

4. Seneca, *Moral Epistle* 99.12: *Vita nec bonum nec malum est; boni ac mali locus est* (life is neither good nor evil: it is where good and evil happen). Cf. Peter Brooks's conclusion: "Stories, narrative fictions, have no positive or negative valence of themselves. They can be used as tools to advance the worse as well as the better cause" (2022, 120).

5. See, e.g., Fernyhough 2012; Bruner 1986; and White 2007.

6. See McAdams 2019; see, e.g., Turner 1996; Boyd 2009; Dennett 2017 and Cave 2016.

7. Cf. McAdams 2019 on the importance of narrative to human evolution from the perspective of group dynamics. He points especially to Dautenhahn 2002 and Boyd 2009.

8. Zimmer 2021.

9. See, for example, Moore and Jaykus 2018.

10. See Pradeau 2016; cf. Zimmer 2021, 68–69.

11. As Zimmer notes in his chapter "Our Inner Parasites," up to 8 percent of an individual human's DNA is made up of symbiotic inheritance. He concludes, "There is no us and them—just a gradually blending and shifting mix of DNA" (2021, 71). Viruses are part of who we are and part of the story of our becoming. Outside the realm of the biological, it is useful to consider how much we can say the same about narrative.

12. See Roossinck 2015.

13. See Iskra-Caruana et al. 2010.

14. See Zimmer 2021, 67–68.

15. See Dolja 2021.

16. Harari 2015. See also Peter Brooks's citation of Friedrich Schiller's notion of the play drive for narrative and imagination, suggesting that "art [is] the fullest realization of what it means to be human" (2022, 101).

17. Gazzaniga and LeDoux 1978; see also Gazzaniga 2012.

18. On the formation of Homeric epic see Nagy 2004.

19. On paradeigmata in speeches, see especially Willcock 1964 and 1977. Cf. Edmunds 1997 and Nagy 1996, 13–46.

20. See my argument about the end of the *Odyssey* in Christensen 2020, chaps. 8 and 9.

21. See, e.g., Andersen 1987.

22. Paradigms in the *Iliad* include 1.259–74 (Nestor's tale of the Lapiths and Centaurs); 1.393–407 (Thetis's rescue of Zeus); 4.370–400 (the tale of Tydeus); 5.382–404 (Dionē's list of gods harmed by mortals); 7.124–60 (Nestor's one-on-one combat); 18.394–405 (Thetis's rescue of Hephaistos); 9.524–605 (the Meleager tale). To this list we can add Nestor's story to Patroklos (11.669–762), Zeus's erotic catalogue (14.315–28), and Zeus's later warning to Hera (15.18–30).

23. For Nestor as the epic's ideal speaker, see Martin 1989, 81; Dickson 1995.

24. An anonymous ancient critic summarizes: "It is right to be ever-mindful of good men. For singers make their audiences wise through ancient narratives." Schol. A ad. Il. 9.189b ex. 1–2.

25. *Iliad* 9.189.

26. *Iliad* 9.524–26.

27. As an anonymous reader also mentions, audiences could imagine that Achilles knows the other details of the Meleager narrative—for example, that Meleager will die if he fights his uncles.

28. *Iliad* 19.64–65.

29. For the titling function of *eris,* see Christensen 2018a.

30. For Achilles' chairmanship of the games as a step in exploring the institutionalization of dissent, see Barker 2009, 83–88; cf. Elmer 2013, 187–95.

31. *Iliad* 23.490–94.

32. See Brian Boyd's (2009) chapters on Homeric epic for an evolutionary perspective of the tension between tradition and innovation.

33. See Christensen 2020, 115–47.

34. *Odyssey* 1.31–32.

35. For a list of the episodes relating to Agamemnon and Orestes, see Alden 2017, 77–100.

36. Nancy Felson has written well in her *Regarding Penelope* (1994) about how different characters encounter different responses based on their gender or social position.

37. See Richard Martin's essay on Telemachus and the last hero song (1993), in which he argues that Telemachus's own story is shaped without the trickster element to help signal the end of a particular kind of narrative (along with the epic tradition!).

38. Pausanias, *Description of Greece*, 6.9.6–9.

39. A third version, in the Byzantine encyclopedia known as the Suda, seems to be drawn from Pausanias's account. Plutarch, Life of Romulus 4–7; Suda, Kappa 1725.

40. For a detailed history of the Columbine shootings and the individuals and events that produced the tragedy, see Cullen's revised *Columbine* (2016).

41. See Hammack 2008; McLean and Syed 2015; and McAdam 2019 for more on the cultural script of the master narrative.

42. See Cook 1999 for heroes' capacity to suffer and cause suffering.

43. See the discussion in Plato, *Republic* 2.390e–91c and again in 10. 599d–601a; Simone Weil's famous essay *The "Iliad": or, The Poem of Force* (2003).

44. See Philips 1994.

45. See Granovetter 1978 and Gladwell 2015.

46. For cultural differences in narrative emphasis on individual and collective, see McAdams 2019, 11–12.

47. But the threshold explanation is still reductive. In the wake of Columbine, critics noted that the killers were not in fact fans of Marilyn Manson and that attacks on performers like him were driven by "culture wars" and conservative Christians in their "satanic panic." Yet two decades later, Brian Warner—the legal name of the artist behind Marilyn Manson—has been accused of abuse, sexual assault, sex trafficking, and a range of racist and harmful behavior. See Grow and Newman 2021.

48. For the contrast between internal state psychology and intentional state psychology, see Bruner 1986, 35–36, and White 2007, 102–106. See Christensen 2018b for an application of this contrast to the *Odyssey*.

Conclusion

1. For a brief overview of these characteristics, see Ojosnegros and Beerenwinkel 2010.

2. See Krishna and Hervey-Jumper 2023 for an overview, and Krishna, Choudhury, Keough, et al., 2023 for more detail.

3. See Boele et al. 2015 for personality changes in glioma patients.

4. See the overview of lesions and criminal behavior in Darby et al. 2017 and the overview of a few cases in Eagleman 2011. Lupton et al. 2020 caution that the tumor may not be causal in a biological sense and urge research into social and personal histories as well.

5. Fuchs 2023, 225.

6. Fuchs 2023, 245.

7. See Harari 2015, 21–37. See also Wilson 1999, 143–45.

8. Wilson 1999, 289–90.

9. See Boyd 2009, but also consider Wilson 2014, 51; Le Hunte and Golembiewski 2014, 75. Cf. Gottschall 2012, 102.

10. See Armstrong 2020, 150–52, for a critique of the naive proposition offered by scholars like Martha Nussbaum and Stephen Pinker that stories increase empathy or understanding when they often have the opposite effect. Farther on, he summarizes: "My cautionary comments about the moral and social effects of stories are not meant to suggest that they do not have beneficial social consequences—just that these effects are likely to be more variable and heterogeneous and harder to measure than the optimistic claims recognize" (169).

11. See Shiller 2019; Gottschall 2012.

12. Brooks 2022, 152.

13. Strawson 2004, 449.

14. Cioran 1949, 149.

15. Boyd 2009, 232.

16. For a basic overview of mirror neurons and how they function, see Heyes 2010. Garrels (2006) argues that they are reconcilable with Aristotelian notions of mimesis. See Ramachandran 2000 for thoughts on their importance to human development in evolution.

17. Brian Boyd suggests that "just as natural selection has evolved sex for amplifying genetic variation, I suggest it has evolved art in humans—first as a means of sharpening minds eager for pattern, but gradually also for creativity, for amplifying the variety of our behavior. Gene-culture coevolution has refigured art for creativity" (2009, 405).

18. See Plato, *Republic* 6.514a–520a for the famous allegory of the cave.

19. For similar advice, see Brooks: "Our analytic tools for studying narrative are important" (2022, 79).

20. In this language I am inspired again by the work of Jerome Bruner and Michael White. On the difference between internal and intentional states of mind, see White 2007. The internal state as Bruner and White pose it is when we have internalized external narratives to the point of paralysis. In contrast, as White explains, "Intentional state understandings shape people's endeavour to come to terms with the unexpected in life, provide a basis for their effort to address obstacles and crises, and make it possible for them to come to terms with a range of predicaments and dilemmas that confront them in everyday life" (2007, 103).

21. For stories as "simulating social experience," see McAdams 2019, 14. For the importance of art in preparing minds for "open ended learning and creativity," see Boyd 2009, 209.

Bibliography

Abusch, Tzvi. 2001. "The Development and Meaning of the Epic of Gilgamesh: An Interpretive Essay." *Journal of the American Oriental Society* 121 (4): 614–22.

———. 2015. *Male and Female in the Epic of Gilgamesh: Encounters, Literary History, and Interpretation*. Winona Lake, Ind.: Eisenbrauns.

Alberts. B., A. Johnson, J. Lewis, et al. 2002. *Molecular Biology of the Cell*. 4th ed. New York: Garland Science.

Alden, Maureen. 2001. *Homer Beside Himself: Para-Narratives in the "Iliad."* Oxford: Oxford University Press.

———. 2017. *Para-Narratives in the "Odyssey": Stories in the Frame*. Oxford: Oxford University Press.

Alexiou, Margaret. 2002. *The Ritual Lament in Greek Tradition*. 2nd ed. Washington, D.C.: Center for Hellenic Studies.

Andersen, Øivind. 1987. "Myth, Paradigm and 'Spatial Form' in the *Iliad*." In *Homer: Beyond Oral Poetry. Recent Trends in Homeric Interpretation*, edited by J. M. Bremer, I. J. F. De Jong, and J. Kalff, 1–13. Amsterdam: B.R. Grüner.

Arend, Walter. 1933. *Die typischen Szenen bei Homer*. Berlin: Weidmann-sche Buchhandlung.

Arft, Justin. 2017. "Structure as Sēma: Structural and Liminal Middles in the *Odyssey*." *Yearbook of Ancient Greek Epic* 1: 5–45.

———. 2022. *Arete and the "Odyssey"'s Poetics of Interrogation: The Queen and Her Question*. Oxford: Oxford University Press.

Armstrong, Paul B. 2020. *Stories and the Brain: The Neuroscience of Narrative*. Baltimore: Johns Hopkins University Press.

Austin, Emily P. 2021. *Grief and the Hero: The Futility of Longing in the "Iliad."* Ann Arbor: University of Michigan Press.

Bachvarova, Mary R. 2016. *From Hittite to Homer: The Anatolian Background of Ancient Greek Epic.* Cambridge: Cambridge University Press.

Bakker, Egbert J. 1997. *Poetry in Speech: Orality and Homeric Discourse.* Ithaca: Cornell University Press.

Barker, Elton T. E. 2009. *Entering the Agon: Dissent and Authority in Homer, Historiography and Tragedy.* Oxford: Oxford University Press.

Barker, Elton T. E., and Joel P. Christensen. 2013. *Homer: A Beginner's Guide.* London: Oneworld.

———. 2019. *Homer's Thebes: Epic Rivalries and the Appropriation of Mythical Pasts.* Washington, D.C.: Center for Hellenic Studies.

Barthes, Roland. 1977. "The Death of the Author." In *Image, Music, Text,* translated by Stephen Heath, 142–48. New York: Hill and Wang.

Beck, Deborah. 2005. *Homeric Conversation.* Washington, D.C.: Center for Hellenic Studies.

Beckman, Gary. 2019. *The Hittite Gilgamesh.* Atlanta: Lockwood.

Bergren, Ann. 2008. *Weaving Truth: Essays on Language and the Female in Greek Thought.* Washington, D.C.: Center for Hellenic Studies.

Beye, C. R. 1984. "The Epic of Gilgamesh, the Bible, and Homer: Some Narrative Parallels." In *Mnemai: Classical Studies in Memory of Karl K. Hulley,* edited by Harold D. Evjen, 7–19. Chico, Calif.: Scholars.

Boele, F. W., A. G. Rooney, R. Grant, and M. Klein. 2015. "Psychiatric Symptoms in Glioma Patients: From Diagnosis to Management." *Neuropsychiatric Disease and Treatment* 10 (11): 1413–20.

Bohacek, J., and I. M. Mansuy. 2013. "Epigenetic Inheritance of Disease and Disease Risk." *Neuropsychopharmacology* 38 (1): 220–36.

Bond, Sarah E., and Joel Christensen. 2021. "The Man Behind the Myth: Should We Question the Hero's Journey?" *Los Angeles Review of Books,* August 12. https://lareviewofbooks.org/article/the-man-behind-the-myth-should-we-question-the-heros-journey/.

Bonds, Matthew H., et al. 2010. "Poverty Trap Formed by the Ecology of Infectious Diseases." *Proceedings of the Royal Society B: Biological Sciences* 277: 1185–92.

Bonifazi, Anna. 2009. "Inquiring into *Nostos* and Its Cognates." *American Journal of Philology* 130: 481–510.

Boyd, Brian. 2009. *On the Origin of Stories: Evolution, Cognition, and Fiction.* Cambridge: Harvard University Press.

Brooks, Peter. 2022. *Seduced by Story: The Use and Abuse of Narrative.* New York: New York Review Books.

Bruner, Jerome. 1986. *Actual Minds, Possible Worlds.* Cambridge: Harvard University Press.

Burke, Seán. 1998. *The Death and Return of the Author: Criticism and Subjectivity in Barthes, Foucault, and Derrida.* 2nd ed. Edinburgh: Edinburgh University Press.

Burkert, Walter. 1997. "The Song of Ares and Aphrodite: On the Relationship Between the *Odyssey* and the *Iliad.*" In *Homer: German Scholarship in Translation,* translated by G. M. Wright and P. V. Jones, 249–62. Oxford: Clarendon Press.

Campbell, Joseph. 1973. *The Hero with a Thousand Faces.* Princeton: Princeton University Press.

Carson, Anne, trans. 2002. *If Not, Winter: Fragments of Sappho.* New York: Knopf.

Cave, Terence. 2016. *Thinking with Literature: Towards a Cognitive Criticism.* Oxford: Oxford University Press.

Chirigati, F. 2022. "Cultural Diversity Through the Lenses of Ecology." *Nature Computational Science* 2 (137): 765–69.

Christensen, Joel P. 2008. "Universality or Priority? The Rhetoric of Death in the Gilgamesh Poems and the *Iliad.*" In *Quaderni del Dipartimento di Scienze dell'Antichità e del Vicino Oriente dell'Università Ca' Foscari,* 4, edited by E. Cingano and L. Milano, 179–202. Padua: S.A.R.G.O.N.

———. 2018a. "Eris and Epos." *Yearbook of Ancient Greek Epic* 2: 1–39.

———. 2018b. "The Clinical *Odyssey:* Odysseus' Apologoi and Narrative Therapy." *Arethusa* 51: 1–31.

———. 2020. *The Many-Minded Man: The "Odyssey," Psychology, and the Therapy of Epic.* Ithaca: Cornell University Press.

Cioran, E. M. 1949. *A Short History of Decay.* Translated by Richard Howard. New York: Viking.

Clay, Jenny Strauss. 1994. "Sex, Drugs and . . . Poetry?" In *Epic and Epoch: Essays on the Interpretation and History of a Genre,* edited by Steven Oberhelman, Van Kelly, and Richard Golsan, 40–48. Lubbock: Texas Tech University Press.

———. 2003. *Hesiod's Cosmos.* Cambridge: Cambridge University Press.

Cohen, Sheldon, et al. 2006. "Socioeconomic Status Is Associated with Stress Hormones." *Psychosomatic Medicine* 68 (3): 414–20.

Collins, D. 2004. *Master of the Game: Competition and Performance in Greek Poetry.* Washington, D.C.: Center for Hellenic Studies.

Combellack, Frederick M. 1960. Review of *Homer and the Heroic Tradition* by Cedric H. Whitman. *Comparative Literature* 12 (2): 159–66.

Cook, Erwin F. 1999. "'Active' and 'Passive' Heroics in the *Odyssey*."
    Classical World 93: 149–67.
———. 2014. "Structure as Interpretation in the Homeric *Odyssey*." In
    Defining Greek Narrative, edited by Douglas Cairns and Ruth Scodel,
    75–102. Edinburgh: Edinburgh University Press.
Csapo, Eric. 2005. *Theories of Mythology*. London: Wiley-Blackwell.
Cullen, David. 2016. *Columbine*. Rev. ed. New York: Twelve Books.
Darby, R. Ryan, Andreas Horn, Fiery Cushman, and Michael D. Fox.
    2017. "Lesion Network of Criminal Behavior." *Proceedings of the
    National Academy of Sciences* 115 (3): 601–6.
Darshan, Guy. 2016. "The Calendrical Framework of the Priestly Flood
    Story in Light of a New Akkadian Text from Ugarit (RS 94.2953)."
    Journal of the American Oriental Society 136 (3): 507–14.
Dautenhahn, Kerstin. 2002. "The Origins of Narrative: In Search of the
    Transactional Format of Narratives in Humans and Other Social
    Animals." *International Journal of Cognition and Technology* 1 (1):
    97–123.
Dawkins, Richard. 1987. *The Blind Watchmaker*. New York: Norton.
Dennett, Daniel C. 2017. *From Bacteria to Bach and Back: The Evolution
    of Minds*. New York: Norton.
Dickson, Keith. 1995. *Nestor: Poetic Memory in the Greek Epic*. New York:
    Garland.
Dolija, Valerian V. 2021. "Rapid Emergence of Virus-Host Mutualism
    Under Stress." *Biological Sciences* 118 (10): e2100936118.
Douglas, Mary. 2007. *Thinking in Circles: An Essay on Ring Composition*.
    New Haven: Yale University Press.
Drout, Michael C. 2011. "Variation Within Limits: An Evolutionary
    Approach to the Structure and Dynamics of the Multiform." *Oral
    Tradition* 26 (2): 447–74.
Dué, Casey. 2002. *Homeric Variations on a Lament by Briseis*. Lanham,
    Md.: Rowman & Littlefield.
———. 2015. "The Invention of Ossian." In *The Homerizon: Conceptual
    Interrogations in Homeric Studies*, edited by Richard Armstrong and
    Casey Dué. Special issue, *Classics@* 3. http://nrs.harvard.edu/urn
    -3:hlnc.jissue:ClassicsAt.Issue03.The_Homerizon.2005.
———. 2019. *Achilles Unbound: Multiformity and Tradition in the Homeric
    Epics*. Washington, D.C.: Center for Hellenic Studies.
Dué, Casey, and Mary Ebbot. 2009. *"Iliad" 10 and the Poetics of Ambush*.
    Cambridge: Harvard University Press.
Eagleman, David. 2011. "The Brain on Trial." *The Atlantic,* July/August.
Edmunds, Lowell. 1997. "Myth in Homer." In *A New Companion to
    Homer,* edited by I. Morris and B. Powell, 415–41. Leiden: Brill.

Elmer, David. 2013. *The Poetics of Consent: Collective Decision Making and the "Iliad."* Baltimore: Johns Hopkins University Press.

Felson, Nancy. 1994. *Regarding Penelope: From Character to Poetics.* Princeton: Princeton University Press.

Fenik, Bernard. 1968. *Typical Battle Scenes in the "Iliad."* Wiesbaden: F. Steiner.

———. 1974. *Studies in the "Odyssey."* Wiesbaden: F. Steiner.

Fernyhough, Charles. 2012. *Pieces of Light: The New Science of Memory.* New York: Profile Books.

Finglass, P. J. 2021. *The Cambridge Companion to Sappho.* Cambridge: Cambridge University Press.

Finnegan, Ruth. 1977. *Oral Poetry: Its Nature, Significance, and Social Context.* Cambridge: Cambridge University Press.

Fish, Stanley. 1980. *Is There a Text in This Class? The Authority of Interpretive Communities.* Cambridge: Harvard University Press.

Fletcher, Angus. 2022. *Wonderworks: Literary Invention and the Science of Stories.* New York: Simon and Schuster.

Foley, John Miles. 2002. *How to Read an Oral Poem.* Urbana: University of Illinois Press.

Ford, Andrew. 1992. *Homer: The Poetry of the Past.* Ithaca: Cornell University Press.

Foster, Benjamin R. 1993. *Before the Muses: An Anthology of Akkadian Literature.* 2 vols. Bethesda, Md.: CDL Press.

Frame, Douglas. 1978. *The Myth of Return in Early Greek Epic.* New Haven: Yale University Press.

Frank, Roslyn M. 2008. "The Language-Organism-Species Analogy: A Complex Adaptive Systems Approach to Shifting Perspective on Language." In *Body, Language and Mind,* edited by Roslyn M. Frank, René Dirven, Tom Ziemke, and Enrique Bernárdez, vol. 2: *Sociocultural Situatedness,* 215–64. Berlin: De Gruyter.

Frog and William Lamb, eds. 2022. *Weathered Words: Formulaic Language and Verbal Art.* Cambridge: Harvard University Press.

Fuchs, Florian. 2023. *Civic Storytelling: The Rise of Short Forms and the Agency of Literature.* New York: Zone Books.

Fuentes, Augustín. 2019. *Why We Believe: Evolution and the Human Way of Being.* New Haven: Yale University Press.

Garrels, S. 2006. "Imitation, Mirror Neurons, and Mimetic Desire: Convergence Between the Mimetic Theory of René Girard and Empirical Research on Imitation." *Contagion: Journal of Violence, Mimesis, and Culture* 12–13: 47–86.

Gazzaniga, Michael S. 2012. *Who's in Charge? Free Will and the Science of the Brain.* New York: Harper Collins.

Gazzaniga, Michael S., and Joseph LeDoux. 1978. *The Integrated Mind.* New York: Springer.

George, A. R. 1999. *The Epic of Gilgamesh.* New York: Penguin.

———. 2003. *The Babylonian Gilgamesh Epic.* Oxford: Oxford University Press.

———. 2007. "*The Epic of Gilgameš:* Thoughts on Genre and Meaning." In *Gilgameš and the World of Assyria,* edited by J. Azize and N. Weeks, 37–66. Leuven: Peeters.

Gill, Christopher. 1996. *Personality in Greek Epic.* New York: Oxford University Press.

Gladwell, Malcolm. 2015. "Thresholds of Violence." *New Yorker,* October 12. Available at https://www.newyorker.com/magazine/2015/10/19 /thresholds-of-violence.

González, José M. 2013. *The Epic Rhapsode and His Craft: Homeric Performance in a Diachronic Perspective.* Washington, D.C.: Center for Hellenic Studies.

Gopinath, Arvind, Michael F. Hagan, M. Cristina Marchetti, and Aparna Baskaran. 2012 "Dynamical Self-Regulation in Self-Propelled Particle Flows." *Physical Review E* 85 (June 1). DOI: 10.1103/PhysRevE.85.061903.

Gottschall, Jonathan. 2012. *The Storytelling Animal: How Stories Make Us Human.* Boston: Houghton Mifflin Harcourt.

———. 2021. *The Story Paradox: How Our Love of Storytelling Builds Societies and Tears Them Down.* New York: Basic.

Gould, Stephen Jay. 1977. *Ever Since Darwin: Reflections on Natural History.* New York: Norton.

Graeber, David, and David Wengrow. 2021. *The Dawn of Everything: A New History of Humanity.* New York: Macmillan.

Granovetter, Mark. 1978. "Threshold Models of Collective Behavior." *American Journal of Sociology* 86 (3): 1420–43.

Grant, Catherine. 2012. "Analogies and Links Between Cultural and Biological Diversity." *Journal of Cultural Heritage Management and Sustainable Development* 2 (2): 153–63.

Graziosi, Barbara, and Johannes Haubold. 2005. *Homer: The Resonance of Epic.* London: Duckworth.

Griffin, Jasper, ed. 1995. "*Iliad*": *Book Nine.* Oxford: Clarendon.

Grow, Kory, and Jason Newman. 2021. "Marilyn Manson: The Monster Hiding in Plain Sight." *Rolling Stone,* November 14. Available at https://www.rollingstone.com/music/music-features/marilyn-manson -abuse-allegations-1256888/.

Guo, Y., J. Shachat, M. J. Walker, et al. 2021. "Viral Social Media Videos Can Raise Pro-Social Behaviours When an Epidemic Arises." *Journal of the Economic Science Association* 7: 120–38.

Hammack, Phillip L. 2008. "Narrative and the Cultural Psychology of Identity." *Personality and Social Psychology Review* 12 (3): 222–47.

Harari, Yuval Noah. 2015. *Sapiens: A Brief History of Humankind.* New York: Harper.

Haubold, Johannes. 2002. "Greek Epic: A Near Eastern Genre?" *Proceedings of the Cambridge Philological Society* 48: 1–19.

Havelock, Eric A. 1986. *The Muse Learns to Write: Reflections on Orality and Literacy from Antiquity to the Present.* New Haven: Yale University Press.

Heiden, Bruce A. 2008. *Homer's Cosmic Fabrication: Choice and Design in the "Iliad."* Oxford: Oxford University Press.

Heijmans, B. T., et al. 2008. "Persistent Epigenetic Differences Associated with Prenatal Exposure to Famine in Humans." *Proceedings of the National Academy of Sciences* 105 (44): 17046–49.

Helle, Sophus. 2021. *"Gilgamesh": A New Translation of the Ancient Epic.* New Haven: Yale University Press.

———. 2023. *Enheduana: The Complete Poems of the World's First Author.* New Haven: Yale University Press.

Heyd, David. 2010. "Cultural Diversity and Biodiversity: A Tempting Analogy." *Critical Review of International Social and Political Philosophy* 13 (1): 159–79.

Heyes, Cecilia. 2010. "Where Do Mirror Neurons Come From?" *Neuroscience and Biobehavioral Reviews* 34: 575–83.

Hitch, Sarah. 2009. *King of Sacrifice: Ritual and Royal Authority in the "Iliad."* Washington, D.C.: Center for Hellenic Studies.

Hunter, Richard, ed. 2005. *The Hesiodic Catalogue of Women: Constructions and Reconstructions.* Cambridge: Cambridge University Press.

Iser, Wolfgang. 1974. *The Implied Reader: Patterns of Communication in Prose Fiction from Bunyan to Beckett.* Baltimore: Johns Hopkins University Press.

Iskra-Caruana, Marie-Line, et al. 2010. "A Four-Partner Plant—Virus Interaction: Enemies Can Also Come from Within." *Molecular Plant-Microbe Interactions* 23 (11): 1394–1402.

Jackson, Zakiyyah Iman. 2020. *Becoming Human: Matter and Meaning in an Antiblack World.* New York: New York University Press.

Johnston, Sarah Iles. 2018. *The Story of Myth.* Cambridge: Harvard University Press.

Jiang, Shui, et al. 2019. "Epigenetic Modifications in Stress Response Genes Associated with Childhood Trauma." *Frontiers in Psychiatry* 10: 808.

Jung, C. G. 1981. *The Archetypes and the Collective Unconscious.* Translated by R. F. C. Hull. Princeton: Princeton University Press.

Kakridis, Johannes. 1949. *Homeric Researches.* Lund: C.W.K. Gleerup.

Kanigel, Robert. 2021. *Hearing Homer's Song: The Brief Life and Big Idea of Milman Parry*. New York: Knopf.

Kelemen, D. 2004. "Are Children 'Intuitive Theists'? Reasoning About Purpose and Design in Nature." *Psychological Science* 15 (5): 295–301.

Kolbert, Elizabeth. 2014. *The Sixth Extinction: An Unnatural History*. New York: Picador.

Konstantopoulos, Gina, and Sophus Helle. 2023. *The Shape of Stories: Narrative Structures in Cuneiform Literature*. Leiden: Brill.

Krishna, S., A. Choudhury, M. B. Keough, et al. 2023. "Glioblastoma Remodelling of Human Neural Circuits Decreases Survival." *Nature* 617: 599–607.

Krishna, Saritha, and Shawn Hervey-Jumper. 2023. "Brain Tumors Are Cognitive Parasites—How Brain Cancer Hijacks Neural Circuits and Causes Cognitive Decline." *The Conversation*, June 7, 2023. https://theconversation.com/brain-tumors-are-cognitive-parasites-how-brain-cancer-hijacks-neural-circuits-and-causes-cognitive-decline-205901.

Kwapisz, Jan. 2014. "Behaghel's Club." *Classical Quarterly* 64 (2): 615–22.

Labatut, Benjamin. 2020. *When We Cease to Understand the World*. Translated by Adrian Nathan West. New York: New York Review Books.

Lakoff, George, and Mark Johnson. 2006. *Metaphors We Live By*. 2nd ed. Chicago: University of Chicago Press.

Lauring, Adam S., and Kayla Peck. 2018. "Complexities of Viral Mutation Rates." *Journal of Virology* 92: 1–17.

Le Hunte, Bern, and Jan A. Golembiewski. 2014. "Stories Have the Power to Save Us: A Neurological Framework for the Imperative to Tell Stories." *Arts and Social Sciences Journal* 5 (2): 73–76.

Lesser, Rachel H. 2022. *Desire in the "Iliad."* Oxford: Oxford University Press.

Lloyd, G. E. R. 2021. "Demystifying the Greek Miracle." In *Expanding Horizons in the History of Science: The Comparative Approach*, 32–43. Cambridge: Cambridge University Press.

Lohmann, Dieter. 1970. *Die Komposition der Reden in der "Ilias."* Berlin: De Gruyter.

Lord, Albert. 2000. *The Singer of Tales*. Cambridge: Harvard University Press.

Lupton, Ashleigh, Huda Abu-Suwa, Glen C. Bolton, and Charles Golden. 2020. "The Implications of Brain Tumors on Aggressive Behavior and Suicidality: A Review." *Aggression and Violent Behavior* 54 (September–October).

Lynn-George, Michael. 1994. "The Stem of the Full-Blown Flower: Homeric Studies and Literary Theory." Review of *The Poetry of the*

Past; Man in the Middle Voice: Name and Narration in the "Odyssey"; and *The Homeric Narrator* by H. A. Ford, J. Peradotto, and S. Richardson. *Phoenix* 48 (3): 226–53.

Madigan, Stephen. 2010. *Narrative Therapy.* Washington, D.C.: American Psychological Association.

Martin, John Jeffries. 2022. *A Beautiful Ending: The Apocalyptic Imagination and the Making of the Modern World.* New Haven: Yale University Press.

Martin, Richard. 1989. *The Language of Heroes: Speech and Performance in the "Iliad."* Ithaca: Cornell University Press.

———. 1993. "Telemachus and the Last Hero Song." *Colby Quarterly* 29 (3): 220–40.

Matute, H., F. Blanco, I. Yarritu, M. Díaz-Lago, M. A. Vadillo, and I. Barberia. 2015. "Illusions of Causality: How They Bias Our Everyday Thinking and How They Could Be Reduced." *Frontiers in Psychology* 6 (888): 1–14.

McAdams, Dan P. 2019. "'First We Invented Stories, Then They Changed Us': The Evolution of Narrative Identity." *Evolutionary Studies in Imaginary Culture* 3 (1): 1–18.

McCandlish, Samuel, Aparna Baskaran, and Michael F. Hagan. 2012. "Spontaneous Segregation of Self-Propelled Particles with Different Motilities." *Soft Matter* 8: 2527–2534. DOI: 10.1039/c2sm06960a.

McLean, Kate C., and Moin Syed. 2015. "Personal, Master, and Alternative Narratives: An Integrative Framework for Understanding Identity Development in Context." *Human Development* 58 (6): 318–49.

Mermelstein, Spencer, and Tamsin C. German. 2021. "Counterintuitive Pseudoscience Propagates by Exploiting the Mind's Communication Evaluation Mechanisms." *Frontiers in Psychology* 12. doi.org/10.3389/fpsyg.2021.739070.

Michalowski, Piotr. 1990. "Presence at the Creation." In *Lingering over Words: Studies in Ancient Near Eastern Literature in Honor of William L. Moran,* edited by T. Abusch, J. Huehnergard, and P. Steinkeller, 381–96. Leiden: Brill.

Minchin, Elizabeth. 2001. *Homer and the Resources of Memory: Some Applications of Cognitive Theory to the "Iliad" and the "Odyssey."* Oxford: Oxford University Press.

Mitchell, Lynette. 2007. *Panhellenism and the Barbarian in Archaic and Classical Greece.* Swansea: Classical Press of Wales.

Moore, Matthew D., and Lee-Ann Jaykus. 2018. "Virus-Bacteria Interactions: Implications and Potential for the Applied and Agricultural Sciences." *Viruses* 10 (2): Article 61. doi: 10.3390/v10020061.

Muellner, Leonard. 1990. "The Simile of the Cranes and Pygmies: A Study
    of Homeric Metaphor." *Harvard Studies in Classical Philology* 93:
    53–101.
———. 1996. *The Anger of Achilles: Mēnis in Greek Epic.* Ithaca: Cornell
    University Press.
———. 2019. "Metonymy, Metaphor, Patroklos, Achilles." *Classica:
    Revista Brasileira de Estudos Clássicos, [s. l.],* 32 (2): 139–55. doi:
    10.24277/classica.v32i2.884.
Nagy, Gregory. 1979. *The Best of the Achaeans: Concepts of the Hero in
    Archaic Greek Poetry.* Baltimore: Johns Hopkins University Press.
———. 1996. *Poetry as Performance: Homer and Beyond.* Cambridge:
    Cambridge University Press.
———. 2004. *Homer's Text and Language.* Urbana: University of Illinois
    Press.
———. 2008. *Homer the Classic.* Washington, D.C.: Center for Hellenic
    Studies.
———. 2013. *The Ancient Greek Hero in 24 Hours.* Cambridge: Harvard
    University Press.
———. 2016. *Masterpieces of Metonymy: From Ancient Greek Times to
    Now.* Washington D.C.: Center for Hellenic Studies, 2016.
———. 2017. *Homer the Pre-Classic.* Berkeley: University of California
    Press.
Oberhelman, Steven M., Van Kelly, and Richard J. Golsan, eds. 1994. *Epic
    and Epoch: Essays on the Interpretation and History of a Genre.*
    Lubbock: Texas Tech University Press.
Ojosnegros, S., and N. Beerenwinkel. 2010. "Models of RNA Virus
    Evolution and Their Roles in Vaccine Design." *Immunome Research* 6:
    1–14.
Ong, Walter J. 2012. *Orality and Literacy: The Technologizing of the Word.*
    3rd ed. London: Routledge.
O'Nolan, K. 1978. "Doublets in the *Odyssey*." *Classical Quarterly* 28 (1):
    23–37.
Ormand, Kirk. 2014. *The Hesiodic Catalogue of Women and Archaic
    Greece.* Cambridge: Cambridge University Press.
Otterlo, W. A. A. van. 1944. *Untersuchungen über Begriff, Anwendung und
    Entstehung der griechische Ringcomposition.* Amsterdam: Noord-
    Hollandische Uitg. Mij.
Pantelia, Maria C. 2002. "Helen and the Last Song for Hector." *Transac-
    tions of the American Philological Association* 132 (1): 21–27.
Parry, Milman. 1971. *The Making of Homeric Verse: The Collected Papers
    of Milman Parry.* Edited by Adam Parry. Oxford: Clarendon.

Philips, Chuck. 1994. "Rap Finds a Supporter in Rep. Maxine Waters." *Los Angeles Times,* February 15, available at https://www.latimes.com /local/la-me-watersphilips15feb1594-story.html.

Pickersgill, Barbara. 2018. "Parallel vs. Convergent Evolution in Domestication and Diversification of Crops in the Americas." *Frontiers in Ecology and Evolution* 6: 1–15.

Pradeu, Thomas. 2016. "Mutualistic Viruses and the Heteronomy of Life." *Studies in History and Philosophy of Science Part C: Studies in History and Philosophy of Biological and Biomedical Sciences* 59: 80–88.

Preston, J. L., and F. Shin. 2021. "Anthropocentric Biases in Teleological Thinking: How Nature Seems Designed for Humans." *Journal of Experimental Psychology* 150 (5): 943–55.

Propp, Vladimir. 1968. *Morphology of the Folktale.* Translated by Laurence Scott. 2nd ed. Austin: University of Texas Press.

Prothero, Donald R. 2017. *Evolution: What the Fossils Say and Why It Matters.* New York: Columbia University Press.

Pryke, Louise M. 2019. *Gilgamesh.* London: Routledge.

Pucci, Pietro. 1998. *The Song of the Sirens: Essays on Homer.* Lanham, Md.: Rowman & Littlefield.

Ramachandran, Vilayanur. 2000. "Mirror Neurons and Imitation Learning as the Driving Force Behind the Great Leap Forward in Human Evolution." *Edge,* May 31. https://www.edge.org/conversation /vilayanur_ramachandran-mirror-neurons-and-imitation-learning-as -the-driving-force.

Rank, Otto. 1909. *Der Mythus von der Geburt des Helden: Versuch einer psychologischen Mythendeutung* [The Myth of the Birth of the Hero: A Psychological Exploration of Myth]. Leipzig: Deuticke.

Ready, Jonathan. 2011. *Character, Narrator and Simile in the "Iliad."* Cambridge: Cambridge University Press.

———. 2018. *The Homeric Simile in Comparative Perspectives: Oral Traditions from Saudi Arabia to Indonesia.* Oxford: Oxford University Press.

Reece, Steve. 1993. *The Stranger's Welcome: Oral Theory and the Aesthetics of the Homeric Hospitality Scene.* Ann Arbor: University of Michigan Press.

Reiss, J. O. 2005. "Natural Selection and the Conditions for Existence: Representational vs. Conditional Teleology in Biological Explanation." *History and Philosophy of the Life Sciences* 27 (2): 249–80.

Richards, I. A. 1965. *The Philosophy of Rhetoric.* Oxford: Oxford University Press.

Roberts, Alice. 2014. *The Incredible Unlikeliness of Being: Evolution and the Making of Us*. London: Heron Books.

Rogers, Brett. 2011. "Heroes ~~Un~~Limited: The Theory of the Hero's Journey and the Limitation of Superhero Myth." *Classics and Comics,* edited by G. Kovacs and C. W. Marshall, 73–86. New York: Oxford University Press.

Roossinck, Marilyn J. 2015. "Move Over, Bacteria! Viruses Make Their Mark as Mutualistic Microbial Symbionts." *Journal of Virology* 89 (13): 6532–35.

Russo, Joseph, and Bennett Simon. 1968. "Homeric Psychology and the Oral Epic Tradition." *Journal of the History of Ideas* 28: 43–58.

Sammons, Benjamin. 2013. "Narrative Doublets in the Epic Cycle." *American Journal of Philology* 134 (4): 529–56.

———. 2014. "A Tale of Tydeus: Exemplarity and Structure in Two Homeric Insets." *Trends in Classics* 6 (2): 297–318.

Sanders, Seth. 2015. "What If There Aren't Any Empirical Models for Pentateuchal Criticism?" In *Contextualizing Israel's Sacred Writings,* edited by Brian Schmidt, 281–304. Atlanta: SBL Press.

Sasson, Jack M. 1972. "Some Literary Motifs in the Composition of the Gilgamesh Epic." *Studies in Philology* 69: 259–79.

Saussure, Ferdinand de. 2011. *Course in General Linguistics.* Translated by Wade Baskin. Edited by Perry Meisel and Haun Saussy. New York: Columbia University Press.

Saussy, Haun. 1996. "Writing in the *Odyssey:* Eurykleia, Parry, Jousse, and the Opening of a Letter from Homer." *Arethusa* 29: 299–338.

Schachner, A., L. Zhu, and D. Kelemen. 2017. "Is the Bias for Function-Based Explanations Culturally Universal? Children from China Endorse Teleological Explanations of Natural Phenomena." *Journal of Experimental Child Psychology* 157: 29–48.

Scodel, Ruth. 2001. "Poetic Authority and Oral Tradition in Hesiod and Pindar." In *Speaking Volumes: Orality and Literacy in the Greek and Roman World,* edited by Janet Watson, 109–37. Mnemosyne Supplements 218. Leiden: Brill.

———. 2002. *Listening to Homer: Tradition, Narrative, and Audience.* Ann Arbor: University of Michigan Press.

Scorza, P., C. S. Duarte, A. E. Hipwell, J. Posner, A. Ortin, G. Canino, and C. Monk. 2019. "Program Collaborators for Environmental Influences on Child Health Outcomes. Research Review: Intergenerational Transmission of Disadvantage: Epigenetics and Parents' Childhoods as the First Exposure." *Journal of Child Psychology and Psychiatry* 60 (2): 119–32.

Scott, William C. 2009. *The Artistry of the Homeric Simile.* Hanover, N.H.: University Press of New England.

Shiller, Robert J. 2019. *Narrative Economics: How Stories Go Viral and Drive Major Economic Events.* Princeton: Princeton University Press.

Snodgrass, A. M. 1971. *The Dark Age of Greece: An Archaeological Survey of the Eleventh to the Eighth Centuries BC.* Edinburgh: Edinburgh University Press.

Sperber, D. 1994. "The Modularity of Thought and the Epidemiology of Representations." In *Mapping the Mind: Domain Specificity in Cognition and Culture,* edited by L. A. Hirschfeld and S. A. Gelman, 39–67. Cambridge: Cambridge University Press.

———. 1996. *Explaining Culture: A Naturalistic Approach.* Oxford: Blackwell.

Stamatopoulou, Zoe. 2017. *Hesiod and Classical Greek Poetry: Reception and Transformation in the Fifth Century BCE.* Cambridge: Cambridge University Press.

Stanley, Keith. 1993. *The Shield of Homer: Narrative Structure in the "Iliad."* Princeton: Princeton University Press.

Stewart, Douglas J. 1976. *The Disguised Guest: Rank, Role and Identity in the "Odyssey."* Lewisburg, Pa.: Bucknell University Press.

Strawson, Galen. 2004. "Against Narrativity." *Ratio* 17: 428–52.

Tigay, Jeffrey H. 1982. *The Evolution of the Gilgamesh Epic.* Philadelphia: University of Pennsylvania Press.

Tomasello, Michael. 1999. *The Cultural Origins of Human Cognition.* Cambridge: Harvard University Press.

Turner, Mark. 1996. *The Literary Mind.* New York: Oxford University Press.

Van Prooijen, J. W., and K. M. Douglas. 2018. "Belief in Conspiracy Theories: Basic Principles of an Emerging Research Domain." *European Journal of Social Psychology* 48 (7): 897–908.

Wachter, Rudolf. 2001. *Non-Attic Greek Vase Inscriptions.* Oxford: Oxford University Press.

Warwick, Celsiana. 2019. "We Two Alone: Conjugal Bonds and Homo-erotic Subtext in the *Iliad.*" *Helios* 46 (2): 115–39.

Weil, Simone. 2003. *The "Iliad": or, The Poem of Force.* Edited by James P. Holoka. New York: P. Lang.

Weiner, Jonathan. 1994. *The Beak of the Finch: A Story of Evolution in Our Time.* New York: Knopf.

West, M. L. 1997. *The East Face of Helicon: West Asiatic Elements in Greek Poetry and Myth.* Oxford: Clarendon.

———. 2001. *Studies in the Text and Transmission of the "Iliad."* Munich: De Gruyter.

White, Michael. 2007. *Maps of Narrative Practice*. New York: Norton.

———. 2011. *Narrative Practice: Continuing the Conversations*. New York: Norton.

Whitman, Cedric H. 1958. *Homer and the Heroic Tradition*. Cambridge: Harvard University Press.

Willcock, M. M. 1964. "Mythological Paradeigma in the *Iliad*." *Classical Quarterly* 14 (2): 141–54.

———. 1977. "Ad Hoc Invention in the *Iliad*." *Harvard Studies in Classical Philology* 81: 41–53.

Willis, Matthew. 2022. "Crabs Have Evolved Five Separate Times—Why Do the Same Forms Keep Appearing in Nature?" *The Conversation*, December 6. https://theconversation.com/crabs-have-evolved-five -separate-times-why-do-the-same-forms-keep-appearing-in-nature -195739.

Wilson, Donna F. 2002. *Ransom, Revenge, and Heroic Identity in the "Iliad."* Cambridge: Cambridge University Press.

Wilson, Edward O. 1999. *Consilience: The Unity of Knowledge*. New York: Vintage.

———. 2014. "On Free Will and How the Brain Is Like a Colony of Ants." *Harper's*, Aug. 20, 2014.

Wimsatt, W. K., and Monroe C. Beardsley. 1982. *The Verbal Icon: Studies in the Meaning of Poetry*. Lexington: University Press of Kentucky.

Wolf, F. A. 1795. *Prolegomena ad Homerum*. Edited by Anthony Grafton, Glenn W. Most, and James E. G. Zetzel. Princeton: Princeton University Press.

Wolfe, Joanna, Javier Luque, and Heather D. Bracken-Grissom. 2021. "How to Become a Crab: Phenotypic Constraints on a Recurring Body Plan." *BioEssays* 43 (5): 1–14.

Worthington, Martin. 2020. *Ea's Duplicity in the Gilgamesh Flood Story*. London: Routledge.

Zimmer, Carl. 2021. *A Planet of Viruses*. 3rd ed. Chicago: University of Chicago Press.

Zipes, Jack. 2023. *Buried Treasures: The Power of Political Fairy Tales*. Princeton: Princeton University Press.

Acknowledgments

This book could not have been written without the serendipity of my education, and countless conversations with teachers, colleagues, and friends over the course of three decades. Sections of the book were improved by talks given at the Greek Literature and the Environment Workshop, University of California, Santa Barbara, the University of Chicago Rhetoric and Poetics Homer Lecture, and work presented at the Brandeis Psychology Department colloquia series. I cannot recall all the participants who were involved in discussions during these talks, but I know they helped enrich my thinking. Some of the ideas and passages also appeared in pieces for *The Conversation* and *Neos Kosmos*. Research grants from Brandeis University provided support for this book from 2021 to 2023.

I owe a debt to many for help with bibliography and subjects beyond my expertise, including Joseph Cunningham, Sophus Helle, Prasad Jallepalli, Dan Perlman, Seth Sanders, Claudio Sansone, and Mario Telo. I cannot thank Eric Blum, Becca Frankel, and Talia Franks enough for editing and bibliographical assistance. Among the many friends who have supported my flights of fancy over the years, I would be remiss not to thank Justin Arft, Elton Barker, Larry Benn, Sarah Bond, Anna Hetherington, Mimi Kramer, Lenny Muellner, Paul O'Mahony, Julio Vega-Payne, and Celsiana Warwick, all of whom read drafts of or discussed various parts of this book and provided needed encouragement. Special thanks are due to my editor Heather Gold, who provided the focus and the framework to help turn a half-baked idea into a full manuscript. Elizabeth Sylvia also provided invaluable editorial support, and Susan Laity's careful eye improved the book's prose and style immeasurably. Varsha Venkatasubramanian prepared the index with accuracy, speed, and good humor. The anonymous reviewers were especially kind in their suggestions for revision and additions to the bibliography. I apologize directly to them that I could not take all their good advice for fear of writing a different, much longer book. If there are virtues to this current text, they come from the relationships that have enriched the life that led to it.

And, as always, my spouse, Shahnaaz, deserves the final word—my belief in the future and any confidence I have starts with her.

Index

Abusch, Tzvi, 103

Achilles, 1, 33, 52–55, 165; and
Agamemnon, 46, 50, 73, 124,
153–54; and audience reception,
32; characterization of, 123, 173;
and dactyl, 33; death of, 118;
and deaths, 170; as enemy,
56; and epigraphs, 135; and
epitaphs, 134; and epithets,
45; and Gilgamesh, 103; and
Hektor, 157; and Herakles, 98;
Kleomēdēs compared to, 2,
167; and *kleos*, 103, 117, 120–25;
language of, 117; and narrative,
154–55, 157–58; and Nestor,
155–56; and *paradeigmata*, 140;
and Patroklos, 102, 157; and
Peleus, 27, 31, 38, 45, 51, 75; and
Phoinix, 85–86, 155–56; rage
of, 13, 27, 31, 38; speeches of, 56,
121, 125; and story versions, 12;
strife of, 164; and "swift feet,"
44–46, 48; and Thetis, 106; and
Zeus, 2

adaptation, 45, 49, 66, 70, 80, 105,
118, 131, 134, 177; and epigraphic
formulas, 118; and Greek

poetry, 69, 77, 119; and
narrative, 11, 82, 86, 116, 119, 145,
156, 158, 162; and natural world,
64; and rituals, 66; and simile,
144; and species, 59

Aegisthus, 160–61

Aeschylus, 160

aesthetics, 11, 14, 17–18, 23–24, 60,
62–63, 72, 74, 79, 82, 138

Agamemnon, 45–46, 50, 55, 73–75,
124, 153–54, 157, 160, 173

Ajax, 51–53, 75, 157

a-kleiēs, 129

Alcman, 47–48

Alexiou, Margaret, 132

Althaia, 85

Amphinomos, 125

Anaktoria, 83–84, 134

analogy, 9, 15, 17, 41, 180; and
biodiversity, 112; biological, 48,
56, 86, 92; and crab evolution,
100–101; of DNA expression, 39,
43, 179; and evolution, 106; and
homology, 95; and meaning
making, 21; and morphologies,
33; and music, 26; and narrative
function, 182; phenotypic, 99;

analogy (*continued*)
   and poetry, 30, 60; and syntax,
   31, 37; virus, 181
Andromache, 75–76, 124
antiquity, 4–5, 26, 40, 104
Aphrodite, 118
Apollo, 113, 115, 153, 160
Ares, 118
Argos, 126
Aristophanes, 90
Aristotle, 16, 90
Armstrong, Paul, 82
artificial intelligence, 11–15, 43, 182
Astupalaia, 165–67
Astupalaians, 1, 165–68, 170, 172,
   176
Athena, 1–2, 161, 163, 166
Athens, 6, 90, 105, 117, 135, 139–40,
   160
Atrahasis, 101
Atreus, 27, 73, 161
Augustine, Saint, 15
Austin, Emily, 132

Babylon, 101, 103–5, 107, 109
Bacchylides, 129–30, 133
Bachvarova, Mary, 105
bacteria, 148
Bakker, Egbert, 29
Balkans, 29, 41
Barker, Elton, 46, 77
Baskaran, Aparna, 10
battles, 45–46, 66, 68, 78, 85–86,
   122, 135, 142–43, 155, 157
Bentley, Richard, 35
biology, 20–21, 36, 39, 93, 97, 118,
   148, 192; and analogy, 30, 43, 48,
   56, 86, 92, 156; and cells, 31,
   58–59; and ecosystems, 86; and
   evolution, 106; and gender, 99;
   and language, 20, 41, 43, 56; and

metaphor, 141, 144; and models,
   32, 40, 141, 181; and relation-
   ships, 120; and systems, 30, 49
birth narratives, 90–91, 97, 149
Boyd, Brian, 185, 189
Briseis, 50, 55
Brooks, Peter, 186–87
Bruner, Jerome, 175, 187

ChatGPT, 11–14
children, 36, 97, 108, 115, 130, 135,
   161, 166–71, 173–74, 177
Cioran, E. M., 188–89
cognition, 5, 72
cognitive bias, 9–10
cognitive blend, 82, 84
cognitive ecology, 20
cognitive linguistics, 42–44
cognitive metaphor, 141
cognitive psychology, 146, 184, 188
cognitive science, 8, 42, 175
cognitive transformation, 97
Combellack, Frederick M., 60,
   63–64, 79, 86
Cook, Erwin, 72, 170
crabs, 93–94, 96, 106; evolution of,
   100–101; features of, 95, 97–98;
   morphology of, 93–94, 100
culture, 6, 19, 78, 86, 89, 98, 147,
   183; and aesthetics, 63; athletic,
   47; and cognitive biases, 10; and
   dialects, 104; of Greece, 106, 112,
   120; and language, 20, 42, 99,
   105, 111, 135; literate, 29; song, 18,
   110, 113, 141; and storytelling, 2;
   transformations of, 100;
   warrior, 134

death, 97, 107–8, 134–35, 148, 165,
   167, 170; of Achilles, 46, 118;
   analytical, 90; and anxiety, 116;

attitudes toward, 109; of
Gilgamesh, 102; of Hektor, 75,
157; heroic, 103, 106; of Meleager, 85; and memory, 122; and
Odysseus, 124, 162; and Orestes,
160; of Patroklos, 102, 157
digamma, 34–35
DNA, 30–31, 36, 38–40, 43–44, 46,
56, 90, 118, 148–49, 151, 153, 168,
175, 179
doublets, 59, 71, 76–80, 87, 162,
180
Dué, Casey, 19, 132

ecosystems, 34, 39, 49, 55–56, 58,
64, 69, 80, 86, 123, 161; communicative, 179; cultural, 113;
development of, 100; and *kleos*,
122; of meaning, 23; and
monocultures, 112; natural, 112;
and new species, 136; of
performance, 118–19; and
specialization, 34. *See also*
narrative
epigenetic effects, 30, 36–38, 119,
156
epigenetics, 35–36, 39

fame, 102, 106, 116–18, 122–34,
136–37, 140, 163. See also *kleos*
Fenik, Bernard, 77
Foley, John Miles, 29

Gazzaniga, Michael, 151
George, Andrew, 104
Gilgamesh and Gilgamesh poems,
91–92, 96, 107–8; and accomplishments, 103; and Achilles,
98; and function, 104; and
Homeric epics, 89, 101–2, 105–6,
111; and reception, 103; and

translations, 104; versions of,
109–10
gods, 5, 33, 46, 74, 101, 114–15, 117,
124, 133, 144, 153, 159–60
Greece, ancient, 6, 34, 45, 104, 113,
128, 135
grief, 106, 113–14, 124, 132, 165, 172

Hagan, Michael, 10
Hektor, 25–26, 32, 46, 68, 75–76,
122–24, 142, 144, 157
Helen, 78, 83–85, 160
heroic narrative, 2, 89, 101, 171–72;
and cultural presence, 97;
evolution of, 98; Greek, 102, 116;
and memory, 114; parts of, 99,
168; and plot patterns, 90;
traditional, 170
Hesiod, 5, 77–78, 80, 113–14
Hitch, Sarah, 65–66
Homeric epics. *See* Homeric
narratives
Homeric Greek (dialect), 32–35, 37,
40, 50, 157
Homeric narratives, 2, 7, 19, 24, 59,
87, 139–40; and Achilles, 98;
aspects of, 15; characters of, 67,
125, 153; and children, 108; as
closed system, 45; and cultural
expectations, 152; duals, 53; and
Gilgamesh poems, 89, 101–3,
105–6, 108, 111; impact of, 164,
191; interpretations of, 13,
118–19; and *kleos*, 103, 121, 126,
128; and language, 23–24, 44,
56, 89, 117, 136, 140, 143–44, 179;
line breaks in, 75–76; and
linguistics, 30; morphology of,
86; origins of, 23; and Peisistratid recension, 139; performance
of, 16–18, 55, 71; reception of, 82;

Homeric narratives (*continued*)
recitation of, 16; and rhetoric,
73; and sacrifice, 140; and
translation, 3, 17; as vaccine,
165, 191; and values, 117; and
war, 140. *See also* Homeric
poetry; *Iliad, Odyssey*
Homeric poetry, 21, 26, 37, 41, 58,
62, 69–72, 118, 139, 165; and
Achilles, 32; and arboreal
metaphors, 15; and audiences, 37,
142; and aural metaphors, 15;
authorship of, 19; building
blocks of, 25, 34, 39, 69;
characters of, 119; conventions
of, 67; and cosmic relationships,
151; development of, 60; and
digamma, 34; and epithets, 29;
function, 7, 39, 62; and Gilgamesh poems, 104; and *Ion*, 6;
and language, 23, 61, 89; line
breaks in, 28; and linguistics, 25,
41; metonymic nature of, 70; and
modern readers, 79; and myth, 7,
151; and narrative, 21; and nature,
79; and Odysseus, 32; paratactic
nature of, 72; recitations of, 16,
37; and repetition, 25; and ritual,
66; and similes, 142; structure of,
58, 64, 87–89, 102, 164, 179; and
type-scenes, 65; and words, 27;
and Zeus, 32
Homeric Question, 4, 7
Homeric studies, 5, 24, 41
honor, 1, 86, 134, 157, 166–67,
170–72, 174–75
human beings, 8–10, 13, 62,
145–46, 185–86; and anxiety, 116;
brains of, 10; and cognition, 88;
and consciousness, 14; and
emotions, 114; grammar of, 17;

and memory, 8; minds of, 8, 11,
89, 93, 147, 182; and neurology,
43, 97
human communities, 7, 139, 180,
189–91; and audiences, 21, 116;
and languages, 12, 43, 99, 147, 151
human life, 2, 187–88; and
agriculture, 112; and culture, 63,
92, 98, 100, 183; and narrative,
90, 110, 132, 148, 150; parameters
of, 98; and reason, 24; and song,
60
human nature, 96

identity, 115, 137, 159–60, 169,
174–75, 186
Iliad, 2–4, 23, 37, 54, 113, 118–19,
129, 136, 143; Achilles in, 13, 27,
31–32, 45–46, 85, 102–3, 117, 123,
140, 155, 167; Agamemnon in,
74; and Alcman, 47–48; and
Athenian epigraphs, 135; and
classical Greek, 50; and death,
106, 108; editions of, 35; and
evolution, 7; and Gilgamesh
poems, 92, 102, 109, 111; Hektor
in, 131–32; and heroes, 142; and
kleos, 122, 125–26; and language,
66; and life, 107; Nestor in, 73;
Odysseus in, 67–68, 70, 121; and
the *Odyssey*, 60, 128, 130, 139,
151, 163–65, 168, 176; and
paradigms, 153–54; and
persuasion, 153; Phoinix in, 156;
snow metaphor in, 143; and
song, 115; and symbiogenesis,
158; Thetis in, 109; and Trojan
War, 152; and violence, 173
inscriptions, 34, 116–18, 122,
132–34, 136–37, 140
Ion (Plato), 6

Kakridis, 75
katabasis, 90
Kleomēdēs, 1–2, 165–72, 175–76
Kleopatra, 85
kleos (fame), 103, 116, 140; and
   Achilles, 120, 122, 125; articulations of, 118; and collocation,
   134; and deeds, 133; and
   esthlon, 121; and *euru,* 125;
   function of, 122, 126, 131–32;
   and Greek culture, 120; in the
   Iliad, 125, 129; impact of, 128;
   kleos aphthiton (imperishable
   fame), 117; meanings of, 121;
   motifs, 134; as narrative
   pattern, 127–28, 135; in the
   Odyssey, 124; and *pothē*
   (longing), 132; transferability
   of, 123; variability of, 126; and
   victory poems, 129

Lakoff, George, 42
languages, 22, 29, 40, 47–48, 59,
   73, 103–4, 122, 145, 151, 188–89;
   adaptability of, 31, 147; capacity
   of, 20, 42; and culture, 20;
   European, 45, 105; flexibility of,
   35; formulaic, 66, 69–70;
   foundations of, 88; function of,
   35–36, 45; and genealogies, 20;
   Greek, 37–38, 49, 111–12, 135–36,
   169; Homer's use of, 23–26, 28,
   32, 34, 39, 44, 55–56, 61, 89, 117,
   126, 144, 179; and *langue,* 41–42;
   and legibility, 14; of memorialization, 140; and narrative, 185;
   native, 17; as organism, 21; and
   parole, 41–42; and rules, 26;
   and selection, 93; and storytelling, 99
Lesser, Rachel, 132

linguistics, 20, 24, 29–30, 34,
   39–44, 53, 56, 66, 92, 98, 106
Lord, Albert, 24, 29, 65

Martin, John Jeffries, 185
Martin, Richard, 54
Meillet, Antoine, 24, 41
Meleager, 85, 119, 155–56
memory, 8, 16, 97, 113–14, 121–22,
   140, 188
metaphor, 6, 42–43, 100, 127, 156,
   191; arboreal, 15, 17, 19; and
   authorship, 19; biological, 141,
   144; cultural, 8; and language
   development, 21, 56; and music,
   16; and narrative development,
   15, 19–20; and Plato, 6, 14; and
   scientific discourse, 86
metonymy, 70, 80, 122, 145, 157
monoculture, 112, 138
monomyth, 89–90, 96–97, 99–101,
   106, 110–11
mortality, 47, 98, 102, 108–10, 149
motifs, 65, 70, 77, 79, 91, 101, 105,
   107, 110–11, 127, 131–34, 136
Muellner, Leonard, 38, 142, 145
Muses, 6, 113–14, 129
mutualism, 120, 148, 150–51

Nagy, Gregory, 29, 54, 121
narrative, 10–11, 70, 108, 148, 150,
   178, 180, 184; and Achilles,
   46–47, 86, 121; action, 54; and
   agency, 20–21; aural nature of,
   19; character, 93; and cognitive
   science, 8; development, 7, 15,
   98; doublets, 76–77; ecosystems,
   44, 64, 87, 92, 110, 112, 118–19,
   133, 135–37, 144–45, 156, 186;
   environment, 3, 65, 118–19, 186;
   epic, 48, 58; evolution of, 53;

narrative (*continued*)
  evolutionary, 149; forms, 71, 88,
    96, 109, 156, 171–72, 174, 183;
    functions, 80, 88, 123; and
    gender, 109; and Gilgamesh
    poems, 101–5; grammar of, 90;
    Greek, 77–78, 83–85, 102, 116,
    179; and human intervention,
    100; and the *Iliad*, 45–46, 54,
    102, 156–58, 163, 165, 167–68; and
    individual power, 134; inset,
    75–76; and interiority, 67; and
    kleos, 122, 125–27, 132, 135; and
    language, 21, 44, 147, 185; and
    metastasis of language, 21;
    monocultures, 112; and the
    Odyssey, 46, 77, 102, 115, 124,
    158–63, 165, 168; and the
    Oresteia, 160–62; patterns,
    89–90, 93, 95–96, 99–101, 116,
    131, 136, 169; as persuasion, 59;
    power of, 114, 190; purpose of,
    100, 155, 172, 181–82, 187–90;
    reception of, 72, 191–92;
    relationships with, 152–54; of
    selfhood, 175–76; and similes,
    81, 83; structures, 78, 82, 90, 98,
    116, 119, 121, 175; theory, 8, 145;
    time, 58; traditions, 109, 140,
    151, 153, 157; and viruses, 148,
    163, 191; worlds of, 146. *See also*
    heroic narrative; Homeric
    narratives; Homeric poetry
Natural Language Processing,
    12–13, 43
Nestor, 50–51, 53, 73, 153–54, 161
noun-epithet combinations,
    44, 48

Odysseus, 1, 32–33, 52, 74–75, 119,
    163; and Achilles, 124; and Ajax,
    53; and *akleiēs*, 124; and
    Calypso, 67; characterization
    of, 46; and deaths, 170; and
    Gilgamesh, 103; homecoming
    of, 2, 115, 126, 162, 165; in the
    Iliad, 67–68; and Kleomēdēs, 2;
    and *kleos*, 125; as narrator,
    114–15, 158–59; and Phoinix, 54;
    and Polyphemos, 12–13;
    rehabilitation of, 61; and
    Telemachus, 77; and Tiresias,
    188; transgressions of, 47–48;
    and vengeance, 162
Odyssey, 4, 135, 164; Achilles in,
    134; Agamemnon in, 115;
    characters in, 46, 66–67, 69,
    160; doublets in, 76; function
    of, 176; and Gilgamesh poems,
    102–3, 111; and heroic narrative,
    2, 165, 168; and human
    emotion, 114; and the *Iliad*, 60,
    73, 118, 139, 151; *kleos* in, 121,
    124–26, 130; and metastructure,
    61–62; and narration, 152–53,
    159; and *Oresteia*, 161–62;
    performance of, 3; stratigraphy
    of, 7; and symbiogenesis, 158;
    Telemachus in, 97; and
    Theogony, 113; transmissions of,
    23; and vengeance, 162–63;
    versions of, 13. *See also*
    Odysseus
oracle at Delphi, 1, 160, 166–67,
    169–70, 172
Oresteia (Aeschylus), 160–62
Orestes, 126, 160–62
organicism, 20–21

parasitism, 120, 148–50
Parry, Milman, 24–25, 28–29, 41,
    44–45, 54

"particular epithet," 41
Patroklos, 12, 52, 54, 102, 157
Pausanias, 1, 165, 169, 178
Peleus, 27, 31, 38, 45, 51, 75
Penelope, 13, 125–26
Phoinix, 51–55, 85–86, 119, 155–56
Pindar, 85, 129–30, 133
Plato, 6, 14, 173
Pliny, 15
Plutarch, 1, 166, 169–70
popular culture, 2, 137–38, 174
Priam, 26, 75–76

race, 159
racial trauma, 37
racism, 105, 169, 175
rage, 1, 13, 27–28, 31, 38, 85, 102, 157,
    165, 169–71
repetition, 59, 71, 79–81, 87, 102–3,
    136, 180; and Homeric epics, 25,
    45, 47, 69, 76, 158; and narra-
    tive, 59, 89; and ring structure,
    73–74
ring composition, 70–74, 81,
    102
ring structures, 59, 71–73, 79, 84,
    87–88
RNA, 30–31

Sappho, 83–84, 86, 119, 134
Schleicher, August, 20
scripts, 15, 169, 183, 186–87
sex, 107, 109, 159, 189–90
similes, 81–83, 142–45, 177
social change, 96
social conventions, 68, 86
social Darwinism, 20
social discourse, 168, 183, 187
social environment, 36
social power, 97
social relationships, 66, 169

social status, 22
social structures, 2, 91, 99, 139,
    175–76
species, 136, 180, 185; adaptation
    of, 59; and convergent evolu-
    tion, 92, 106; dominant, 151; and
    ecological system, 150; and
    environmental change, 34, 48,
    94, 110, 164; and evolution, 33;
    and form, 63; interdependence,
    147; invasive, 123, 127; and
    monomyth, 90; and mutualism,
    148; narrative, 172; parallel
    evolution of, 106; and pheno-
    types, 100; and ring structure,
    71; and storytelling, 120, 145;
    and traits, 95
Strawson, Galen, 187, 189–90
"swift feet" metaphor, 44–48, 52
symbiogenesis, 150, 153, 158
symbiosis, 116, 120, 123, 126–27,
    148–49, 151, 171
symbiotic relationships, 120, 132,
    147–54, 156, 159, 171

Telemachus, 61, 77, 97, 124–25,
    161
Thebes, 78
Theogony (Hesiod), 77, 113, 115
Tomasello, Michael, 40
"traditional epithet," 25, 29, 32, 41,
    45–46, 76
trees, 17–20, 58, 60–61, 69,
    161
Trojans, 26, 75, 117, 120, 124, 133,
    143, 155
Trojan War, 78, 125, 152, 160
Troy, 6, 46, 48, 78, 83, 105, 153, 160,
    162, 165
Turner, Mark, 42, 82, 84
Tyrtaeus, 130–31

vestigial structures, 34, 49–50, 56
violence, 2, 46, 78, 110, 113, 159, 162, 167–68, 171, 173–76, 183
viral growth, 127–28, 148
viral infection, 127
virality, 21, 131, 150
viruses, 7, 21, 127–28, 148–51, 180–81, 190

White, Michael, 175
Whitman, Cedric, 60, 63–64, 79, 86, 181
Wolf, Friedrich August, 23

Zeus, 2, 25, 32–33, 51, 113–14, 129, 132, 143, 159–60, 165
Zimmer, Carl, 147